Soccer City

Denis Campbell & Andrew Shields

SOCCER CITY

The Future of Football in London

Mandarin

A Mandarin Paperback
SOCCER CITY

First published in Great Britain in 1993
by Mandarin Paperbacks
an imprint of Reed Consumer Books Ltd
Michelin House, 81 Fulham Road, London SW3 6RB
and Auckland, Melbourne, Singapore and Toronto

Copyright © 1993 Denis Campbell and Andrew Shields
The authors have asserted their moral rights

A CIP catalogue record for this book
is available from the British Library
ISBN 0 7493 1651 9

Photoset by
Photoprint, Torquay, S. Devon
Printed and bound in Great Britain
by Cox & Wyman Ltd, Reading, Berkshire

To Margaret and Arthur Campbell,
and Lorna and John Shields.
And to Elaine Burgess, a Tottenham fan
– but we won't hold that against her.

Contents

Acknowledgements		ix
Introduction		1
ONE:	**Facing Up to the Future** *The challenge to London football*	5
TWO:	**Sky's the Limit?** *BSkyB, and the 'Whole New Ball Game'*	27
THREE:	**American Football?** *Arsenal, David Dein, and the 'total leisure experience'*	50
FOUR:	**The Great Dictators?** *Ken Bates, Ron Noades, and the cult of the individual*	74
FIVE:	**The Building of Barnet** *Flashman, Fry, and soccer strife in suburbia*	95
SIX:	**Forward with the People** *Millwall, Brentford, and a sense of community*	121
SEVEN:	**Young, Gifted – and Free!** *Leyton Orient, and the search for schoolboy stars*	142
EIGHT:	**From the Pitch and the Dugout** *George Graham, Terry Howard, Clive Allen, Julian Dicks, John Fashanu and Gerry Francis*	161
NINE:	**Perverse Passion** *London fans who even sing when they're losing*	193

TEN:	**Ten Thousand are Missing** *West Ham: loyalty, betrayal,* *and the lessons of 1991–93*	214
ELEVEN:	**Spurred into Action** *From fanzines to full-time lobbyists:* *the rise and rise of fan power*	238
TWELVE:	**London Football in the 21st Century** *Survival of the fittest?*	252
EPILOGUE:	**The Final Whistle**	271

Acknowledgements

This book would not have been possible without the help so generously given by the supporters, players and officials of London's football clubs. We extend our grateful thanks to all those who assisted, regrettably too numerous to credit individually, and who dispensed wisdom, insight and their considered opinions on the future of the game, plus a constant supply of tea. Our suspicion has been entertainingly confirmed that any worthwhile conversation about football is, indeed, endless.

Our thanks are due also to three individuals at *Time Out*: managing director Mike Hardwick, who claims an undying love of Spurs despite the fact that he hasn't set foot inside White Hart Lane since the days of Gilzean and Greaves; editor Dominic Wells, for readily allowing us leave (unpaid, sadly) to write 80,000 words on one of the few subjects he confesses to know nothing about; and particularly to executive editor Steve Grant, an Arsenal fan for even longer than Nick Hornby, for countless constructive comments and endless encouragement.

Geoff Brown's early criticisms were useful, Tracey Harrison helped with research and Razi Mireskandari was an eagle-eyed law-man. Clemency Keegan patiently bore being a temporary football widow, and perfected the art of the soothing midnight phone-call.

Special thanks go to Neil Tunnicliffe and Tony Pocock, our editors, for spotting a good idea amid a jumbled proposal and backing it all the way.

And last, we must thank the following for their kind permission to reproduce the following photographs: Action Plus (nos 2, 3, 7, 8, 9, 13), Allsport (4, 5, 10, 16), BSkyB (1), Barry J. Holmes (6), Simon Norfolk/Select (11, 12, 15), and Jon Spaull (14).

Denis Campbell
Andrew Shields

Introduction

He doesn't know it, but Brendan McKeown is responsible for this book, in a roundabout sort of way. If he hadn't taken so long to retrieve the ball from the school playground behind one of the goals at Coram Fields, the astroturf in genteel Bloomsbury which *Time Out*'s no-hopers used to grace every Tuesday lunchtime, then we probably wouldn't have begun one of those interminable conversations about the state of football.

It was the first week of January 1992, three days after West Ham had been held at home in the FA Cup by non-league Farnborough Town. We had both stood on the North Bank at a game which proved to be exceptional for every reason other than what happened on the pitch. Sitting on the astroturf while Brendan clambered over the railings to atone for a miss more worthy of Tony Adams than his hero Paul Merson, we reached the conclusion that the spontaneous, popular anger aimed at the Upton Park directors, the sheer venom and feeling of betrayal behind the chants of 'Sack the Board!' we had heard the previous Saturday, was the start of some kind of revolution.

After years of frustration, something had suddenly snapped. Fans were used to seeing good players sold, poor ones bought as replacements and their beloved club apparently declining due to a lack of dynamism and direction. They were not, however, used to being asked to dig deep into pockets, regularly emptied in support of their side, in order to buy a right they already possessed: a Hammers Bond, giving them permission to keep on watching their team. The outrage at such an iniquitous and ill-judged idea was motivated by more than the understandable concern that future generations of West Ham followers would be barred from Upton Park for being unable or unwilling to find £500–£975. It was also borne of a general unease that football was slipping away from its fans; that the regular supporters who paid the players' wages and provided the vocal support were no longer considered important.

An eighteen-month interlude which has seen massive price rises, the creation of a laughably-titled Premier League, and the signing of a television deal which deprived 95 per cent of the population of the chance to see the country's leading teams and the national side in live action, has confirmed this depressing trend. While innovation is to be welcomed, not all 'progress' is necessarily beneficial. Squatting on our haunches at Coram Fields, we agreed that with football in unprecedented turmoil, at stake was the very feature which had ensured its survival for more than a century: its unique appeal as a mass spectator sport.

Having written several articles together about the uncertain future of football, we felt that only a full-scale book could do justice to the complexity of the subject. Unlike the creators of the Premier League, our interest lay in the game as a whole – from the glamour clubs whose affairs dominated the sports pages of the papers to the smaller set-ups which received scarcely a column inch. London, a near-perfect microcosm of the state of the game nationwide, fitted the bill. Britain has numerous rightly famous 'soccer cities' – Manchester, Glasgow,

Liverpool, Newcastle, Edinburgh, Birmingham, Sheffield – but none boasts the sheer number of clubs, thirteen in all, to be found in the capital. Nor does any other metropolitan centre have clubs at every level of the professional game: from the European Super League aspirations of Arsenal and Tottenham Hotspur to the eternal battle for survival of Fulham and Leyton Orient to the discreet ambitions of QPR and Brentford. The confusion over the game's future is reflected in the stories that have recently seen all thirteen clubs make the national news, whether it be West Ham's difficulties with their Bond scheme, Charlton's return to the Valley, or the wrangles between Alan Sugar and Terry Venables at Spurs.

As fans concerned about football's direction, we are interested in the broader picture, not just the teams we support – which both happen to be in London. Thus we viewed all thirteen clubs as of equal importance, believing that, like it or not, the fate of Wimbledon is as worthy of attention as that of Chelsea. However, we haven't attempted to write an equal amount about each club. Instead, we have approached our subject thematically, examining the various survival strategies being adopted and, in particular, where the most important people of all – the supporters – fit into the future scheme of things. Thus Orient's investment in youth is just as significant as Arsenal's Napoleonic designs towards Europe. We have written at length about West Ham, believing its extraordinary recent history serves as a testing ground for the future relationship between a club and its followers, and as a cautionary tale to those who take the punters for granted. In a game dominated more than ever before by larger-than-life characters, we have also profiled Chelsea's Ken Bates and Crystal Palace's Ron Noades, and recounted in detail how, for Barnet, benevolence turned into tyranny under the regime of the infamous Stan Flashman.

Although we received generous help from almost everyone we approached, we were disappointed that Terry Venables, Ron Noades and the reclusive 'King of the Touts' failed to make themselves available in the way that George Graham, Gerry Francis, Barry Fry and John Fashanu, among many others, had done. As a pre-eminent figure in London football, we were more interested in Venables's thoughts on the game in general than Tottenham's own prospects. White Hart Lane's 'back from the brink' saga and recent dispute have already been amply chronicled in a clutch of books, articles and television documentaries, leaving no angle unexplored. Given his recent problems, we understand why he was so busy.

In this book, we have tried to make sense of the present – no easy task – and point a constructive way forward. We fervently hope that, unlike Aldershot, all of London's thirteen clubs will be alive and well and still causing third-round FA Cup upsets in the 21st century.

London
May 1993

Denis Campbell
Andrew Shields

ONE

Facing Up to the Future

The challenge to London football

Upton Park, E13. Saturday, 4 January 1992.

They came in their thousands, pouring out of Upton Park tube station, nudging past the shoppers looking for bargains in the January sales, stopping off for a burger, buying a fanzine from a stall set up in a front garden. It was a gorgeous day, perfect weather for the fans to greet the start of another West Ham FA Cup run. For who, after all, would expect anything else from the side that had capped their promotion year with a glorious surge to the semi-finals the previous April?

West Ham, however, were not having things all their own way during their first season back in the top flight after two years' exile from what the fans considered their rightful home. It was clear to most observers that the Hammers had needed to boost their promotion squad with at least two players, but manager Billy Bonds had received no book of blank cheques to ink in during the summer months. In a summer of hectic transfer activity, when fifteen English players changed clubs for fees of more than £1 million, West Ham were content to pay £400,000 for an unproven second-division forward,

£500,000 for a defender struggling in the reserves at his former club, and £20,000 for a young striker saddled with the same name as crooner Dean Martin. Little wonder, then, that Hammers fans began to accuse the board of starving the team of resources.

The result was inevitable: the boys in claret and blue were now stuck at the wrong end of the league table and, if truth be told, were drawing greater inspiration from the schoolyard of the local comprehensive than the self-styled Academy of Football. But this was the FA Cup – a competition in which a good run by the Hammers was supposed to be as much a feature of East London life as a plate of pie, mash and liquor. And their opponents were Farnborough Town.

It all began with Dean Coney's unbelievable miss. Twenty minutes into the game, the Hammers had produced nothing while their visitors from the GM Vauxhall Conference looked assured, confident even. Then Farnborough broke away, and Coney – who had once fringed the big time as an England Under-21 cap with Fulham and Queen's Park Rangers – headed one of the easiest chances of his entire career straight into West Ham 'keeper Ludek Miklosko's arms. It was all too much for the supporters to bear. 'Sack the board, sack the board, sack the board' came an instant chorus from the terraces. On the North Bank, the Christmas spirit had evaporated. The mood was bitter; the talk was of betrayal.

Coming out for the second half in front of the West Ham kop, Farnborough's 'keeper got a genuinely rousing reception. And when the chant of 'Sack the board' rose again, the visiting fans – not quite certain of what was going on, but determined to enjoy it all the same – joined in too. The final score, 1–1, suggests it was an even contest. In fact, despite Julian Dicks putting them ahead, the Hammers were lucky to escape with a draw.

The home goal did not rattle the non-leaguers and, after Dean Coney had atoned for his earlier howler, they could easily have snatched a famous victory.

The unusual atmosphere – almost jovial in spite of adversity – vanished at the final whistle. After West Ham's players had slunk off the pitch, heads hung low, and Coney & Co. had told their tale to the tabloids, around 1,000 West Ham supporters staged a sit-in in front of the directors' box. Rather than call the police to break up the demo, club managing director Peter Storrie did an unexpected thing. He invited half-a-dozen of the crowd's representatives into his office to discuss their grievances.

West Ham's six directors, sitting apart in the stand and unknown to the public except through snapshots in the match-day programme, were finally being called to account over their previously unquestioned right to rule. Storrie's decision was a moral victory for the fans – and tacit recognition by the club that the views of its supporters could no longer be ignored.

In truth, there had been discontent from the very start of the season. Remember 'Chirpy, Chirpy, Cheep, Cheep,' the No. 1 hit record by the 1970s pop band Middle of the Road? Down at Upton Park, the tune was matched to the words, 'Where's the money gone?' How could the eighth-best supported club in the land, which had enjoyed near sell-out crowds right through their second-division stay, which had got to two Cup semi-finals in that time, be pleading poverty? The club's 6,000-selling fanzine, aptly named *Fortune's Always Hiding*, had caught the mood when it declared, 'Never has there been a greater sense of depression, resignation and apathy at Upton Park. It's a sense of powerlessness borne of watching possibly the worst group of individuals ever to play in claret and blue.'

Three months into the season, West Ham's announcement that they were launching the Hammers Bond scheme to pay for the redevelopment of Upton Park stretched an already taut relationship with their fans to breaking-point. The supporters' initial disbelief at being asked to pay between £500 and £975 just for the right to buy a season ticket when Upton Park became an all-seater stadium – as it would, according to the demands of the Taylor Report – soon turned to fury. They denounced the Bond plan as a rip-off, claiming that the club was, in effect, asking fans to make them a gift of large sums of money. *Fortune's Always Hiding* commented that: 'The idea of being asked to pay £500 in advance for more of the rubbish we currently have to watch would be funny if it wasn't so unforgivable. If the board of directors at this club can't be bothered to put their hands in their well-lined pockets, then why the hell should we? Once again they have demonstrated how they pay lip-service to our loyalty and then take liberties with it.'

On the Monday morning after the Farnborough sit-in, West Ham's directors announced that they were, after all, able to find money for new players. A day later, they had changed their minds again. There was cash available, but only if players were offloaded first. Billy Bonds announced that his entire first-team squad was up for sale: 'We will listen to offers for anybody,' he said. The prospect of the handful of genuine stars being pushed out of the door to raise a few thousand pounds simply became too much for the faithful. Come Saturday, and a crucial relegation battle against Wimbledon, resentment against the board reached fever-pitch. Yet another dismal performance by the Hammers, who equalised only in the eighty-eighth-minute, provoked the second sit-in within a week. At the final whistle of the 1–1 draw, two teenagers were cheered as they leapt from the terraces, made for the centre circle, sat down and folded their arms. Another 3,000 took that as their cue, congregating on the pitch in front of the directors box.

Although the mood was good-humoured, the chants were unequivocal. To the board, 'Resign'; to the club chairman Martin Cearns, 'Cearns Out!' A waggish cry of 'Let's all storm the boardroom', an instant hit with the crowd, led twice to brief pushing and shoving between protestors and police, but no arrests were made. A public appeal for calm by Billy Bonds went unheeded and, in a remarkable display of solidarity, the fans continued to occupy the pitch for two hours.

Next morning, the usual big-match reports had disappeared from the back pages of the Sunday tabloids. 'Uprising!' proclaimed the *Mail on Sunday*, almost as if the paper was reporting the people of Berlin's destruction of the hated wall. For once, the press had picked on the really important football story of the day.

Upton Park wasn't the only place where fans were turning discontent into direct action. At White Hart Lane, for example, Spurs supporters, disgruntled at their team's mediocre season, had hoisted banners and chanted a simple message against their manager: 'Shreeves Out!' The last day of the season at Highbury saw some North Bank regulars don mourning garb and turn Arsenal's game against Coventry City into 'a funeral for a friend'. This was the last time they would ever stand on their beloved kop; the bulldozers were due very soon to turn the terrace into a 12,000-seat stand financed by the hated Arsenal Bond scheme.

Nor was this unprecedented uproar an exclusively London phenomenon. All over Britain, fans were starting to channel the energy, humour and dedication usually reserved for following their team into challenging the arrogant, 'we know best' attitude of the game's establishment. West Bromwich Albion's faithful, incensed at new manager Bobby Gould's imposition of the alien creed of Route One tactics, mounted a vocal campaign for the return of *proper* football. In Manchester, more than 2,000 United followers attended the inaugural meeting of HOSTAGE (Holders of Season Tickets Against Gross Exploitation), formed to oppose ticket price rises of up to 50 per cent. In Glasgow, rallies organised by the Save Our Celts campaign drew thousands of devotees of the green and white hoops, disturbed at the club's apparently relentless decline.

Yet the tensions exposed by such discontent, dramatic though they were, were only one aspect of the most strife-ridden season in the game's history. Football in the early 1990s was a game divided against itself, split right down the middle. Rumours of a formal rupture had been rife for years. England's 'Big Five' glamour clubs – Arsenal, Tottenham Hotspur, Manchester United, Liverpool and Everton – had long been pressing for a bigger share of soccer's multi-million pound income. By the spring of 1992, they had encouraged the other seventeen clubs in the first division to break their historic ties with the Football League and establish an élite Premier League.

The new set-up, as enshrined in the Football Association's revolutionary document, the 'Blueprint for the Future of Football', published early in 1991, sounded great. A top flight comprising eighteen clubs: restructuring, everyone agreed, was long overdue. Fewer, better-quality games: players would be fresher, matches would have more meaning, and bigger crowds would be lured by a renaissance in skill. More preparation time for the England team before major internationals: a long-awaited practice, already common abroad and in Scotland.

Within days, however, all this was revealed as a sham,

as these laudable aims were supplanted by more mercenary motives. Fewer clubs meant fewer home games, and fewer home games meant less income. Most club chairmen realised that they did not like that equation, so one of the Premier League's fundamental ideals was dumped almost immediately. Others soon followed.

The appointment of Sir John Quinton, chairman of Barclays Bank, and Rick Parry, an accountant, as chairman and chief executive respectively, showed the new organisation in its true colours: a money-making enterprise, pure and simple. Parry accepted that the plan was, as he put it, 'to maximise the game's commercial potential'. But this, he insisted, would ultimately be good for everyone, not just for the few. The one-time Liverpool trialist played down suggestions that the gap between the haves (Premier League clubs) and the have-nots (the rest) would grow ever wider. Instead, he offered a footballing version of the classic Conservative belief: that the new era of increased prosperity enjoyed by the top clubs would rub off on their poorer relations. However, Brian Glanville, the *People*'s pungent and widely respected football observer, spoke for the sceptical and cynical majority of soccer-lovers when he christened the new set-up the GIG League – the Greed Is Good League.

* * *

When the history of English football is written in years to come, the Great Room of Park Lane's Grosvenor House Hotel will surely occupy a central place, to rival the famous steps outside the Football Association's HQ in Lancaster Gate and the tunnel-end goal at Wembley breached twice by Geoff Hurst one July afternoon in 1966. Five days before the first whistle of the 1992–93 season, it hosted the media launch of the soon-to-be Premier League. Tottenham captain Gary Mabbutt, resplendent in a vivid amber blazer, was among dozens of players on show. The journalists mingled in the foyer, deep tans separating those just back after three weeks covering the Barcelona Olympics from the unfortunates left at home to write about transfer deals.

Strangely, though, the most important people in the room were also the most anonymous. When the notables took their seats on the stage, more than one player was heard to mutter, 'Who the hell are this lot?' Rick Parry was instantly recognisable, but it was still a fair question. Who, after all, had ever heard of Gary Davey or Richard Keys, much less David Hill or Jonathan Martin? They were, in fact, as crucial a quintet to the future of English football as Graham Taylor's faltering five-man defence. For the record, these others were, respectively: Gary Davey, MD of BSkyB, the satellite TV company; Richard Keys, anchorman for the station's match coverage; David Hill, the Sky Sports supremo, who had engineered a controversial five-year, £304-million deal to show live Premier League action exclusively to the nation's satellite dish-owners; and Jonathan Martin, head of sport at the BBC, Sky's unlikely co-conspirators.

The line-up offered a neat synopsis of the new balance of power in domestic football. No longer was the sport to be controlled by those genial chaps at Lancaster Gate; the people who mattered now were this breed of sharp-suited TV executives, schooled in the belief that football should be entertainment with a big E. As Gary Davey put it, 'The rich, magnificent past of this great game we will always respect. To this will be added the dazzle of the modern era.' Davey's dazzle, however, owed more to Dallas than to the fading glamour of the domestic game.

During questions from the media, Parry emerged as the main spokesman for the new set-up. Indeed, its alleged *newness* appeared to be its chief virtue. Never mind that it was just last year's first division under a different name; there were some genuine innovations. Well, two. In the old days, ITV's live football coverage had concentrated on the big names, ignoring the little clubs like Coventry, Norwich and the dreaded Wimbledon. BSkyB would change all that, and give everybody – yes, even Wimbledon – their chance. Something else was new too. ITV had introduced the concept of the live Sunday afternoon match; now Sky was taking the idea further, giving the world 'Monday Night Football'.

Parry insisted it would soon catch on. Presumably he was referring to the fans in the armchair and in the pub. He certainly didn't mean the Premier League clubs, who accepted the Monday night novelty reluctantly; perhaps the £60,000 match fee helped them reach their decision. In fact, the various reservations voiced by the Premier League club chairmen – chief among them, that the fans simply wouldn't put up with it – paled into insignificance when they realised the colossal sums on offer. In the case of Crystal Palace, for example, what was the loss of a few thousand paying customers on a Monday, compared to the fat fee for letting the cameras in?

Whether they recognised it or not, the chairmen had chosen to destroy a football-watching habit built up over a century. In place of the Saturday-Wednesday-Saturday routine – so consistent that most regular fans built the rest of their lives around it – they offered empty Saturdays, awkward away trips on Monday nights, and Sunday kick-offs at the strange time of 4 p.m., with no thanks given for your putting up with it all. It might have been new, as Parry insisted, but it posed serious difficulties for the average loyal fan, especially those used to fortnightly adventures round the motorways of England. Parry's 'new partnership in football' was solely between the clubs and

BSkyB; the fans' wishes were not part of the deal. It was a dangerous game, running the risk of severing the umbilical cord between football, a notoriously fickle but curiously addictive form of entertainment, and its legions of devotees.

Sure, there were bound to be initial problems, Parry agreed. There was, for instance, Queen's Park Rangers' strong protest at having their first game of the season, away to Manchester City, switched from Saturday at 3 p.m. to Monday at 8 p.m. How many fans would be making that trip, then going to Loftus Road forty-eight hours after for the clash with Southampton, and *then* forking out another tenner three days later for the hardly heart-stopping visit of Dave Bassett's Sheffield United? Never mind, said Parry, this wouldn't happen very often. It was, he explained, all part of the new deal. Quizzed further about widespread concern at the effects of constant fixture disruption, his reply was blunt: 'They will just have to get used to it.'

Only time would tell whether the Premier League and a restructured, three-division Football League was the best way for the game to develop. But earnest debates about administration and format soon took second place as the big kick-off approached, and fans of London's thirteen clubs prepared for the fray. The run-up to the new season is always the most peculiar time of the year in the football calendar: in spite of not having spent any money, club chairmen will still insist that they expect their team to be fighting for honours; while fans, ever ready to swap the rational for the romantic, really do believe that this year – yes, definitely this year – anything is possible for their boys.

Despite Rick Parry's insistence that this was the start of football's bright new dawn, a cursory examination of the health of the capital's clubs provided plentiful evidence to the contrary. All the old problems – like crummy grounds and often crummy football – were still there; to them were now added potentially serious new ones.

Let's start in the East End. West Ham's claret and blue army – both revered and mocked in equal measure for their legendary devotion to unreliable heroes – had got used to the fact that the season's away trips would once more be to the likes of the Abbey Stadium, where the dreaded long-ball hoofers of Cambridge United plied their trade, and Molineux, home to perpetual under-achievers Wolverhampton Wanderers. No more Highbury, Old Trafford or Anfield – except, perhaps, in one of those mythical Hammers Cup runs. What's more, the team was now minus the exciting young winger, Stuart Slater, sold to Glasgow Celtic for £1.5 million, while Southend United's Peter Butler and the Spurs cast-off, Mark Robson, were the only pre-season arrivals at Upton Park. Although the results of warm-up friendly games should never be relied upon as a guide to future form, the sight of a full-strength Hammers line-up struggling to beat a Leyton Orient side containing four teenage debutants by 3–2 did not augur well for their attempts to regain their rightful place. If there was to be a crumb of comfort for Irons fans as they consulted their road maps for the opening trip to Barnsley, it was that the league's reorganisation meant West Ham had enjoyed the dubious honour of becoming the first team ever to be relegated from division one . . . to division one.

'£195,000 for Castle but nothing to spend', a headline in the *Evening Standard* in late July, hinted at deep financial problems at Brisbane Road, home to West Ham's near-neighbours Leyton Orient. Steve Castle, the club's tough-tackling captain, had been sold to Plymouth Argyle, who two months previously had paid £250,000 for the O's top-scoring striker Kevin Nugent. The fans – the 4,000 regulars at least – were appalled. They viewed the sales as depressing evidence that Orient's traditional 'sell to survive' policy was set to continue, despite the team's encouraging progress on the pitch the previous season: a league berth just outside the third-division play-off positions, and a valiant run to the fifth round of the FA Cup. The sale of two other first-teamers soon afterwards reinforced the fans' belief that the club had little ambition to shake off its small-time image and claim a place in the new first division.

Six miles away, through Hackney and into Islington, Arsenal ran out against Norwich City as everybody's tip to bring the inaugural FA Premier League trophy back to Highbury Stadium, N5. At 2–1, the Gunners were the shortest-priced favourites for years. They had ended the previous season in blistering fashion, showing off the imperious, goal-happy form that had made them champions twice in the previous three years. Even the departure of David 'Rocky' Rocastle, a midfielder whom the North Bank recognised as Arsenal through and through, was softened by the arrival of John Jensen, who had just helped Denmark to their unexpected victory in the European Championships. With Arsenal being title favourites, an upset was almost inevitable: the first embarrassment of the season duly arrived in the shape of a 2–0 up, 2–4 down scoreline against the Canaries. That's football for you.

Far more acute embarrassment came on the back page of the *Sun* three days later: 'All white! Gunners told to paint fans black.' The problem was Arsenal's North Bank mural. It had appeared during the close-season, to hide the bitterly opposed transformation of the 16,000-capacity terrace beloved by fans and players alike into a 12,000-seater stand, financed by the equally unpopular 'rip-off' Arsenal Bond scheme. The mural was meant to look like any other football crowd. Certainly, it featured 12,000 fans – but none were women, and none were black. The boob, rumoured to have been spotted by one of Arsenal's own stars, was explained away amid technical printing jargon, and then hastily rectified.

Another alarming indication of the Gunners' future plans was their American football-style 'every game is all-ticket' policy, brought about by the drastically reduced capacity at Highbury. Despite Arsenal's protestation that the policy was fair to their fans, many of the die-hards who had never needed a season ticket warned that the unprecedented move would destroy the club's large pay-on-the-day following.

Arsenal fans like little better than to gloat at Tottenham's misfortunes, and the season promised rich pickings for the cruel of tongue. In replacing Gary Lineker, Paul Gascoigne and Paul Stewart, stars to rival Ardiles, Villa and Hoddle of a decade earlier, Spurs had raised eyebrows with their choices. Where White Hart Lane regulars demanded skill, deftness and subtlety, they got Andy Gray, Neil Ruddock and Jason Cundy, a trio of modestly gifted pros not hitherto renowned for the beauty of their technique. In keeping with the fans' habit of expecting miracles from mere mortals – Blanchflower, Greaves, Waddle – newcomer Darren Anderton, bought from Portsmouth for £1.7 million, was cast in the role of saviour. It was a heavy burden to impose on anyone's shoulders, let alone those of a teenager in only his second full season in the game. Few fans expected 1992–93 to feature many of the famed glory, glory days.

Tottenham fans were anxious about the lack of quality players in N17. So what else was new? Up the road at Barnet, a *real* crisis had been brewing over the summer. Several crises, in fact. First, manager Barry Fry had been sacked by larger-than-life club chairman Stan Flashman in the middle of the fourth-division play-offs, which would decide whether North London's most suburban outfit gained a second successive promotion. No sooner was Fry dismissed than he was reinstated following a revolt by his players, whose energies might have been better directed towards beating Blackpool the following Wednesday night. 'The sparks fly when Stan and I get together,' said Fry with considerable understatement. None of this was new: Fry and Flashman had broken up then made up umpteen times before. What *was* new, however, was Flashman's seemingly deliberate underpayment of his players' wages, which sent the entire first-team squad round to their chairman's Totteridge mansion demanding the balance. While such antics led wags to dub Barnet 'Football's Keystone Cops', and to constant ridicule in the press, the Football League had its eye on much more serious goings-on at the club. Alleged 'contractual irregularities' and illegal payments to players led the League to ban Barnet from dealing in the transfer market until the matter was settled. Some light relief was needed, and fast. The new season could not come soon enough at Underhill.

Down at Loftus Road, Queen's Park Rangers fans were looking forward to the action, too. Results the previous season had fitted Rangers' usual pattern – claiming the scalps of the two glamorous Uniteds, Leeds and Manchester, then losing heavily to no-marks such as Southampton and Chelsea. But a strong finish to the campaign seemed to justify club captain Ray Wilkins's belief that, 'We have seen the start of an exciting new era at Rangers. I think we could get among the honours next year.' Behind the talk of 'Rangers reborn' was a new spirit instilled by manager Gerry Francis, whose appointment the previous year had met with delight bordering on delirium among fans who remembered his exploits in the blue and white hooped No. 8 shirt during the 1970s. He sent out for the first game a team featuring many of the capital's brightest prospects, such as Les Ferdinand and Bradley Allen, the latest member of London's most famous football family. The only blight on a promising season was Rangers' traditional Achilles' heel: the lack of a decent crowd. This stubborn refusal of West Londoners to go and watch a team praised by many for playing the most entertaining football in the capital was highlighted by a statistic more telling than wins, draws or losses: the average attendance, 13,592.

Half a mile away, Ken Bates was finally proclaimed 'King of the Bridge'. 'It's home sweet home for Chelsea', trumpeted the *Daily Mirror* during the close-season as it announced that Bates's eight-year struggle to buy Stamford Bridge had, at last, ended in triumph. After endless public haggling with landlords Cabra Estates, the chairman paid a sum close to the original asking price of £22.85 million for the freehold of the ground. A master of the one-liner, Bates wryly described his quest as 'a saga lasting longer than Coronation Street'. A famous ground that once held 60,000 fans cheering on Osgood, Cooke and Hutchinson had, during the intervening trophy-less years, become London football's most unpopular venue. The pitch was too far away from much of the crowd, while the notorious Chelsea supporters were scarcely renowned for the warmth of their welcome to friend and foe alike.

Bates, however, had a vision for the future. In keeping with Lord Justice Taylor's urging that football grounds offer more than a fortnightly fixture, the Bridge was set to become 'a multi-million-pound, multi-purpose sports and leisure centre which will be the most exciting leisure site in London'. Determined to build a team that would restore Chelsea to their once illustrious position, Bates let manager Ian Porterfield splash out £3 million on a trio of new strikers.

Fulham v Bradford City on 2 May, the last day of the 1991–92 season, had seemed an anonymous and irrelevant match. Yet 8,671 fans paid to watch, some even forsaking their favourite team just to be there. It was an occasion steeped in football nostalgia: Fulham's last game at Craven Cottage, the charming Thames-side ground which had been home to the club since 1896. The turf, once graced by Johnny Haynes in his heyday and George Best in his decline, was due to be ripped up and replaced by 280 mock-Edwardian houses and flats. It didn't happen, though.

Instead, the ground's owners, Cabra Estates – soon to be ousted at Stamford Bridge – postponed their housing scheme, citing the recession-induced plunge in property prices as the reason why their plan had been put on ice. The Cottagers, resigned to becoming soccer nomads with no ground to call their own, had a home again – but only for a year, when their lease would finally expire. Away from the headlines about the club's precarious future, the mood was of quiet optimism. Fresh from being removed as manager at mega-rich Blackburn Rovers to make way for Kenny Dalglish, the much-travelled Don Mackay demolished the apathetic regime he had inherited from his predecessor Alan Dicks and took the team almost to the third-division play-offs. Even the club's magazine for malcontents, *There's Only One F in Fulham*, predicted a promising season ahead.

The result that had shattered Fulham's promotion dream was a 0–4 pasting at high noon one Sunday in late April by neighbours Brentford. The massacre at Griffin Park, watched by a sell-out 12,000 crowd, decided one other issue – that the Bees, for the first time since 1955, were back in the second division. Even better, the advent of the Premier League meant they had actually leapt into the *first* division. Promotion for Brentford was no accident. Rather it was the latest product of a long-term plan hatched by the chairman Martin Lange to turn the unfashionable club in the shadow of the M4 into a serious rival to Chelsea and QPR.

The key to the plan was stability, as witnessed by the reappearance of sponsor KLM's logo on the players' shirts for a record thirteenth unbroken year. At a time when clubs such as Arsenal were demolishing their kop to comply with Lord Justice Taylor, Brentford actually managed to increase their capacity to 14,250. On the first day of the new season, at home to Wolves, expectation among the all-ticket crowd was understandably high. But fears that the loss to Wimbledon of the thirty-eight-goal terrace hero, Dean Holdsworth, might prove costly grew after the Bees had crashed 0-2, a rude reminder that their hardest work was yet to be done.

If devotion was any yardstick, Wimbledon – Holdsworth's new home – should have shrivelled and died years ago. Rarely in the annals of English football had a club been so utterly unloved. The long-ball dogma first inflicted upon the Football League by manager Dave Bassett's self-styled 'Crazy Gang' in the early 1980s had earned the Dons a special kind of loathing. By August 1992, little had changed. A derisory 4,954 turned up for Wimbledon's first home game, albeit a Tuesday-night clash with anonymous Ipswich, prompting the *Daily Mirror* to run a photo of an empty terrace with the accusing headline, 'So this is the Premier League'.

Had the Dons been playing at Plough Lane, the ground which had witnessed their meteoric rise from Southern League to Premier League, they might have hoped for a few more fans to click through the turnstiles. The problem was, they weren't. They were beginning a second year of temporary residence at Selhurst Park, putting ten grand a game into the coffers of hated rivals – now landlords – Crystal Palace. If the Dons' few fans already suspected that there was a conspiracy against their team, conclusive proof of dark forces ranged in opposition appeared in the form of Merton Borough Council. Although the authority publicly professed to want Wimbledon back within its boundaries, its councillors had rejected four successive proposals for sites which the nomads could call home. Plough Lane, a poky little ground by a dog track in suburban SW19, was now obsolete. No matter that the Dons had played there since 1912; it simply didn't match up to the ambition of supremo Sam Hammam for his Wimbledon to complete an unlikely transformation from perpetual outsider into a respected member of the game's establishment. Splashing out a cool million on Dean Holdsworth seemed to show that Sam was serious.

But, within weeks, cold financial realism intruded. Thoughts of building a squad of stars were forgotten, as Hammam reluctantly admitted that every player had his price. A faxed £3 million formal bid for key striker John Fashanu, seriously entertained where all others had been binned, was the symbolic end of Hammam's struggle to fund high ambition with low income. Unsurprisingly, rumours of a merger with Palace re-emerged. For his part, the supremo vowed: 'I would rather die than merge Wimbledon. I would not be able to live with myself; my name would be tarnished throughout the world.'

One man already uncomfortably familiar with having his good name tarnished was Hammam's Crystal Palace counterpart, the outspoken Ron Noades. Derogatory comments about black players, aired early the previous season in a Channel 4 television documentary, had earned him instant notoriety and plunged a club noted for producing a steady stream of exciting black talent into by far the most serious crisis of its eighty-six-year history. Not the least of a number of violent reactions was that many of the Palace players – white as well as black – threatened to resign *en bloc*, and the FA considered charging Noades with bringing the game into disrepute.

As if the psychological trauma of what turned into an unpleasantly long-drawn-out affair was not enough, more trouble soon followed. Detectives from Scotland Yard's Fraud Squad visited Selhurst Park more than a dozen times, taking away account books and documents during an inquiry into the alleged disappearance of some £200,000 in proceeds from the Palace lottery; its manager, Graham Drew, was subsequently charged with 'lottery deceit'. No wonder one critic talked of Crystal Palace 'cracking up'. The simmering discontent at the club, poor results, and the sale of striker Ian Wright, took their toll at the turnstiles as well. Attendances dropped perilously close to four figures – prompting Ron Noades to castigate the stay-aways for 'disloyalty'.

All was not gloom, however. There was the Palace juniors' appearance in the final of the FA Youth Cup. And, when England was selected as host nation for the 1996 European Championships, pride in SE25 swelled with the unexpected choice of Selhurst Park as one of the venues. For the sole remaining pride *of* SE25, midfielder Geoff Thomas, the close-season seemed to promise lucrative pastures new. Arsenal and Blackburn Rovers both wanted to sign him. The Gunners offered £2.5 million; Ron Noades demanded £3m. Where George Graham cooled, Kenny Dalglish cooed. A £3 million deal to bring Thomas to Ewood Park was lined up. But fate intervened in the shape of the Premier League's fixture computer. Out popped Palace v Rovers, 15 August, first game of the season. Football being football, Rovers won without him, Thomas played a stinker, and the deal fell apart. It really was a nightmare start, Brian.

In the decaying former dockland of South-East London, meanwhile, Millwall were embarking on the last of their eighty-three seasons at the Den. As a football ground, its day had long gone. Sandwiched between rows of Victorian terraces and the train lines into Waterloo East, its reputation as one of the bloodiest battlegrounds for feuding London fans had been overtaken by frustration at its sheer impracticality. The poor view of the pitch, for example, generally prompted anything from dozens to hundreds of fans to save their cash and instead watch the variable standard of entertainment for free from a grassy bank behind the Den's exposed south-east corner.

After this campaign, the Lions were due to start afresh in a purpose-built, 20,000-seat stadium half a mile down the road at Senegal Fields – again, part-financed by the fans. Just as Canary Wharf across the Thames was billed as a beacon of economic revitalisation, so Millwall's new ground was a model of football planning for the year 2000 and beyond. 'The absolute dog's,' as they say in that part of London. All it needed was a team to sustain top-flight football there. That task fell to Mick McCarthy, who had replaced Bruce Rioch as manager in March 1992 after the Lions suffered a humiliating 1–6 defeat at Portsmouth. Despite maintaining a squad of players as large as that at Old Trafford, Millwall's form was erratic and they had finished in fifteenth place – not the most encouraging position from which to launch a bid for Premier League status.

While Millwall had a spanking new ground to look

forward to, hapless Charlton Athletic began the season without a home to call their own. Like Wimbledon, Charlton were nomads, sharing Upton Park for a second season, and suffering at the turnstiles as a result. Only 5,000 regularly made the fortnightly hike through the Blackwall Tunnel, just half the number who used to watch the team when they had last played at their spiritual home, the Valley, way back in 1986. Throughout the years of exile, this hard core had stayed loyal to a club torn from its roots. Their dream was to see the Valiants back at a ground which had once held more than 70,000 fans, but more recently had been condemned by the fire brigade, the police and the local authority as too dangerous to use. But proof that dreams do sometimes come true, even in football, arrived early in the season. Charlton's chairman, Roger Alwen, announced that the club had managed to raise enough money finally to reopen the Valley, and named the day, 6 December. After countless false dawns, this time it was for real – thanks to the generosity of their loyal fans, who had contributed more than £1 million through the Valley Investment Plan. Although at first it seemed that only the two ends of the ground would be reopened, gone were the worries of the slow death by financial strangulation which would have occurred if Charlton had been forced to stay at Upton Park.

That triumph against the odds was remarkable enough; what happened next *on* the pitch was almost as unlikely. A year earlier, the departure of long-time manager Lennie Lawrence – who used to perform an annual miracle by keeping the club in the first division on a shoestring budget – had led to predictions that Charlton would fall into a rapid spiral of decline. In August 1992, however, the new managerial duo of Steve Gritt and Alan Curbishley, both promoted straight from the playing staff, were in charge of a team at the top of the table . . . if only for a fortnight.

Events on and off the park combined to make Charlton a rare beacon of success, when the mood of football almost everywhere else was growing increasingly sombre.

TWO

Sky's the Limit?

BSkyB, and the 'Whole New Ball Game'

The 1992–93 season kicked off on 15 August amid the sort of sunshine that the first day of a fresh campaign always seems to bring. Although fans filed into grounds in time-honoured tradition, some wearing T-shirts and shorts, many talking up their team's chances way beyond the realistic or the rational, the general atmosphere within football was, however, curiously downbeat. Less than two months before, an England side lacking the inspiration of Paul Gascoigne had caught an early plane back to Luton from the European Championships in Sweden after three utterly miserable performances and one scraped goal. Yet absurdly that ignominy did not stop BSkyB from billing 15 August as the start of a bright new dawn in English football – 'A Whole New Ball Game', as their brash adverts put it. Their friends in the tabloid press, who should have known better after condemning England's stumblings in Scandinavia, joined in the frenetic hype.

Just as supporters took what they read on the back pages with a large dose of salt, so many Premier League managers voiced their anxieties about the new set-up. Queen's Park Rangers boss Gerry Francis, for example, protested long and hard in the pre-season build-up about his team becoming the first victim of that new incarnation, 'Monday Night Football'. Exercising their costly acquired right to meddle with the fixture-list to accommodate the station's apparently insatiable desire for live games, BSkyB ordained that Rangers would play their first match of the season more than forty-eight hours after everyone else, away at Manchester City. Francis was incensed – his players were scheduled to meet Southampton just two days later, and would have little time to recharge their batteries – but he was powerless to act. He fumed at the unfairness of foisting such a schedule upon his players so early in the season, and would doubtless have sympathised with the view of one cynical fan that BSkyB had the Premier League fixture-list in roughly the same sort of grasp that Vinnie Jones had been so infamously captured demonstrating on Paul Gascoigne a few seasons previously.

Then Francis widened his complaint to the structure of the Premier League in general, which he lambasted as a wasted opportunity to engineer lasting, beneficial change. 'We had a chance here to put the game right for the next five years, but they've blown it,' he lamented. 'There will be saturation television coverage, and football will end up like snooker. No one will want to watch it.'

No amount of BSkyB publicity could disguise the fact that, while root-and-branch revolution had been necessary in English football, the only things which had actually changed by 15 August were the names of the four divisions. As David Lacey pointed out in the *Guardian*, 'The Premier League is nothing more than a costume drama working from a borrowed script. An assortment of fairly ordinary players will appear in new colours, having changed clubs for fees compared to which soccer's previous extravagances were mild bouts of impulse buying.' The Professional Footballers' Association secretary, Gordon

Taylor, also viewed the Premier League as mutton dressed up as lamb. He reminded those in the game that the new structure had ostensibly been created to improve the standard of football, but instead was being used as little more than a means of making money. 'The last twelve months have seen too heavy an emphasis on the commercial aspects,' he warned. 'We have lost sight in the end of what any Premier League should have been about, which is quality.' The fans, characteristically, were more blunt about the fare due to be offered up: 'Same old shit, different shirts.'

Suspicions that the league was primarily geared towards making money grew with the announcement of massive price rises by almost all its twenty-two clubs. In the past, fans had always accepted that, as addictions go, football could never be relied upon to provide the guaranteed high of other more conventional stimulants. Buy a bottle of single malt Scotch or some high-purity cocaine, and you know what you're getting for your money. The Saturday afternoon fix is different, though; its intrinsic unpredictability can delight or depress. Every regular knows that each season will have its ups and downs – perhaps a shock 4–0 win over Manchester United one week, then a home defeat by non-league opposition in the Cup the next – but mostly it is a wearisome slog through an unchanging, often mundane routine of forgettable matches. Historically, however, football's relative cheapness had always ensured that this mysteriously enduring habit was passed on through the generations. But the advent of the Premier League, which saw Stamford Bridge usher in the era of the £30 seat, threatened to end this tradition. Gordon Taylor was among those who warned that fans simply could not afford such dramatically hiked-up prices, and he reminded the game's authorities that spectators still poured more money into football through the turnstiles and souvenir shops than any sponsor ever could. 'It is important to remember that last year, in a recession, spectators contributed £120 million-plus in gate receipts to the Football League,' he pointed out. 'Grateful though the game should be for BSkyB's commitment, the fans' figure is still far in advance of that and any other sponsor. Quite clearly, the game hasn't got too many laurels to rest on and really needs to get its act together and make sure that spectators are going to get value for money.'

Taylor's alarm at a potential haemorrhage in live support stemmed from the fact that, at all seven of London's Premier League clubs, the cost of the cheapest adult non-member's seat had risen by anything from a just-above-inflation 5 per cent (Arsenal) to a whopping 50 per cent (Crystal Palace). 'It's pure greed', blasted Craig Brewin, chairman of the Football Supporters' Association, the organisation recognised by the government as the official voice of the fans. 'It's totally indefensible to put up prices like this on top of the money they get from television. Ground improvements have given them the excuse, but they are getting more from television than they ever dreamt of'.

The tabloids also condemned the increases; the *Sunday Mirror*, for example, ran a 'Fair Play for Fans' campaign, and enlisted the all-party Parliamentary Football Committee to table a motion in the House of Commons deploring what they saw as moves which would price many fans away from football. Even the *Sunday Times* believed the issue was sufficiently important to devote one of its influential editorials to the subject. 'The capacity of football clubs to shoot themselves in the foot appears limitless,' it thundered. 'Their latest lunacy is the decision of the clubs which make up the new Premier League to hike up the gate prices for their long-suffering supporters, just as they have become the beneficiaries of the biggest television deal in British sports history. This is not merely greedy. It is also stupid and self-defeating: football appears to be intent on pricing itself out of the entertainment market.' The paper gave an example of the rapidly rising cost of watching football compared to another popular activity, cinema-going. 'To take two teenagers to Chelsea next season, in the cheapest seats, will cost more than £50. To take them to the nearby Chelsea Cinema, in the King's Road, costs less than £15. The cinema's most expensive ticket is £4.50. The football club's cheapest standing ticket is £10.' And it quoted Terry Neill, the former Arsenal and Tottenham manager, and one of the senior statesmen of London football, who remarked pithily: 'I see more renovations of hospitality suites, boardrooms and guest-rooms than improvements for the people who are the lifeblood of the game, the fans on the terrace and in the stand.' Commenting on close-season rises of 56 per cent for the best seats at Queen's Park Rangers, Neill jibed: 'Look at that, that's not worth the money – I'd rather go and play golf.' Evidence that thousands of London fans felt the same way was just around the corner.

Despite the mounting dissatisfaction among supporters, the twenty-two clubs in the Premier League were still apparently united by common financial interest. Or at least that was the theory. But the opening of the season was overshadowed by a fresh outbreak of the feuding which had led to the formation of a breakaway league in the first place: arguments about the division of the spoils. A self-styled 'Platinum Collection', ultimately comprising eight of the league's richest clubs – Arsenal, Manchester United, Liverpool, Everton, Aston Villa, Nottingham Forest, Leeds United and QPR – had hatched a plan to introduce Continental-style revolving perimeter advertising at their grounds. With every club in the Premier League set to enjoy unprecedented wealth from their membership of the new élite, surely it wasn't out of order for eight of them to cash in further on the cachet of their name?

The other fourteen clubs, however, saw it differently. They feared that this plan would, in effect, create a 'league within a league', based essentially on wealth. Sam Hammam, supremo of hard-up Wimbledon – with annual gate receipts of just £700,000 – summed up their disgruntlement when he stated, 'I have always believed that Arsenal and Liverpool were our big brothers, that we could look up to them and respect them. I am devastated that we appear not to be one big family.' Within a few tense weeks, though, the 'Platinum Collection' scheme fell apart. Although the Premier League had promised to dispense with the traditional acrimony over the way the rewards were divided between the richer and poorer clubs – the age-old blight on the game – this episode clearly showed it was as distant a prospect as ever. The FA's 'Blueprint' had so grandiosely declared: 'The end of the power struggle will bring with it the dawn of a new era of progress and development throughout the game.' The *Guardian's* David Lacey noted the intention but added tartly: 'Not much sign of daylight yet.' New set-up; same old rows.

Two more rows followed, both reinforcing the general impression that the collaborators, having pulled off their coup, were now busy stabbing each other in the back. The first concerned a sponsor for the Premier League. In theory, this should have been one of the major new money-spinners – Bass and Ford were among those interested in coming up with the £10 million required – but conflicts of interest with some of the clubs' individual sponsors soon materialised. Liverpool and Nottingham

Forest objected to Bass as both were already backed by brewers, while Coventry were against Ford as they were supported by a rival car manufacturer. Once again, the eight 'Platinum Collection' clubs acted in concert to ensure that neither the brewing giant nor the car company won the contract. QPR chairman Richard Thompson said the league was worth more than was being offered: 'I felt we were selling the league too cheaply. The way we worked it out, it was worth little more than £85,000 to each club'. Both Bass and Ford were duly rejected and the Arsenal vice-chairman, David Dein, recommended an urgent search for a non-conflicting sponsor. Thus, when the Premier League kicked off on 15 August, deprived of a well-known backer, the only initials placed in front of the competition's name were, rather appropriately, FA.

If it was easy to understand the twenty-two clubs' failure to agree on a package worth £10 million, it was harder to fathom BSkyB's insistence on screening live Gazza's early-season debut for his new club, Lazio of Italy, in a friendly against his former outfit, Tottenham. Rightly hoping to catch the nation's interest in the long-awaited return from horrendous injury of English football's only genuine superstar, BSkyB paid for the privilege of beaming every kick of the match in Rome on 23 September – giving no heed whatsoever to the long-standing tradition, honoured thus far by both broadcasters and the FA, that no live games be shown on any Wednesday when fixtures in a domestic competition were being played. This tacit agreement was designed to maintain the attraction of football seen from the terraces, not the armchair. But BSkyB, in their ravenous hunger to show as much soccer as possible, regardless of its relevance, demonstrated their contempt for such gentlemen's agreements. They even went to the High Court to win the right to screen the match, arguing that 'People have been waiting for seventeen months to see Gascoigne's comeback. And if we couldn't show it, then all the emotion that goes with that wouldn't have been seen.' The FA, furious but impotent, retaliated by threatening to pull the plug on a proposed five-year, £72-million deal with BSkyB to show all of England's games at Wembley and one FA Cup-tie per round. Trevor Phillips, the Association's commercial director, felt they had been betrayed. The High Court legal battle 'makes you think twice about doing a deal with someone who takes you to court at the drop of a hat,' he said. 'I now have an uneasy feeling about signing contracts with them.'

The row appeared trivial – protecting attendances at that night's Coca-Cola League Cup games against what Phillips called 'a meaningless friendly' – and was certainly unseemly. However, its true significance lay in its status as an undeclared test case of the power relationships within the game's new order. BSkyB's victory served as a sharp illustration to the bureaucrats of Lancaster Gate that their days of omnipotence were fading fast, and gave them a rude reminder that, despite the £304-million deal with their supposed allies at the satellite channel, the tough-talkers in charge at Sky Sports were ruthlessly pursuing interests which only spasmodically coincided with those of the sport's historic guardians. If the Gazza row had been a football match, the final score would have read: BSkyB 2 FA 0.

Over at Highbury, Arsenal manager George Graham added his voice to those expressing reservations. Asked in an interview whether he thought the Premier League would be a success he replied bluntly, 'No.' He regretted the lost opportunity to slim down the top flight to just sixteen or eighteen teams, believing that skill would suffer and fans would get disillusioned with mediocrity. He highlighted the danger as 'too much football. We have four domestic competitions while, in the rest of Europe, they only have two. Nothing has changed in England – and the product will suffer. People in the game want quality, not quantity.'

His views were undoubtedly coloured by the sobering experience less than a year before of having seen Arsenal, the then English champions, crash out of the European Cup to Benfica at only the second-round stage. A 1–1 draw in the famous Stadium of Light had given the Gunners some cause for optimism. But a 1–3 humiliation at Highbury, with his side totally outclassed, provided Graham – an ambitious man who craved success for his team at the highest level – with a stark illustration of how far the domestic game had to improve before its representatives could compete with the best on the Continent. Graham was furious that Arsenal's aspirations of becoming heirs to the glorious European tradition established by Glasgow Celtic, Manchester United and Liverpool had been ruined by the short-term, self-interested determination of most Premier League chairmen to play twenty-one money-spinning home games – a marathon-like league programme wisely avoided by the rest of Europe. 'We are sacrificing the product for finance,' he railed. 'Little wonder', said the Arsenal boss, 'the foreigners think we are crazy in playing the number of games we do.'

His words were echoed by Howard Wilkinson, the plain-speaking and highly regarded manager of Leeds United, whose players were now carrying the tattered standard of English football in the European Champions' Cup. But a 0–3 reverse in the first round in Stuttgart to the German champions – only three days after a further example of sensitive BSkyB scheduling had compelled Leeds to face Aston Villa in a televised league tussle – gave a clear indication that the skewed priorities in

English football's new order were causing chaos. 'We are playing far too many matches. The situation is bloody ridiculous,' opined Wilkinson. He blamed the two goals conceded in the final stages of the Stuttgart on the sheer tiredness of his players, who were already knackered after playing eight high-pressure games in the previous month. Even worse, he felt moved to warn that much of the football Leeds had to play 'is of such a breakneck, physical, intimidating nature that I cannot believe the players will survive a whole season of it'.

An appalling casualty list comprising some of the Premier League's biggest names bore Wilkinson out: in the first month alone, Manchester United's Dion Dublin and Everton's Mark Ward both suffered broken legs; Chelsea's Paul Elliott found his season ended due to severe knee ligament damage; and Sheffield Wednesday's England centre-forward David Hirst missed a month's action from a cracked ankle bone. Peter Reid, Manchester City's pugnacious player-manager, and no stranger to midfield tussling, pulled no punches: 'Nowadays, everything is so fast and frenetic. Some games are more of a battle than a football match.'

Like George Graham and Howard Wilkinson, Eamon Dunphy's views on the game were formed in the late 1960s and early 1970s, widely believed to be the most recent golden age in English football – a period when all three were playing, with varying degrees of success. Even allowing for a touch of dewy-eyed nostalgia, this was an era when full-backs never ventured beyond the half-way line, wing-halves had time and space to create, and centre-forwards *always* wore the No.9 shirt. Football still kicked off at three o'clock on Saturday, and the game's administrators would have been shot if they had allowed FA Cup-ties to be staged on Sunday afternoon or Monday night.

Dunphy, a stylish midfielder with Charlton and Millwall and capped twenty-three times for the Republic of Ireland, took up journalism when his playing career ended. Not for him, however, the Emlyn Hughes-style ghosted condemnations of modern football so often found in the tabloids. He established his reputation in 1976 with *Only a Game? The Diary of a Professional Footballer*, a vivid insider's account of Millwall, since regarded as the definitive portrait of a season at a club. More recently, *A Strange Kind of Glory* allowed him to examine past and present at Manchester United, through the personality of Sir Matt Busby. Looking back, Dunphy is appalled when he compares the football on offer today with what he, George Graham – nicknamed 'The Stroller' for his languid, intelligent contribution to Arsenal's double-winning side of 1970–71 – and Wilkinson would remember. He derides contemporary football as the equivalent of the no-brand goods found on the bargain shelves of supermarkets: 'In Ireland, we call such things "yellow-pack", meaning cheap and standard. Yellow-pack peas, yellow-pack tea, yellow-pack football.'

To Dunphy, the whole notion of the Premier League as raising quality is laughable. In his opinion, élitism in football is good, because it sets continually higher standards; the problem is that a twenty-two-team division which includes both lowly Wimbledon and would-be European champions such as Manchester United cannot justly be termed an élite. The result of a forty-two game slog is that mediocrity – lowest-common-denominator football – triumphs. 'The structure of the Premier League is against élitism,' Dunphy believes. 'There seems to be a caucus of people who want to hurt Liverpool, Arsenal, Manchester United, Spurs – the great clubs. And if the great clubs are hurt, if the Premier League has to be run in a certain way simply so that Wimbledon can stay in it, then it has to be no good.'

His caustic comments reflect a conscious harking-back to a bygone age. However, in demeaning Wimbledon, the whipping-boys of English football, Dunphy clearly did not appreciate what had come to appear to be the one definite achievement of the Premier League so far: that the for-once equitable distribution of the money involved was helping produce the most evenly balanced and open contest between the top clubs for years. 'You may say that's anti-romantic,' he adds, referring to the Dons' amazing ascent from non-league obscurity to the top flight within a mere handful of years. 'I am, in fact, deeply romantic about soccer. But what's good for Wimbledon can't possibly be good for Manchester United. And what matters for the future of English football is Manchester United, not Wimbledon.'

Like Gerry Francis, Dunphy believes that the chance to make lasting beneficial changes to the game was wasted. His opinion is that the twenty-two-club structure of the Premier League dictates the style of football most teams must adopt simply to get through the season. 'If the league was administered wisely,' he says, 'then those who run it would see that the system works against skill and free expression, so therefore the system must be changed.' Dunphy demands one amendment above all: 'I would like to see a Premier League with sixteen clubs.'

Little more than a month into the 'Whole New Ball Game', even David Dein – who had been the driving force behind the creation of the Premier League – was forced to admit that things were not turning out as expected. 'The end product so far,' he told the *Mail on Sunday*, in an article headlined "New world to civil war in just six weeks", 'is nowhere near what we had hoped. Naturally, we are disappointed.' He, too, regretted the lost opportunity to create a slimline league designed to achieve what its proponents had sought from the start: a set-up which was 'in the best interests of football and the national team'. Dein did not hide his disgust that the motivations which had inspired the breakaway had now been consigned to the dustbin. Perhaps significantly, he also let slip his opinion that the goal was still 'a reduced league with strict criteria' – an ominous hint that a further convulsive shake-up, again initiated by the big clubs, and intended to set football on a progressive path once and for all, might not be far away.

At the same time, the premonition expressed by George Graham and Gerry Francis – that too much football, especially of the erratic, high-cost variety, would sap the fans' enthusiasm for attending the live event – appeared to be coming true. Figures for the first six Saturdays of the season showed that crowds were down by 11.7 per cent compared to the first division a year before. The fall was all the more alarming because, for five years previously, football had been steadily winning back its paying customers. Crowds had been going up since 1986; now, in mid-September 1992, they were suddenly falling again. The average attendance, 19,895, was the first time in five seasons it had dipped below 20,000. Club chairmen were at pains to deny that the drop was due either to the hefty price rises many had seen fit to impose at their grounds in the close-season; to the game's drastically reduced exposure thanks to its link-up with satellite TV; or, heaven forbid, to public recognition that the 'Whole New Ball Game' was no improvement on the old one. Declining to acknowledge these danger signs, they instead took the easy option and simply blamed the recession. Yet that analysis ignored the statistics for division one, two and three of the cast-off Barclays League, which showed crowds *up*, in the second division by no less than 11.5 per cent.

Rick Parry, notably, failed to share in the Premier League chairmen's complacency. He expressed his disappointment at the figures for the top flight, but said he hoped that the twenty-two members would now set their differences aside and unite to confront the problem. 'We have been given the chance of a brand new start and the opportunity to put right all that was wrong before, and so far we are not achieving,' he admitted. Another Parry comment was more cryptic, however: 'When you are up to your neck in alligators, it's difficult to remember you were there to drain the swamp.' What could he mean? Sadly, he didn't identify exactly to whom this intriguing remark referred, though more than a few chairmen will have wondered if they were being cast as Parry's snappers.

A day later, worse news followed. Not only were fewer people handing over good money to witness Premier League action, research showed that neither were they sitting at home or in pubs, watching it on BSkyB. 'It's a turn-off,' rand the back-page headline in the *Evening Standard*, above a story showing that, despite the massive advertising campaign, satellite football was drawing pitifully small numbers of viewers. The season before, ITV's *The Match* programme had regularly pulled in audiences of more than eight million for live first-division games. BSkyB, by contrast, attracted a mere 468,000 viewers for the first ever Premier League clash screened live on a Sunday afternoon, Nottingham Forest v Liverpool. It was not exactly an auspicious kick-off for the 'Whole New Ball Game'. An early-season nadir was reached when Middlesbrough and Sheffield United, despite the added attraction of dancing girls and fireworks, pulled in a mediocre 107,000. To be fair to BSkyB, its awful viewing figures were largely due to the fact that only 14 per cent of homes in Britain possessed a dish. But even if every man, woman and child in every dish-owning house in the land had been tuned in, the inescapable truth was that the maximum possible audience was 6.5 million. It was a statistic which led many to ask the obvious question: why, if satellite TV's penetration was so low, had the Premier League done a deal with them in the first place? How could the next generation of fans be enthused about the game if so few were able to watch it on television? Once again, those in charge of football were sacrificing long-term health for short-term wealth.

In contrast, the BBC's revamped *Match of the Day* programme on Saturday night, featuring a package of highlights from three of that day's games, was drawing 4.5 million. Spurned by the Premier League, ITV had ended up able to offer only action from the Barclays League; but even LWT's Sunday-afternoon *The London Match* – seen only in the capital and featuring such dubious delights as Luton v Watford – consistently earned higher ratings than BSkyB's much-hyped glamour ties. One Sunday early in the new season, LWT's screening of West Ham v Derby drew 870,000 viewers, almost twice as many as the 465,000 who tuned in to the Manchester City v Chelsea game on BSkyB – even though the proceedings at Upton Park were televised solely in the London area.

However, three weeks into the campaign, the Sunday afternoon head-to-head contest between ITV and BSkyB had turned into a three-way battle. Totally undetected, Channel 4 had stolen in and landed the right to show live matches from Italy's *Serie A*. A station whose previous football experience extended no further than the Women's FA Cup and the African Nations Cup had struck a deal to screen live action from what is generally regarded as the finest league in the world – and a snip at the cost of £1.5 million per year. Where BSkyB had Vinnie Jones and Tony Adams, Channel 4 now boasted Baggio, Papin, Van Basten and, of course, Paul Gascoigne. Zappers in hand, armchair fans were suddenly spoiled for choice; they would become judge and jury in the ultimate footballing free market. It was no contest: many viewers quickly decided that they preferred Continental flair and finesse to the breakneck battles regularly witnessed on English fields, and some two million regularly turned to Channel 4 each Sunday afternoon. Any thought that Italian football would appeal solely to the cappuccino-drinking pseuds among London's trendier-than-thou élite disappeared when that week's exploits of AC Milan and Juventus joined the royals, the recession and immigration as the favourite conversational gambits of the capital's taxi drivers.

The early results of this ongoing three-way contest must have alarmed the executives at BSkyB's HQ in unfashionable Isleworth, underneath the Heathrow flight path. It is almost impossible to exaggerate just how vital Sky Sports' massive investment in Premier League football was to the very survival of the innovative satellite station. A year before, its coup of winning exclusive rights to show the 1991 cricket World Cup from Australia had done wonders for sales of dishes; now it was expecting an even bigger breakthrough. At the same time, however, there was no doubting BSkyB's genuine enthusiasm to present football – and lots of it – in a totally new style, which owed much to the razzmatazz of American sports broadcasting and nothing at all to what BSkyB saw as the staid, outdated presentation offered by the BBC and ITV. It promised 'a brave new era in television coverage'. David Hill, BSkyB's Head of Sport, said the station had an ambitious target: 'We want to educate, inform and explain, as well as question, amuse and entertain.'

Suggestions that BSkyB was most interested in amusing

and entertaining appeared to be borne out by its treatment of the first 'Monday Night Football' transmission from the capital, an Arsenal v Manchester City clash at the end of September. Sky Sports had promised that such occasions would serve up 'spectacular family entertainment at the grounds as well as for armchair viewers'. And so it came to pass at Highbury that evening: former Page Three pin-up Sam Fox took part in a pre-match penalty shoot-out. Cartoon hero Bart Simpson turned up and did the Bartman, his signature tune. As he mimed, the Sky Strikers, a troupe of dancing cheerleaders apparently dressed for an energetic aerobics class, showed off their latest steps; they were met by inevitable chants of 'Get your tits out for the lads' and, because they were wearing blue, white and yellow, 'Are you Tottenham in disguise?'

Half-time brought fireworks, the return of the Sky Strikers – obviously undaunted by their coarse reception earlier – and the arrival of the Shamen. These four earnest and drably-attired young musicians, then top of the charts with their elliptical drug homage 'Ebeneezer Goode', appeared on the pitch to mime to their hit, only to be met by derisive choruses of 'What a load of rubbish' and 'Who're the wankers in the black?'

This, in all its glory, was a perfect illustration of BSkyB's vision of the future of football. One Highbury regular remarked, at least half-seriously, that the booing of the band was the loudest noise he had heard in N5 since Arsenal last won the league. He, like almost everyone in the ground, was unimpressed with the half-time show; it seemed to him an unwelcome reminder of the 1970s, when football's powers-that-be made risible attempts to persuade potential trouble-makers that watching a marching band, motorcycle display or dogs jumping through burning hoops really was more fun than laying into opposing supporters. 'Not one person went to a game then to see such vacuous trash, and nobody goes now to see a pop group or a Sky Striker,' he snorted. 'Those things don't add one iota to the entertainment.'

Oh yes, and there was a game as well. But it wasn't very good. Writing in the match programme, George Graham had hardly fired up the fans' enthusiasm for the ensuing clash when he admitted with refreshing honesty: 'I'd like to promise a TV spectacular tonight. I'd be dishonest if I did.' He attributed his low expectations to the unexpectedly poor start to the season made by the Gunners and City, both of whom had finished the previous campaign strongly. Graham's candour proved well founded: the dismal quality of the action prompted one journalist, Donal Conaty of the *Irish Times*, to observe: 'The football was hard and fast but also tedious, as the frantic pace forced errors. Towards the end, it left one or two players looking as ungainly as three-legged mules in a race.'

Conaty's commentary was interesting, because he had not gone to Highbury that wet and windy Monday night simply to report the match, but to stand on the Clock End and check the health of English football's 'Whole New Ball Game'. His diagnosis doubted the patient's vitality. The football, he said, 'should have been exciting. This was Highbury – home to one of the truly great English clubs. It was a Premier League match – and the Premier League was supposed to deliver quality football. As Arsenal emerged with a deserved victory, the view from the terrace was bleak. Fans could be forgiven for thinking that they were witnessing the slow, certain death of soccer – with Bart Simpson dancing attendance.'

Maybe it was the weather. Maybe it was the fact that the game was live on BSkyB. Or maybe the fans were flummoxed by the still novel phenomenon of

Monday-night football. Whatever the reason, only 21,504 spectators felt compelled to part with their money. Even given the ground's drastically reduced capacity of 29,000 because of building work, it was a pretty poor turn-out – 13,505 down on the same fixture the previous season.

The goings-on at Highbury were certainly less than thrilling, both on and off the pitch. But they left fans in no doubt that football had been yanked – perhaps literally – into an era where no expense was spared trying to reinvent every game as 'spectacular family entertainment'; where BSkyB's coverage of a ninety-minute tussle somehow stretched to fill a five-hour programme; and where the week's action was deemed fascinating enough to justify its dissection and debate every day for the next seven days. The Arsenal v Manchester City encounter did, however, provide some genuine amusement, albeit after the event. Inspired by the Highbury debut of the Sky Strikers, the next issue of the Arsenal fanzine *One-Nil Down, Two-One Up* published a full-page, *Private Eye*-style piss-take of all things BSkyB. 'That Sky TV schedule in full!', ran its headline. Underneath, it spoofed a typical week's football viewing on BSkyB thus:

SUPER SUNDAY, 12 noon-midnight: Sky pads out twelve hours with special reports on 'the groundsman's grass cuttings' and 'the ref's half-time cuppa', followed by LIVE AND EXCLUSIVE coverage of a top Premier League fixture – OLDHAM v EVERTON. With Richard Keys and Andy Gray. Sponsored by Ford and Fosters: 'Drinking and driving, you know it makes sense.'
MONDAY: San Marino v Canvey Island LIVE AND EXCLUSIVE.
TUESDAY, 9 pm-everybody gets fed up and goes home: 'The Footballers' Football Show'. Four cerebrally-challenged personalities (managers, players, tabloid hacks

etc.) get round a table and waffle on for hours, where the following questions are posed: Did any of these people go to school? Are they all pissed or what? Host – Richard Keys.

WEDNESDAY: Canvey Island v San Marino – the return fixture LIVE AND EXCLUSIVE.

THURSDAY: 'The Bootroom'. Andy Gray and Richard Keys play draughts on a Subbuteo pitch and pretend it's something to do with football.

FRIDAY: 'Pro-Celebrity game'. Richard Keys and Andy Gray lead the Sky Scrubbers against Canvey Island/San Marino Select XI.

SATURDAY: RICHARD KEYS's and ANDY GRAY's day off. Sally Gunnell takes over live and exclusive etc., etc.

Unbeknown to its authors, this amusing fantasy schedule bore an uncanny resemblance to a genuine BSkyB document which they could never have seen. A press release, headlined 'Soccer Seven-Days-A-Week: Programming Plans for Season 1992–93', had been dispensed to journalists attending the station's glamorous media launch at the Grosvenor House Hotel – a function to which mere club fanzine editors were definitely not invited. In fact, upon inspection of both 'schedules', the main difference between them appeared to be *One-Nil Down*'s underestimation of just how many shows really would be hosted by the previously low-profile Mr Richard Keys.

Clearly, there could be little doubt that the satellite channel was planning abundant coverage. The station proudly boasted that, as well as 'exploring new avenues in broadcast technology and giving the viewer more choice and input', it would be screening 'more football than could ever have been imagined just a few years ago. This coming season, Sky Sports will show more live football than British viewers have ever had before, with sixty live matches on Sundays and Mondays from the all-new FA Premier League.'

While BSkyB made a virtue of the sheer *quantity* of its coverage, the station's critics argued that this would be at the expense of the *quality* of the action. Gerry Francis, George Graham and Howard Wilkinson had quickly made known their fears on this score, as summed up in the QPR manager's warning that saturation coverage would leave football as overexposed as snooker: 'No one will want to watch it.' Although it was hard to disagree with the opinion of three such eminent figures, it had to be remembered that they were speaking on the basis of gut instinct, albeit complemented by decades of experience. Interestingly, a similar view, but this time the product of more than twenty years spent in market research, came from an unlikely source: the smart Charlotte Street offices of advertising giant Saatchi & Saatchi.

Alex Fynn, who joined Saatchis in 1971, has become one of the game's most quixotic observers. A Newcastle United fan since the era of Jackie Milburn, the deadly centre-forward whose photograph adorns his office to this day, Fynn was lucky enough to find his professional life and personal passion for football beginning to merge in 1982. It was then that he became involved with Tottenham, helping to plan a TV advertising campaign to encourage the public along to White Hart Lane, a technique which had never been tried before. The scheme was the first of many footballing innovations with which Fynn has been associated. He quickly established himself as the leading authority on one of the 1980s' major growth industries, the spiralling value of live football to television; in that capacity, he has advised both Arsenal and the Football League. By 1991, Fynn – whose proposal for a European Super League had found favour with UEFA and been detailed in a book, *The Secret Life of Football* – was the FA's obvious choice to write the all-important commercial section of its revolutionary 'Blueprint for the Future of Football', which led directly to the breakaway Premier League.

An engaging enthusiast whose contempt for football's rulers knows few bounds, Fynn concedes that his maxim throughout his advertising career – that 'the consumer is not a moron' – has special difficulties when applied to football. The trouble, he acknowledges, is that fans disprove his golden rule because they exhibit unique brand loyalty in supporting their team through thick and thin. That, however, does not mean that the tolerance of supporters, their willingness to put up with being miserably treated and poorly entertained, is infinite. Football *can* escape the consequences of treating its consumers like morons, but it *cannot* ignore the fact that, like any other commercial enterprise, it depends on repeat business. This, says Fynn, leads a marketing man to look at the game in a different way to a football administrator and conclude that: 'In football, you have to respect your audience, which is primarily the paying fan, and that means giving them what they want. The first thing to do is to find out what the fans want, but nobody in football has done that. Making an educated guess, what the fans want are: entertaining football, played in a safe environment; not to pay through the nose for it; and to be treated as a respected customer should be treated.'

Fynn's thesis is an implicit challenge to BSkyB's philosophy, because he firmly believes that fans desire *quality* from their football, not just a vast *quantity* of it. The only way to achieve this, he suggests, is to have fewer matches than at present, but games which are both meaningful and relevant. In an unconscious echo of boyhood memories fondly recalled, Fynn often refers to something which seemed always to exist then but is too frequently missing now: the 'event-like quality that is present – or *should* be present – in all football. With an event comes scarcity value, because you can't have an event if it's commonplace. What we need are more events and fewer non-events. Arsenal v Spurs, for example, is both a local derby and a major national event. But Arsenal v Sheffield United is a complete non-event.' The familiarity born of a forty-two-game Premier League campaign breeds understandable contempt.

Fynn's concern is that *all* of football may suffer because of what he regards as an historic misjudgement, that is, the Premier League chairmen's decision to back a 'never mind the quality, feel the width' policy. 'Every manager of every major club, and Graham Taylor and Gary Lineker, said a twenty-two-club division was nonsense. They were all ignored.' One of the nineteen chairmen who vetoed a reduction in size was Wimbledon's supremo, Sam Hammam. Curiously, when a record low crowd of just 3,386 bothered to turn up for the Dons' early-season clash with Oldham – a measly attendance prompting headlines such as 'Home Alone' – Hamman was uncharacteristically lost for words.

THREE

American Football?

Arsenal, David Dein and the 'total leisure experience'

Where the FA had a 'Blueprint for the Future of Football', David Dein has something much grander: he has a *vision*. Typical of a man who projects himself as the saviour of the game, this 'vision' is bold, dynamic and ambitious: a futuristic picture of English soccer emerging into the 21st century revitalised after decades of gloom, at last ready to reoccupy its historic place as one of world football's most potent forces. It is a vision of Arsenal, Tottenham and their ilk being able to entertain realistic hopes of victory if they meet AC Milan or Barcelona in European competition, and of England's once proud name again inspiring fear even in Germany and Brazil. But it also is a vision of ultra-modern, all-seater stadia banishing the rain-swept terraces and wooden stands known to past generations. Of smiling families enjoying ninety minutes of high-class entertainment in a friendly atmosphere. Of soccer being run by a powerful American football-style commissioner. Of a European Super League, radical rule changes making the game more exciting, and fans eating ice-cream at summer matches. In short, it is a vision that believes English football must adapt or die; that it must undergo painful, tradition-defying, but ultimately life-saving upheaval, both on and off the pitch, if it is to thrive beyond the turmoil that now appears to be its almost permanent state.

Fans confronted with the name of David Dein, the architect of this apocalyptic scheme, could be forgiven for shaking their heads and asking, 'David *who*?' He is not, after all, a household name like Jack Walker, Ken Bates or Alan Sugar. Regulars at Highbury Stadium, though, will nod in recognition at the mention of their club's vice-chairman. In football parlance, the term 'vice-chairman' often denotes the meaningless honorary position bestowed on a local businessman happy to part with thousands of pounds a year in return for a little reflected glory. Not so David Dein. Despite his innocuous title, he is in fact one of the most powerful, influential and controversial figures in English football, and one of the deepest thinkers about its uncertain future.

Dein's power base lies at Arsenal, where he has effective control thanks to the 42 per cent stake he has gradually accumulated since joining the board in August 1983; it is the largest individual shareholding in the club. Faithful to the Highbury dictum of team effort over individual enterprise, Dein goes out of his way in public to stress the collective decision-making which has laid the foundations for league and cup successes, placing the Gunners alongside Manchester United and Glasgow Rangers as British football's biggest money-spinners. He is especially fulsome about the contribution of Ken Friar, the one-time Highbury turnstile-operator who is now Arsenal's managing director. Despite this professed spirit of co-operation, however, Dein is undoubtedly the man in charge, the one driving Arsenal forward with an entrepreneurial zest previously unseen at this most staid and traditional of clubs. To borrow a phrase from the

American dictionary of business-speak – something the vice-chairman himself has been known to do – he is the man calling all the shots.

For example, Dein began and has presided over an astounding commercial revolution at the club. When he arrived in 1983, Arsenal's turnover was just £2 million; now it is around £16 million. Significantly, almost half comes from non-gate revenue, notably the scores of official club products on sale at its massive Arsenal World of Sport shop outside Finsbury Park station – the largest outlet of its kind in Europe. Until the mid-1980s, Arsenal had only one tiny club shop built into a wall at the Clock End, into which a mere five people could fit at any one time; now they have the World of Sport, another shop called the Bootroom, and they employ two marketing managers. All this has provided a steady flow of funds for manager George Graham to buy talent and build a winning side. Thus, in some ways, Dein deserves at least as much credit as Graham, Michael Thomas or Ian Wright for the pre-eminent position which the club enjoys today.

Dein has run into controversy several times since joining the Arsenal board. In the early days, it surrounded his habit of appearing in the home dressing-room minutes before kick-off to urge the Gunners to 'get stuck in', and of taking selected players out on the town. More recently, his zealous championing of the Arsenal Bond as the best way to finance the new North Stand at Highbury earned him ill will from the fans, who felt the club was trying to rip them off. But it is in his role as the self-styled saviour of English football that he has received most attention, and inspired roughly equal amounts of anger and admiration.

Yet getting to meet David Dein, a restless character you might perhaps expect to be keen to promote his challenging ideas, is not altogether straightforward. A man highly skilled in using the media to publicise his latest brainwave, he is also deeply suspicious of journalists as a breed; he is convinced, perhaps justifiably, that they are usually out to malign, misquote or otherwise do harm to Arsenal, their players or himself. After one particular profile appeared in print, he stopped giving interviews altogether. That incident, plus a flurry of legal actions, either threatened or undertaken, seems to portray Dein as a man easily provoked and suffering from something of a siege mentality. He has been known to treat journalists expecting an hour of his views on football to a twenty-minute diatribe on wilful distortion by the press, and to invite up to Highbury hacks whose articles have offended him for a line-by-line explanation of where they went wrong.

To get an interview with Dein, you have first to send him a letter detailing the subjects you want to cover. A tip: it's wise not to mention the hitherto, er, modest success of the Arsenal Bond scheme or the vociferous protests it sparked off. Then, if he agrees to a meeting, you must promise to honour a series of unusual conditions, including checking direct quotes with him before publication. Only when you have done all that will the Arsenal vice-chairman invite you to share coffee, biscuits and his thoughts about how he would save the game – if only the ungrateful world of football would let him. Or, as he has cautioned at least one interviewer: 'I don't want to talk about me, but I'm happy to talk about my vision.'

You reach David Dein's office by turning up at reception in the gleaming new South Stand complex of offices off Avenell Road, N5, and taking the lift to the fourth floor. All around are photographs of famous Arsenal teams of the past, notably the 1970–71 double-winning side of Wilson, McLintock and Armstrong, Graham, Radford and Kennedy. While Highbury is better known for its magnificent marble halls and the bust of Herbert Chapman, both situated around the corner in the art-deco masterpiece of the East Stand, the South Stand is a much more appropriate setting for the vice-chairman's executive suite. Built on the site that, until 1988, was the historic Clock End terrace, the stand – a multi-purpose commercial complex containing fifty-three hospitality boxes, offices, restaurants, conference facilities and an indoor sports hall – is a symbol of a new era in Arsenal's history, and of Dein's belief that football clubs should diversify into other commercial activities to guarantee their financial future. Not for the last time in the Highbury vice-chairman's controversial career, the arrival of the bulldozers in 1988 signalled that the rebuilding of Arsenal, both literally and metaphorically, was well underway.

Visionaries in football have not enjoyed a great reputation since David Icke, the former Coventry City goalkeeper, took to wearing purple shell-suits and announced that he was the son of God. Dein, however, is unfazed by accusations of pomposity from his critics. He remains convinced that if he is not a prophet or a messiah, then he is at least a man ahead of his time, a born leader in a sport urgently needing a powerful figure to end its constant squabbling and push it into the next century. And he is utterly unmoved by the most common criticism levelled against him: that his 'vision' of football, if implemented, would turn it into a pale imitation of the National Football League in the United States, which he admires so much, and destroy it as mass live entertainment. A man used to being the target of unkind words, Dein consoles himself with the conviction that history will prove him right, that before long the doubters and sceptics will be queing up to applaud his ideas, courage and foresight.

So who is David Dein, and what exactly is his football masterplan – the 'vision' which he insists he has got? What are his ideas? And why does he divide his critics so fiercely? The key to answering much of this can perhaps be found in his first publicly recorded utterance, words which have since assumed the status of a personal mantra: 'Business comes first'. That was the answer he gave when asked by *The Times* in 1964 why he had dropped out of a degree course at Leeds University to start a business with his older brother, Arnold, importing tropical fruit. Although just twenty-two at the time, Dein was already showing signs of the aggressively commercial approach that was to become his hallmark. Selling then exotic fruits such as yams, mangos and avocados, Dein Brothers (Food Importers) Ltd was a spectacular success; within five years, it had achieved a turnover of £2 million. A few years later, another Dein quote – describing himself as being 'always optimistic' – provided further insight into what makes him tick. He expects to succeed, whatever his chosen mission.

However, it was not until nearly twenty years later that Dein got the chance to apply his commercial expertise to the one area of business which really intrigued him – football. Not just any old football club, mind you; but Arsenal, the team he had supported since boyhood. 'I remember being taken to Highbury by my uncle when I was about five', he recalls. 'We stood on the North Bank, and I saw Tommy Lawton score with a header from virtually the edge of the penalty area. I also remember vividly the match in 1958 before the Munich air disaster when we played Manchester United – a sensational game, even though we lost 4–5.' Supporting Arsenal, he says, 'was a way of life for me. One week I'd go to see the first team and the next week, if I wasn't travelling to the away game, I'd go and see the reserves. So I've been going regularly since the early 1950s. Saturday isn't Saturday without seeing Arsenal play.'

On 30 August 1983, Dein finally realised his ambition of getting involved in football. The *Daily Mail* reported how Dein, 'a 39-year-old commodity broker', had spent £290,250 to acquire 1,161 shares in Arsenal at £250 each, giving him an instant 16 per cent stake in the club. At a stroke, he had transformed himself from an ordinary fan who held four season-tickets into the single largest shareholder at Highbury. Although Dein's arrival did not alter the overall control exercised by the Carr family and chairman Peter Hill-Wood, his purchase meant that he now owned 145 more shares than even the chairman. Asked why he had sunk his money into the club, Dein was uncharacteristically coy: 'Speak to me in a year's time,' was all he told reporters.

Dein to this day denies that his move represented an investment. 'I didn't go into it for commercial reasons. Getting a return was very much at the back of my mind,' he insists. 'I didn't think, "Well, here is an opportunity." That was not the point. For me, it was a dream come true. I loved the game. Arsenal was a passion, a love affair. I was passionately involved with Arsenal in any event; I was a one-club man. Whereas in life you may change the brand of beer you drink or the cigarettes you smoke or the car you drive – and men change their wives occasionally – people never change the allegiance of the football club they support as a kid. Once they've got an allegiance, 99.9 per cent of the time it stays with them for life. I've been on the board for ten years now, and I'm still just delighted to be here. I still get a buzz when I walk through the marble halls. I get a tingle if I go into the dressing-rooms and think, "This is where my heroes – Jimmy Logie, Liam Brady, Charlie Nicholas – pulled on their shirts." It's all hero-worship, isn't it? It's a schoolboy thing; it's something that's ingrained in you early on and, with me, it's still there.'

Peter Hill-Wood certainly thought Dein's move was curious. 'Some rich men like to buy yachts or fast cars,' he said. 'He [Dein] chooses to put his money into a football club. It is dead money really, and I think he is crazy, but we are glad to have him.' The chairman's comments illustrated perfectly the dominant psychology among Highbury's powers-that-be at the time: that football did not represent a wise business proposition, that it was more of an indulgence than an investment. However, although Old Etonian Hill-Wood had no way then of knowing it, his judgement could scarcely have been wider of the mark. Once David Dein joined the Highbury board, Arsenal would never be the same again.

Being reminded of Hill-Wood's reference to 'dead money' brings a rare smile to Dein's face. He accepts that the £290,250 was indeed dead money, but only 'in the sense that I expected no dividend, which normally you would expect if you put money into most other companies.' Pressed for a fuller explanation, though, Dein concedes that there *was* in fact more to it than simply the fulfilment of one ex-schoolboy's very expensive dream. He had a plan. 'I wanted to be involved, to be part of the decision-making process,' he admits. 'And I felt I could contribute something' – something which, by implication, he felt the club was lacking. But contribute what, exactly? 'I thought I had a certain amount of commercial expertise.' Ah, commercial expertise: David Dein's forte.

Presumably, then, he saw potential in the club? 'I thought it was a sleeping giant,' he responds in a flash. 'I saw opportunities for expansion. I wanted to see Arsenal being positioned in its true place – at the top, the pinnacle. I have always believed that Arsenal should be the flagship of English football. Arsenal's voice must be heard around the table. Why? Because we've got a tremendous history, a tremendous heritage: we've been in existence since 1886, we've had the longest continuous run in the top division, and we've won so many trophies.'

These comments reveal stage one of the Dein masterplan: to make Arsenal the biggest, most influential and most successful team in English football. There was a problem, however. When he arrived, the club was in the doldrums, mainly because of the poor form of Terry Neill's team. Despite boasting stars such as Kenny Sansom, Tony Woodcock and Charlie Nicholas, by the late autumn of 1983 erratic league performances had left them well off the pace in the first division; and, in late November, they lost 1–2 at home to lowly Walsall in the League Cup. The fans' agitation mounted: a brick was thrown through a downstairs window at Highbury, and a group of supporters called for the entire board to resign – 'including me, and I'd only just joined the board!', recalls Dein, who describes that period as 'a bit of a torrid time, one way or another'.

Not only that, but football as a whole appeared to be deep in crisis. 'One of the first things I did when I came here in 1983 was to have a look at the way football was going as an industry. Was it in a healthy state? The answer was a resounding "No". In 1968, two years after we won the World Cup, thirty million people watched league football. Do you know how many people watched it in the 1991–92 season? Seventeen million,' he says with disgust. 'And that figure had come up from fifteen million. So you could say that, in less than a quarter of a century, football had lost half its audience at the grounds. I'm not saying that people are no longer interested in football, but people have stopped going.'

'When I take a black cab in London, as I do fairly often, I do a bit of market research with the cab drivers, 95 per cent of whom are football fans. I ask them, "Who do you support?" They say, "Arsenal, West Ham, QPR," or whoever. "Do you go?" "No." "Why don't you go?" "Too much of a hassle. It's a hassle getting a ticket; it's a hassle getting in; I'm a bit worried about whether the kids are going to be safe. I've got other things to do on a Saturday now. I go shopping, I stay home and watch television. There's videos." He's got 1,001 reasons why he doesn't go. So I come out of his cab feeling depressed. But I think, "Well, hang on, we've got to change all that." If we are captains of our own industry, we've got to make the game ultimately more conducive to the fans to bring them back to the stadia.'

Talking to taxi drivers is not perhaps the most reliable basis for devising an entire philosophy of the future of football. But to be fair to Dein, he cites the cabbies' observations not as cast-iron proof of some hitherto undiscovered social phenomenon, but as supporting evidence for his already firm belief that primitive conditions at grounds and appalling treatment of fans have done more than anything else to drive millions of people away from attending football regularly. More, he believes, than rising prices, more than the diminishing quality of the entertainment on offer, and more than the several economic recessions since 1968. 'It's a nonsense,' he fumes. 'These are the 1990s, and we're still living in Dickensian times.' He then launches into a detailed diatribe about the miserable standard of catering facilities and toilets, dressing-rooms and press boxes found in football, even at many grounds in the top flight. He cites – though diplomatically does not name – the case of a Premier League club 'at which its press facility is currently in a terraced house outside the ground!'

His sermon quickly merges into a post-facto explanation of why the Premier League was created – because, as he says with feeling, 'things are still Dickensian in the 1990s, and we intend to change all that.' To prove that he has not just recently arrived at this conclusion, Dein produces from a drawer in his desk a discussion paper, entitled 'The Case for Restructure', which he circulated on 24 March 1986 to the chairmen of the clubs then in the first division. His presentation that day fired the opening shot in what was to prove a lengthy and determined campaign to persuade the leading clubs to break away from the ninety-two-member Football League and start taking for themselves the decisions which would be in their own best interests. It can be seen in retrospect as an uncannily prophetic document: the beginning of the end of English football's traditional unity, and the precursor of the rupture that would finally take effect in August 1992.

Warming to his theme, Dein returns to the subject of English football's falling attendances after 1968: 'There's not a ray of hope there,' is his gloomy summary. 'It's a straight downward plummet,' he says, jabbing a finger at a graph carrying a line which drops diagonally across the page from left to right. 'How many other businesses could have survived losing almost half their customers over that period?' The answer, of course, is none: any other enterprise would have been forced to close. Football, not for the first or last time, had defied the usual rules of business logic. To Dein, though, the game was living on borrowed time; disaster could not be far away, unless action was taken to halt the slide in its appeal.

Given Dein's pivotal role in setting up what became

the Premier League, it is worth quoting in full his analysis back in 1986 of the decline in attendances, as outlined in 'The Case for Restructure'. '1: Safety. At the time we had the hooliganism rampage. People were scared and nervous about going. 2: Poor facilities within the stadia: catering, toilets, parking, general comfort. 3: The game itself. I'm not sure the way we were playing the game was particularly attractive. 4: Fierce competition for disposable income. 5: Inability of management to manage.'

The last of those reasons for decline, Dein says, became 'the key, the power-play I made to say, "Guys, if we're going to arrest all these things, if we're going to turn this graph around, then we're going to have to have change".' The trouble at the time was the power structure of English football, the ninety-two often-competing individual interests within the Football League which made agreement about what was in the best interests of *football as a whole* almost impossible. 'Arsenal has something that football at the time lacked: strong management,' he believes, before launching into another of his football's-just-like-any-other-business comparisons. 'Take any successful company you like – ICI, Tesco, Boots – and I'll tell you one thing: I bet they've got a strong board. They're run from the top. You can't have the tail wagging the dog – and that's what was happening in football. If that happens, then you're as strong as your weakest member and you will not have a thriving business.' To his mind, football in 1986 was weak and getting weaker simply because the weaker – that is, smaller – clubs were pulling it down. They were acting as a sort of lowest common denominator? 'That's right,' he agrees.

The need for a breakaway by the top clubs to save football from being dragged down any further was thus urgent – and economically justifiable, too, Dein says. Another part of his 1986 document asked: 'What does the first division bring?' At the time, according to Dein's figures, it accounted for 63.4 per cent of match income and 55 per cent of all attendances. From those statistics, Dein deduced another dictum that has stayed with him ever since: 'SURVIVAL requires ACTION. ACTION requires DECISION. DECISION requires CONTROL.' By August 1992, this part of his self-imposed mission was finally accomplished.

'This is what I was proposing,' he says, turning the page of his 1986 would-be masterplan. 'What we were doing was clearly wrong, so I was saying, "Let's be a bit radical in our thinking." I said we should consider:

- 'Stringent criteria for grounds. Don't forget that this was six years ago, and we're only now finally starting to see it coming about – this is how long it takes to effect change!
- Family and segregated areas.
- Safety within grounds.
- Minimum ground capacity.
- Minimum facilities within grounds: catering, toilets.
- Artificial surfaces – were these good? I was on the committee that ultimately banned them.
- Summer football – why don't we think about it? Maybe we should think about playing football when the weather is nicer, when the grass is lush, when you've got bright nights so you don't need to use floodlights, when people can come in with their shirt-sleeves rolled up. A different atmosphere, happier occasion – we can sell ice-cream! Why not? *Why not?* Every other country has a winter break; we don't. Why shouldn't we break the season up a bit?
- Change the rules of the game itself. They've already

introduced a rule banning the back-pass. But I was really thinking about altering the offside rule, which is the most frustrating rule ever, and which tends to kill the game off as a spectator sport. I know people will say, "That's a bit rich coming from the vice-chairman of Arsenal," and they're right. But we only do it because it's a rule that's in place, so we make use of it. I mean, David Seaman doesn't like the back-pass rule, right? But ask most fans, and they think it's good because it makes it more exciting.

- Changes to the league? Not just a Premier League, which we've now got, but do we think about bringing the Scottish clubs in, perhaps? Change the menu a little bit.

'OK, some of these ideas were a bit contentious. All I was trying to do was throw a few firecrackers into the ring and see which ones were going to go bang, right? My argument was: "Let's stimulate discussion at least, because if we don't stop this nonsense, if we don't take radical action, before long the game will have gone right down the pan".'

This, then, was the road along which Dein thought English football should travel if it was to arrest what appeared to be a potentially fatal collapse. His alarm was two-fold: not only was the national game in apparently inexorable decline, but football in England – its traditional birthplace – was falling rapidly behind the rest of Europe, both on but especially off the pitch.

Since then, Dein has fine-tuned his thinking. Despite the advent of the Premier League, he believes further radical change is necessary: a slimmed-down Premier League of eighteen clubs and the scrapping of the League Cup to accommodate the creation of some form of midweek European Super League. Asked if Arsenal have more in common with Sam Hammam's Wimbledon or Silvio Berlusconi's AC Milan, Dein does not answer directly, presumably for fear of upsetting Arsenal's South London would-be rivals. But his message is unmistakable: 'Our challenge must be to become the best team in Europe. George Graham's goal is not only to win the English league but ultimately to win the European Cup or be on top of a European league. I think Arsenal's true place is in some sort of European set-up which would run parallel to our domestic competition. We've got our sights set on AC Milan, on Marseille, on Barcelona.

'But at the moment we play too many games to allow that to happen. In an ideal world, I'd like to see a Premier League of eighteen instead of twenty-two clubs, so Arsenal would play thirty-four instead of forty-two games a season; the scrapping of the League Cup, and the setting up of a European league in which we'd play eighteen games a season. Ideally I would like us to play no more than about fifty-five games every campaign: thirty-four in the Premier League, eighteen in a European league format, and a few more in the FA Cup.' Fewer games and regular sparring with European rivals would improve the whole of English football, Dein says, from the national team downwards.

The key to realising all these ambitions, he concluded a long time ago, lay in dramatically improving the shoddy, decrepit stadia in which the game is played: make English football stadia properly user-friendly for the first time in their history, and the fans would come flooding back. He draws a comparison with how British cinemas, confronted with falling audiences, dramatically refurbished their premises, introduced a choice of food and drinks, and gradually reversed a long-term decline to win back customers. However, Dein's inspiration for what could be achieved in football is not the Nou Camp, the San Siro or the Stadium of Light; rather, it is the stadia of the National Football League in the USA. 'You really have to look across the Atlantic to see how stadiums have developed. I've been over and seen grounds in the States – magnificent,' he enthuses. 'You feel comfortable going to a game, there's no aggression. Now all this seems strange. You say to supporters here, "I want you to sit next to your opposite number," and that's anathema to them. Yet I've been to stadiums in the States where you get home and away supporters mixing, and there's no problem. Don't get me wrong, I'm not advocating that for English football,' he back-tracks suddenly, 'but there is a congenial, harmonious atmosphere at stadiums over there. There is no intimidation.'

To highlight the yawning luxury gap between the two sides of the Atlantic, Dein points out that most NFL grounds have been built within the last twenty years. He then poses another question: 'When was the last major stadium built in England? Wembley, in 1923, for the British Empire Fair. That's *seventy years* in which we have not built a major stadium in this country. Why? Because clubs haven't got the money. To build a 50,000- or 60,000-capacity all-seater stadium, you're looking at well in excess of £100 million. How would you ever get that money back? You can't.'

According to Dein, the second-best option open to English clubs is to do everything they can to make their existing grounds fit for the post-Taylor Report era. Arsenal, he says, are already showing the way with their futuristic new 12,000-seater North Bank Stand, which was due to open in August 1993, a full year ahead of the timetable set by Lord Justice Taylor after his inquiry into the 1989 Hillsborough disaster. With its closed-circuit

TV, modern toilets, shops, crèche, wide variety of fast-food outlets and Arsenal museum, it certainly promised to represent the latest stage of Dein's determination to bring the game – or Highbury, at least – into the next century. It is a textbook example of what American experts term 'the total leisure experience': a full afternoon's entertainment for all the family. 'We think it's unacceptable that fans should have to wait fifty-deep to get to urinals, or that the only hot food they can buy is a soggy hamburger with onions dripping all over the outside.' Thus the new North Bank Stand will incorporate all the American-inspired notions of service, comfort and user-friendliness which Dein believes Arsenal must offer if they are to attract a loyal, paying clientele in the next century.

However, by the early summer of 1993, just three months before the stand was due to open, barely 4,000 of the 12,000 Arsenal Bonds needed to finance the £22.5 million redevelopment had been sold. Given their price (£1,500 or £1,100), and their limited benefits (primarily the right to buy a season ticket for a named seat in the new stand for 150 years), this was hardly surprising. Even after shelling out on a bond, the fans still had to find the money for their season ticket. The bulk of the 4,000 bonds had been sold soon after the scheme was launched in a blaze of publicity when the Gunners won the Championship in May 1991. But early the next season, protests against the scheme grew, with fans such as those in the newly formed Independent Arsenal Supporters' Association denouncing the club's attempted 'rip-off'. Very few new sales were achieved after the initial surge. Many fans complained about what they saw as the effective privatisation of football – charging them exorbitant amounts for something they already enjoyed, the right to go to see Arsenal in action – and, for several months, Highbury witnessed a series of passionate but peaceful anti-Bond demonstrations. These grew more intense as the date for the destruction of the North Bank, Highbury's world-famous kop end, drew nearer; for that was what would make way for the glamorous new North Bank Stand, which the club intended to be occupied solely by those who had bought a Bond.

Fans fought the Arsenal Bond with such intensity because they saw in it a nightmare vision of the future of football: if successful, it would forever restrict access to Highbury to those who had parted with their £1,500 or £1,100. Everyone else – all those either unable to afford a bond or who point-blank refused to buy one on principle – would have to content themselves with second-hand thrills: seeing the Gunners on TV, reading about their exploits in the papers, and buying end-of-season videos. Never again would they be able to enjoy at first hand Ian Wright's spectacular goals or Tony Adams's occasionally disastrous lapses in concentration. Fans argued that *this* was David Dein's true vision of the future of football, an NFL-inspired reality of access to the nation's most popular sport being decided on the depth of a fan's pocket, not his or her devotion.

Tony Willis, editor of the influential Arsenal fanzine *One-Nil Down, Two-One Up*, was prominent in the campaign against the Arsenal Bond and is probably David Dein's chief critic. While sharing several of the vice-chairman enthusiasms – for fewer games, regular European football, and more exciting matches based on skill, not speed – he nevertheless accuses him of trying to pull off the footballing equivalent of social engineering. Willis believes Dein to be dumping many of Arsenal's traditional fans and relocating the Gunners upmarket, with a new, much more affluent crowd forming the backbone of their support in a reduced 37,000 capacity all-seater Highbury Stadium. 'Look at what's happened at Arsenal since Dein joined the board ten years ago,' invites Willis. 'We used to be the cheapest club in London to support: until the mid-1980s it was only £3 to stand on the North Bank, and many fans had pride in the club because the people who ran it seemed to value their support. But prices underwent a series of big rises in the late 1980s, and now we're one of the dearest clubs in the country. In the space of three seasons, for example, the cost of my season ticket in the East Stand went up from £170 in 1989 to £474 in 1992 – that's pretty phenomenal.

'As a kid growing up in Islington in the 1960s, I remember what seemed to be everyone from the area tramping across Highbury Fields on Saturday afternoons to go to watch Arsenal. My grandmother, who has lived in Islington since the turn of the century, tells me that she used to queue outside the North Bank in the 1930s, and they used to lock the gates at 12 o'clock. It was mostly local people then. But if you look at the people who come to Arsenal now, you can see it's not really a community club any more. It's moved away from being Islington's club to being much more cosmopolitan.

'Since the mid-1980s, the type of punter at the ground has changed. Part of that is the fact that we've been the most successful London club, and therefore we have drawn the casual, uncommitted fan who wants to see good football. But it's also a by-product of the big price rises throughout the ground: if you're going to charge a lot more to get in, by definition you're going to attract a wealthier person.'

The Arsenal Bond scheme, argues Willis, was the conclusive proof of this trend: that, encouraged by David Dein, the Arsenal board had decided to seek 'a different audience, a more affluent, more upmarket kind of person.

They're aiming for your well-off, cosmopolitan type, usually a guy in his mid-twenties who perhaps works in the City or in advertising, has a professional background, and maybe has a young family.' He cites as evidence of Arsenal's social engineering a comment at the time of the Bond furore by Peter Hill-Wood that 'the Bonds are not aimed at people who currently stand on the North Bank'.

Willis rejects suggestions that he is a latter-day Luddite, suspicious of progress. In his defence, he raises two objections to Arsenal's recent move upmarket. 'First, I think it's wrong to price ordinary fans out of going to football. There are a lot of kids and unemployed people out there who support Arsenal but who can't afford a Bond, even if they want to. How will they get in if they have to buy a Bond? Second, a practical reservation: I don't think that the middle-class punters they're after are out there in anything like the numbers they think. If these people really existed, why weren't they buying a season ticket a few years ago when we first won the Championship? If they're not going to buy season tickets for £350 or £400, what makes you think these people are suddenly going to start appearing and paying £1,100 or £1,500 for a Bond?

'What worries me is the approach to football of people like Dein. Their attitude is: "We're going to truss football up and market it as a package as we see fit. We're going to try to attract a certain kind of person into the ground, have good TV deals, a European Super League," all that kind of stuff. But there's a voice inside my head which says, "Hold on a second, what about the fans? Where do we fit into all this?".'

Tom Watt, the Arsenal fan better known to millions as the actor who used to play Lofty in *Eastenders*, shares a similar view to Willis's. He fears that the advent of all-seater stadia means 'a complete sea-change in the kind of person who goes to watch football. I think football clubs are looking to a demographic which is more like America, where live sport is the exclusive preserve of affluent professionals and everybody else watches it on telly. I think that's what football's authorities, from club chairmen through to sports ministers, would like to see. Remember that sports ministers, heads of the FA and a lot of club chairmen are *scared* of football supporters. They hate fans because fans are volatile, passionate, irrational; because they're utterly devoted, and because they're a crowd.'

Alex Fynn, the Saatchis' football guru who has regular dealings with Dein, believes Arsenal fans may be right to be concerned about their place in the great Gunners' game plan for the year 2000 and beyond. 'If you look at the principle behind the Arsenal Bond scheme – to make those least well-off pay the most – it shows that David Dein's view is that if Arsenal provide better quality, then they can afford to charge more. That idea of quality includes facilities off the field as well as the football on it. That's why you have this grandiose plan for the North Bank Stand. It hasn't just got to be a *good* stand, it's got to be a *superstand*, because he thinks that is what is expected of Arsenal, and what they expect of themselves, as a very superior club. I think that if they had really wanted to retain the sort of people who used to stand on the North Bank, they would have either pursued a much less ambitious plan, such as a mixture of a share issue and debentures to reduce the financial burden on the club, or built a cheaper stand. I mean, £22.5 million is a lot of money for 12,000 people.'

Fynn says that, whether it is the Arsenal board's deliberate intention or not, the club's regular supporters will increasingly be drawn from those who are better off. 'It's inevitable that the live audience at Highbury will change, because less well-off people will not be able to afford expensive seats in the new North Bank Stand on a regular basis, particularly if they're with families. You will still get working-class supporters, but not on a regular basis: their support will become more spasmodic because they won't be able to afford to go all the time. But if all 12,000 bonds had been sold, it would have been a totally middle-class audience, because nobody else could have afforded them, and the working class would have had no access to Highbury in the future. You would have had a mirror-image of the Joe Robbie Stadium in Miami, where the Miami Dolphins play. Everything in that stadium is either debenture or season ticket; the audience is middle-class and upwards. There are a few cheap tickets there, but only because the capacity is 80,000. Highbury's will be less than half that; therefore even that option seems to be closed off.'

Dein strongly denies any suggestion that Arsenal are trying to change the existing social mix of their supporters. 'We want to keep the fan base! If there's a large proportion of our fans who can only afford £8–£10, somehow we've got to cater for those people because they're hard-core, devout fans. I know. I travel on the train very often with our away supporters and I talk to these guys. I'm not blinkered, I'm not closed-minded, and I know that for these guys their life is following Arsenal. They tell me that the first thing they want, obviously, is a successful team, but they also want to be able to come regularly. So we've got to be careful that we don't outprice football. Our game plan is to do our level best to keep prices to a minimum, to make sure that it's not out of reach of the football fan who's only got a limited amount of disposable income, because they're entitled to come and watch their team. I echo what [Chelsea's] Ken Bates said, that he's catering in his development for people who want caviar and for people who want meat pies.'

It is hard to imagine a more ringing endorsement of Arsenal's commitment to maintaining football as a mass-audience, live spectator sport. But pressed to explain how Arsenal will accommodate all their fans, regardless of income, in a 37,000-capacity stadium, Dein is short on detail. 'You have to respect the regular fan; he's got to be catered for. It's a challenge for us to devise a pricing structure which reflects what I've said. That's our balancing act.'

Alex Fynn believes that, even with demographic shifts in Arsenal's support, David Dein's ultimate ambition – of the Gunners being able to compete on equal terms with the superclubs of European football – is unlikely ever to be realised. 'Dein is in love with Arsenal; that's what drives him. He wants what's best for his club, and he sees their future as being in common with the big clubs in Europe. Now clearly Arsenal *should* be playing in the same league as AC Milan, Barcelona and Bayern Munich. They certainly have more in common with them than with Wimbledon or Coventry City. But Arsenal's problem is that the big European clubs have several distinct advantages over them. Those clubs don't own their own stadium – the city council does – so they don't have the fixed costs of its upkeep. In addition, because they are seen as an asset to the community, they qualify for a subsidy from the council in the same way that the local library does. Also, their grounds have much larger capacities, so they have massive gate revenue. And they also receive massive income from television. None of that goes on here, so obviously the dice are loaded against Arsenal competing on equal terms with clubs with these financial advantages.'

As a loyal Arsenal fan, Tony Willis should perhaps be

thrilled by David Dein's ambitious 'vision' for the club, or at least share it. But he doesn't. It scares him, in fact. 'My fear is that the club will head down a route which ultimately destroys it,' he says. 'I'm worried that either the club will end up in a Tottenham-type situation, where it is saddled with a big debt because of the costs of ground redevelopments, or that Dein will take the club so far away from its natural constituency that it's unrecognisable to its traditional supporters. Now that might not matter to someone who's started to support Arsenal only recently, but it matters to me, and I've been coming for twenty-five years.

'I get accused of being nostalgic and of being afraid of progress in football. But I'll only ever accept that I'm the one who's out of touch when Arsenal get 37,000 people, all paying £20 a head, at Highbury on a cold Tuesday night in February when we're playing Wimbledon. When they do, I'll say, "Dein's won". But I wouldn't hold your breath.'

FOUR

The Great Dictators?

Ken Bates, Ron Noades, and the cult of the individual

Despite the high public profile enjoyed by David Dein, and the impact of his vision in both North London and the country at large, no one would ever suggest that Arsenal is a one-man club. Highbury is certainly not the personal fiefdom of its vice-chairman. Over at Stamford Bridge and Selhurst Park, however, the situation is somewhat different. If you asked a fan of Chelsea or Crystal Palace to list the personalities they most closely associated with their club, it is a fair bet that few players would have been mentioned before the names of Ken Bates and Ron Noades sprang to their lips.

Gone for ever are the days when football club chairmen were largely anonymous figures, sitting aloof in the directors' box and known only to supporters from a line in the programme. These venerable gents were the last remnant of the era of big crowds and small wages, often handing on the position like an hereditary peerage in the belief that it would give their sons the key to a respected place in society. Long-lasting dynasties such as the Hill-Woods at Arsenal and the McKeags at Newcastle have almost all ended; in the place of modestly prosperous local businessmen have come entrepreneurs from the world of high finance, only too aware that clubs these days are run mainly in the public domain and that performances in the boardroom are often scrutinised as closely as efforts on the pitch. 'It was a novel idea ten or fifteen years ago that clubs should be run like businesses,' says Peter Johnson, the millionaire who has steered Tranmere Rovers to the verge of the Premier League. 'Now football *is* business, pure and simple.'

Since August 1992, the chairmen of the top-flight twenty-two have had more to manage than just their clubs, though. With their engineering of the most tumultuous changes ever to take place in English football, the very welfare of the game itself has passed into their hands. Ken Bates and Ron Noades are perhaps the most idiosyncratic of these guardians of football's future: individualistic, media-conscious, energetic, highly opinionated, dogmatic, and never short of a pithy one-liner. They believe in maximising football's money-making potential, yet have needed to spend time on curbing the loss-making activities of their own clubs. Far more than their egos and their acumen have been called into question over the years, but both enjoy some measure of respect on the terraces as well as in rival boardrooms. As fans grow confident enough to challenge the once-unquestioned 'we know best' attitude of their club's directors, Bates and Noades have proved adept at wearing the hats of both supporter and businessman at the same time.

* * *

When the Chelsea chairman asked Blues' fans to uncork the champagne and join him in toasting an early Christmas present, London's longest-running football saga had finally come to an end. On 15 December 1992, Ken Bates announced that Stamford Bridge had been bought by the Royal Bank of Scotland from owners Cabra Estates for an undisclosed sum – quoted by some sources as £16.5 million – and thus secured Chelsea's future at their West London stadium. The deal provided Chelsea with a twenty-year lease, and the option to purchase the ground at a fixed price at any time before the year 2012 in a 'buy now, pay later' arrangement. It represented the best transaction yet made by a man for whom more than thirty years of commerce have earned him notably large rewards.

Born not far from Stamford Bridge itself, in Ealing, the son of a London Transport bus painter, Bates reached the age of 18 with hopes of becoming a professional footballer, despite being hindered by a club-foot. He played as a defender for Arsenal juniors but, as he puts it, 'the imperfection presented limitations'. He switched his attention instead to business, and was running a haulage firm by the time he was 21. He bought himself a Bentley, and within ten years was a near-millionaire from the profits of a ready-mixed concrete company. Football was always a passion and, in 1965, at 34, he became the league's youngest chairman when he bought 24,000 ten-shilling shares and took over at Oldham Athletic. He quickly made his mark; directors Harry Massey and Eric Beard resigned, Massey stating that: 'Bates believes in a committee of two, with one absent.' The situation at Boundary Park was similar to the one he would find at Stamford Bridge seventeen years later: Oldham had been refused further credit at the bank, the ground was a dilapidated mess, and there was little prospect of an upturn in fortunes on the pitch. 'I wanted to be associated with a poor club which had once been successful,' Bates has said of his time with the Latics, but a lack of potential to realise his ambitions saw him leave for a brief directorship at the other Latics, Wigan, before retiring to Monte Carlo.

After travelling the world and engaging in numerous exotic enterprises – growing sugar in Queensland, building houses in South Africa, and reclaiming land in the West Indies among them – Bates moved to a 270-acre dairy farm near Beaconsfield, Buckinghamshire, in 1981. It cost him £900,000, and was valued six years later at £3 million. He claims that the ice-cream made on his farm is the best in England. In April 1982, and for a reported £200,000, he purchased Chelsea from the Mears family, who had founded the club in 1905. 'I'm coming in because it's every fan's aim to have his own club, and Chelsea is one of the most glamorous,' he commented. Yet it was a fast-fading glamour. The fans had enjoyed little to cheer on the pitch since the FA Cup final victory of 1970 and European Cup-Winners' Cup success the year after, while the club was losing £12,000 a week and a cheque for the players' wages had just bounced. Liabilities were around £2 million, but one director was still claiming expenses for turning up at away matches.

'It was a freeloaders' paradise,' Bates said. 'I inherited poseurs, hangers-on and fair-weather friends. Never mind that there were no toilets in the Shed, where was the champagne and gin-and-tonics in the boardroom?' He axed twelve members of staff, including a commercial manager whose projects allegedly cost more than they raised, and had Chelsea in profit within eighteen months. However, Bates did not buy the ground itself from SB Properties, the holding company which had been formed to own it, but purchased instead a seven-year lease. What might have cost less than £1 million in 1982 has been the albatross round Bates's and the club's neck for a decade since. Once former chairman David Mears had sold his share in SB Properties to Marler Estates, making that company the new owner of the ground, and Marler had in 1985 received planning permission to redevelop the site with offices and houses, its value shot up to anything from £20 million to £70 million, depending on which property expert you spoke to. In 1987, Bates submitted an alternative scheme for the site, which placed the football ground at the centre of a multi-sport complex, but two years later Cabra Estates bought Marler for £2.87 million and Chelsea's lease on the ground expired. For three years, the future of Stamford Bridge hung in the balance. Bates had become 'King of the Bridge' in the summer when he acquired the freehold, but it was not until the Royal Bank of Scotland stepped in to buy the ground itself from Cabra, themselves badly affected by the property slump, that the club could consider itself secure in its home.

Now, sitting behind a huge desk in his handsome office on the mezzanine floor of the East Stand – ironically, the stand which saddled Chelsea with debts throughout the 1970s and largely accounted for the financial mess Bates found when he arrived – the chairman is free to reflect on ten years of turmoil. He admits that he did not buy the ground back in 1982 because he was unsure whether the club was a remotely viable business proposition. 'When I came here,' he explains, 'there was no drive or dynamism. There was almost a sense of fatalism about the place. No team, no ground, no hope – simple as that, really. At first, I wasn't sure whether Chelsea *could* be saved. That's why I was cautious in only buying the club, getting a lease on the ground, and seeing if I could pull it round.' Bates sought planning consent for his own blueprint for the future of Stamford Bridge in 1987. He got it three years later. Now, the drawings are hung on the walls around the club offices, one illustration cleverly superimposing action from a real match against Liverpool on to an artist's impression of how the ground will look. Bates is like a child with a new toy as he points out the features of the scheme;

it has, after all, dominated his thinking for more than seven years. 'I had dark hair when I started,' he quips.

Stamford Bridge has enjoyed an unenviable reputation among London soccer fans for the best part of twenty years as the capital's most inhospitable venue. Vast, crumbling terraces and the perfunctory protection offered by the Shed contrast with the East Stand, the largest single free-standing construction at any league ground – but built at ruinous cost in 1972. The pitch, surrounded by a disused greyhound track, is so far away from most of the crowd that the joke is of the high admission prices including the loan of a pair of binoculars. Nor have the fans themselves helped engender a welcoming atmosphere; a well-developed reputation for 'hardness' has, at times, been supplanted by a vicious racism. In 1983, a Chelsea supporter was fined £200 for sending the chairman a letter containing razor blades and a message 'to wog-loving Bates: no more coons playing for Chelsea.' Bates's response was to declare his determination 'to rid Chelsea of the mindless scum and moronic sub-humans who spoil football for everyone.' As for his club's selection policy, he blasted: 'If a three-legged, one-eyed Muslim Red Indian is our best striker, then he will be in the team.'

Will Buckley, the tousle-headed presenter of *Quizbowl*, Channel 4's cult knock-out quiz between teams of sports journalists, has been a lifelong Blues supporter. He believes that the uncertainty over Stamford Bridge has been partly responsible for a growing sense of insularity at Chelsea: 'Ken Bates has a reputation as an iconoclastic chairman, storming in and out of meetings and pulling no punches when he speaks. This goes with the tough image of the fans to create a picture of a difficult, unhelpful club. Chelsea seem to react to that by turning in on themselves. The media still have this vision of Stamford Bridge as the haunt of champagne-swilling celebs, when that actually disappeared with the Osgood era. I think that, since those days, Chelsea have actually become more hated than any other club. As a supporter, it's difficult not to be cynical about them.' Ross Fraser, editor of the respected fanzine *Chelsea Independent*, summed up the feelings of many when he stated in his September 1992 editorial: 'It's not easy being a Chelsea fan. We have to put up with never winning anything, regular lower-league humiliations, a ridiculous ground, and a chairman who courts the kind of tabloid publicity that gives us all a hard time at work the next day.'

Bates sympathises with the fans' view, but is adamant that words like Fraser's only represent half the picture. Nor can he resist a typically sly dig: 'Although our achievements on the playing field haven't been too great, at least to the supporters' eyes – and supporters have very short memory spans – they don't seem to realise that we've had this albatross [the future of Stamford Bridge] round our necks for ten years and more. That has inhibited all our performances. Where we have been spending six or seven hundred thousand pounds each year on legal fees, that money could have been spent on the playing staff. Our London rivals have that advantage on us.'

Although Bates describes himself as 'a natural Conservative' – and there is a framed letter and photograph from Chelsea's most famous fan, Prime Minister John Major, on his wall to support this view – he adds that he is 'a local Socialist'. This was convenient when, in 1986, the political complexion of Hammersmith and Fulham council changed from blue to red, and the incoming officials declared that they wanted Chelsea to remain at Stamford Bridge. This was how Bates obtained planning consent for his redevelopment scheme and, thus fortified, was able to tackle Cabra. His success leaves him convinced that Chelsea can now look forward to a bright new era, even if his North London geography is rather awry: 'Chelsea's happy accident is that we are one and a half miles from Harrods and two and a half miles from Piccadilly. We are in the fashionable Fulham, Knightsbridge, Chelsea, Kensington, Belgravia area, which gives us an ultimate advantage over our North London rivals. Sorry for Spurs, but they are 200 yards from Broadwater Estate, and Arsenal are out in the residential sticks somewhere. In the long term, our position and our planning consent should give us the edge.'

Bates makes little secret of his inbuilt antipathy towards the two giants of North London football, and he is adamant that his redevelopment scheme will place the Blues alongside Arsenal and Tottenham in the top drawer of English clubs. His plans have similarities to Arsenal's rebuilding of the North Bank but, with the advantage of acres of unused space to hand, appear even grander: 'The new Chelsea won't be just a football club. That's only the focal point of it. It will be an all-embracing sports, leisure, residential, eating and drinking complex.' Such pat phrases have been the death-knell of any number of property speculators down the years, but Bates, undaunted, presses on: 'We will have a multi-purpose sports arena, a 160-bed hotel, 120,000 square feet of shops, offices and restaurants, 264 luxury apartments, an underground car park, and the new ground will be state-of-the-art. Better than any other in the country.'

However, in a display of solidarity with fans from what he calls 'the working classes, of which I am a member' – hastily postscripted with the line, 'or at least where I came from, that is' – Bates is determined to ensure a fair deal for all spectators, and to evade the problems that have beset David Dein's Arsenal, for one. 'We're trying to avoid the situation where some clubs have gone too much for the corporate sponsors,' he states. 'We want to cater for everybody, from pie and a pint to caviar and vodka. It's just that they won't be standing up to their knees in slutch, as they call it in Lancashire. The working classes don't stand in the rain on concrete terraces watching a film at their local cinema, do they?' But it is not only Chelsea die-hards who Bates wants to benefit from the new Bridge: 'We want to capture the floating supporters, the people who wake up on Saturday morning and say, "Oh, which football match shall we go to?"' They might be tempted – until Bates adds, with just a hint of a twinkle in his steely eyes, 'And, apart from that, we play the best football . . .'

Will Buckley is only one supporter who would dispute that final claim. For him, Stamford Bridge has in recent years been little more than a resting-home for complacent players on high salaries. 'In the 1970s, there was an excitement because you felt Chelsea were always capable of doing the unexpected. The last good side was the Nevin-Speedie-Dixon team of 1985–86, which gave the impression of being able to take on anyone. At the moment, they're unlikely to win anything. It would be worth going if they at least set out to entertain, but the games have been so drear that you leave feeling deeply depressed.' Indeed, a run of twelve matches without a win led, in February 1993, to the departure of manager Ian Porterfield and his replacement by the cleft-chinned battler and scorer of the winning goal in the 1970 FA Cup final replay, Dave Webb. Three months later Webb, in turn, was replaced by Glenn Hoddle.

Although Buckley is disenchanted by the lack of

progress made on the pitch, he finds himself unable to blame Ken Bates for Chelsea's problems. While other media-conscious chairmen, most notably Irving Scholar at Spurs, have been brought down partly as a result of the criticism which their high public profile attracts, Bates has emerged unscathed from the decade of distress. Indeed, few chairmen around the country can be as popular with their fans as Bates is with Chelsea's dwindling faithful. 'Why do fans revere Bates?' asks Buckley. 'Because he stands up and says, "I am Chelsea". It accords with the siege mentality, the "we are Chelsea, we don't care" image the club gives off.' He might also have mentioned the less serious but endearing fact that Bates is, as far as is known, the only chairman to have posed for a photograph on his club's turf wearing nothing but a pair of white boxer shorts.

However, Buckley – as a football fan whose interest extends further than blind devotion to one club – finds Bates's attitude to the game in general worryingly regressive. He has support in this from the editors of the monthly football magazine *When Saturday Comes* who, on celebrating their fiftieth issue in April 1991, mockingly voted Bates 'Man of the First Five Years'. 'It is perhaps significant that the thirty-sixth and thirty-seventh words ever to appear in *When Saturday Comes* were "Ken" and "Bates" respectively,' they wrote. 'Most of the major talking-points to have occupied the minds of football fans over the past five years have in some way involved him.' A quick resumé of events followed: in 1985, there was Bates's suggestion that a strand of electric wire placed across the top of perimeter fencing might deter hooligans from pitch invasions. That same year, he was instrumental, from his position on the Football League management committee, in foisting upon an already crowded schedule the Full Members' Cup, later to transmute into the Simod Cup, then the Zenith Data Systems Cup, which was only abolished at the start of the 1992-93 season. He played a major role in the organisation – if that is the right word – of the Football League's centenary celebrations in 1990, comprising a shambolic weekend of soccer at Wembley Stadium which few were remotely interested in and even fewer attended. If anyone ever sought evidence that there is one rule for the big clubs and another for the rest, then a possible example came in January 1991, when Chelsea were found guilty by the Football League of making illegal payments to players. Shortly after Swindon Town had been shown to do the same and had their newly-won first-division place withheld – demoted, in effect – Bates regained his seat on the management committee. Although Chelsea had committed only three offences compared to Swindon's thirty-six, the sum of money involved was roughly the same. But Chelsea were not demoted – they were only fined. 'If we were to sit down and choose our "Man of the First Five Years",' concluded *When Saturday Comes*, 'he would have white hair and a beard, and bear a closer resemblance to Captain Birdseye than to Father Christmas.'

Even though the saga of Stamford Bridge had occupied much of his time over the preceding two years, Bates was a prime mover behind the setting-up of the breakaway Premier League. His enthusiasm was no doubt partly stoked up by animosity towards the Football League for the £105,000 fine imposed on Chelsea for contract irregularities. And when, in March 1992, strike action by players was mooted after the PFA had not received assurance from the Premier League that it would be given a place on the new organisation's management board, Bates was straight in there. Speaking on BSkyB's *The Footballers' Football Show*, and clearly alarmed by this potential outbreak of player-power, he blasted: 'The

PFA's job is to protect their members. They pay lip-service to improving football and this, that and the other, but they are there to get the best deal for their members. I don't think it is right for the PFA to have a voice in the running of the game at the level they are looking for.' And with one of the cutting one-liners for which Bates has become renowned, he rapped: 'For Gordon Taylor to have an executive position on the Premier League is rather like making Arthur Scargill chairman of the Coal Board!'

Bates's attitude towards the PFA smacks of the old master-servant relationship. And when the first heads were raised above the parapet to venture the thought that top-flight footballers were playing too many matches, and that quality was being sacrificed for quantity, the Chelsea chairman was having none of it. England manager Graham Taylor's complaint at the end of 1991 that twenty-two clubs were too many for a Premier League was met by a stinging rebuke from the East Stand office at Stamford Bridge: Taylor should 'keep his mouth shut and get on with his job'. Bates has not softened in the ensuing months, either. 'I don't believe there is too much football,' he retorts to the suggestion that a congested and fiercely-contested league and cup programme hinders clubs' chances in European competition and, indeed, passes on clapped-out and patched-up players to Graham Taylor's international set-up. 'Liverpool never complained about playing sixty games a season when they were the most successful club in Europe. And don't forget that they voted for a twenty-two-team Premier League too. We've played forty-two matches since the end of the First World War – that's more than seventy years ago.'

Bates professes a weary incomprehension at the argument that there is too much football for the good of the game itself, but he does so in solely economic terms. 'Football is run on a marginal costing basis. It costs very little more to play forty matches than to play twenty matches. The wages are the same, the overheads are the same, the tax, the insurance, the heating, the lighting, the rates, management salaries. The only additional costs are the actual gate costs: cleaning, turnstiles, stewards, police.' But what about the cost, in physical terms, on the players, the extra wear-and-tear? The reply is blunt. 'I think that's a load of crap.' This is, after all, the man whose club filled a blank weekend in October 1992 by inaugurating the Cross-Channel Cup, a two-leg challenge between Chelsea and those crowd-pulling giants of French football, Le Havre.

No competition, however, has been so pilloried as the knock-out which finally expired in 1992 under the name of the Zenith Data Systems Cup. Not only was Bates instrumental in founding this tournament for those first- and second-division clubs which failed to reach Europe, it is the only honour Chelsea have collected under his chairmanship. For proponents of the 'too much football' school lining up behind Graham Taylor, Gary Lineker and the majority of managers in the Premier League, the ZDS Cup was a sitting duck. The gates it attracted were risible; the commitment from the players often, it seemed, less than wholehearted. True, it had a Wembley final, but there was little glamour or mystique. It was a mercenary exercise, pure and simple, and the fans had its motivations sussed.

During an otherwise amiable talk with Ken Bates, this ill-starred competition is the one subject on which he becomes notably touchy. 'I hope this interview isn't going to turn into a discussion of the ZDS Cup,' he growls forbiddingly. Bates believes that the competition was a useful earner for the smaller clubs. 'Each of them made fifty to one hundred thousand pounds out of it,' he asserts. 'And the finalists made half a million. By the FA abolishing – mistakenly abolishing – the tournament, all they've done is cut off a useful source of income to clubs that missed out on Europe.' What about the argument that few fans could be bothered to go and watch? 'They don't have to turn up – it's the same cost as a friendly, or a testimonial. Gates in the League Cup are small to start off with; gates in the FA Cup are small to start off with. They traditionally build the nearer you get to Wembley.' You get the impression that Bates would be happy for Chelsea to play four or five times a week, as long as each game guaranteed a few extra quid for the coffers.

Tradition – or at least what he regards as antiquated tradition – is one of Bates's bugbears. 'I like innovation,' he declares. He has no problem with the variety of kick-off times now imposed on the Premier League by the schedulers at BSkyB: 'Sunday at 4 p.m.? Why is that peculiar? I think it's better. Some people go out for Sunday lunch. Now they can get back home in time to watch the match.' Same goes for Sky's much-heralded innovation, 'Monday Night Football'. Only custom, he suggests, has decreed Monday evening an unsuitable time to stage games. 'Is it any stranger than Tuesday night or Wednesday night?' he snaps back. 'It's a question of habit. Monday night is actually a good night, because it's when everybody usually stays in.'

He tells a story about when he was chairman of Oldham Athletic, and every Lancashire club still in the 1966 FA Cup bar one was drawn at home in the third round. Oldham had been pulled out of the hat with

Wolverhampton Wanderers, an attractive tie considering the Latics were struggling in the third division and Wolves had only just been relegated from the first. 'I applied to the FA for permission to play our game on the Friday night,' he recalls. 'I thought we'd get a 35,000 crowd, whereas we'd have no chance of reaching that on the Saturday. But the FA turned me down.' He mimics the clipped tones of a brass-buttoned FA official: ' "The third round of the FA Cup always kicks off at 3 p.m. on the first Saturday in January. It always has, and it always will. It's inviolate." It's ridiculous, I said. Just because we kicked off the third round on Saturdays when players wore skull-caps and knickerbockers is no reason to do so today. I told that to a reporter on the *Daily Mirror*, in the days when the *Mirror* was a broadsheet. You know what the headline was? "Knickers, says Bates to the FA". And when do we play the third round of the FA Cup now? Saturday, Sunday *and* Monday. It just goes to show that nothing in football is sacred.'

* * *

In David Hare's play *Murmuring Judges*, an entire scene takes place outside Crystal Palace's Selhurst Park ground. When the National Theatre staged its production at the South Bank, the backdrop to the set was dominated by a view of the South London stadium. Part of the dialogue runs:

Sandra: '... to watch Crystal Palace.'
Irina: 'Is that the sports team?'
Sandra: 'Yes. They play football.'
Irina: 'Ah, yes. I've done my best to understand England, but some of the nuances pass me by.'
Sandra: 'Crystal Palace don't have many nuances.'

Lack of subtlety is a criticism Palace fans have often levelled at their team, as the then manager Steve Coppell continued to instil the virtues of energy, commitment and physical strength – whack-and-chase football – into a squad of workaday players severely weakened by the departure to Arsenal of their star striker Ian Wright in autumn 1991. It is also a phrase that has been directed at Palace chairman Ron Noades since his arrival in SE25 in 1980. During a career which has seen him move from Southall to Palace via Wimbledon, the self-made businessman has shown an upwardly mobile approach to football club chairmanship, although his reaction to the situation in which he found himself as the Premier League gathered pace was something of a contrast to that of Ken Bates.

Noades had initially been attracted by Palace's apparent potential, after Terry Venables had taken his exciting young charges into the top flight in 1979. What Noades actually inherited was financial instability and a squad – fatally dubbed 'The Team of the Eighties', and including such players as Terry Fenwick, Kenny Sansom and Peter Nicholas – sliding back down to the second division. Managerial musical chairs followed, with Dario Gradi, Steve Kember and Alan Mullery all struggling to prevent the Eagles from diving any lower. Noades then appointed his former manager at Wimbledon, Dave Bassett, to try to untangle the Palace allsorts, but even 'Harry', the arch-battler, returned from whence he had come within a matter of days. Finally, in 1984, the Selhurst supremo opted for a 28-year-old ex-player with a university economics degree but no managerial experience whatsoever. Steve Coppell proved an astute gamble. After one more year of struggle, Palace finished the next three seasons in the top six, started 1989 with a home game against Walsall and – promotion duly gained – opened the new decade with a visit to Highbury to face league champions Arsenal.

The start of another bright new era? A 'Team of the Nineties'? Noades was certain of it. But the fans were less sure. 'All supporters have a rose-tinted view of the future; every year a thousand names are on the cup,' wrote Selhurst regular David Clee in the *Independent*'s 'Fan's Eye View' column. 'But only at Palace is the lie so deeply rooted.' According to Clee, Crystal Palace is a club with no clear identity or staunch base of support. After all, where, week in week out, were the tens of thousands who went to Wembley to see the Eagles play Manchester United in the 1990 FA Cup final? Certainly not cheering on the lads from the Holmesdale End. 'We are a club without the tradition of Tottenham; without the tight-knit, jellied-eel support of West Ham and Millwall; the set-in-stone playing styles of QPR and Wimbledon; without even the fake glamour of Chelsea,' Clee went on. 'A club from dull suburbia, all we have is a belief that a new dawn is always waiting, when the masses of Croydon and South London will flock to Selhurst, a time when London's other clubs will bow down to the mighty Palace.' He closed: 'Reality has a habit of pricking our dream balloon.'

Reality certainly did intrude in September 1991. In a Channel 4 television documentary about racism in sport, Ron Noades was quoted – or selectively quoted, as he later claimed – characterising black players as skilful but lightweight and needing 'hard white men' around them, and stating that black players would be unlikely management material. The resulting uproar earned Noades instant personal notoriety, and plunged Palace – a club which, ironically, had unearthed numerous exciting black footballers – into crisis. Several players, white as well as black, threatened to resign. The *Daily*

Mirror spoke for many when it condemned Noades's comments as 'an affront to every decent-minded football fan', while *When Saturday Comes* suggested that the statements had been made 'with the certainty of someone not used to being contradicted'. The appearance of Noades's wife Novello at Palace's next home game in a T-shirt bearing the message, 'My husband is NOT a racist!' only kept the story bubbling. When, six months later, in response to rumours of an internal confrontation between players Andy Gray and Marco Gabbiadini, manager Coppell admitted at a well-attended fans' meeting that 'some of our players have a punch-up in training every week', it seemed that Palace were on the point of imploding. However, at the same meeting, chairman Noades quashed all talk of disintegration. Indeed, he unveiled his long-heralded vision of Selhurst Park as an all-seater, near-30,000-capacity stadium – coincidentally, in line with UEFA requirements for staging European Championship matches. Just one week later, Selhurst Park was in fact chosen as one of the eight venues included in England's bid to host the 1996 competition.

Like his Chelsea counterpart, the Palace chairman was an early supporter of the Premier League principle. Like Ken Bates, too, Noades was a proponent of the twenty-two-club structure. Back in 1990, he had been Bates's chief backer when the old first division reverted back from twenty to twenty-two teams. It was not to last. His complaint early in 1992 that the attendance at his club's Rumbelows League Cup quarter-final tie against Nottingham Forest was 'disgraceful' – fewer than 15,000 turned up to watch – brought sharp words from those same critics who had so provoked Bates's ire over the 'too much football' argument. 'I have been criticised for setting high admission prices,' blasted Noades. 'The charges on Wednesday were rock-bottom at £10 a seat and £6 standing, yet many supporters still did not come. We had the lowest gate of the quarter-finals, and I think it was disgraceful.' Ken Jones, the *Independent*'s acerbic columnist, was one of many writers who ruled Noades's griping out of order. 'Really,' he wrote in response to Ron's rant, 'could it not be that people are putting their heads together and coming to the conclusion that there is too much football?' Picking up the comment made the previous week by the Leeds manager, Howard Wilkinson, who had worried that 'the game is at saturation point', Jones added: 'Other prominent managers share Wilkinson's anxiety, but shortsightedly the clubs go on taking the money.' He quoted a club chief executive, who had told him: 'Unfortunately, you can't afford not to. Most of us are struggling to get by.'

In describing Noades's attack on his fans as 'extremely foolish . . . insensitive, provocative,' Jones concluded: 'Football ignores festering discontent at its peril. There is no guarantee against the game going into recession and, if it does, there won't be enough personalities to pull it round.' Before the year was out, Jones's words had an uncannily prophetic ring down in SE25. 'Palace order 10 per cent pay cut,' ran a December headline in the *Sun*, revealing that administrative and ground staff were all having their salaries sliced in order to keep the club solvent. Average gates were down by 3,000 a match and lottery income had fallen, as Palace slumped towards the Premier League basement. The wage drop applied to Noades, too, though not to Steve Coppell or his players. 'I have to manage Palace in the way I see fit, to keep it in business,' declared the chairman tartly in response.

In his book to celebrate Palace's achievement in reaching the 1990 FA Cup final, *No Fishcakes on Matchdays*, Deano Standing writes: 'In spite of his success, Ron

Noades has by no means overcome the suspicions of fans who question [his] motives. His abrasive nature similarly makes people wary of the man.' Those same supporters must, however, have been surprised to find Noades – only weeks after he had castigated them for disloyalty – defending one of their firmly-held principles in the face of the Taylor Report: the right to stand at matches. Continuing his swing away from his Premier League peers, Noades came down on the side of tradition when he announced that he was in favour of terraces behind the goals being retained. 'Fans can stand behind goals in absolute safety, provided the numbers, the access and the exits are right. Clubs can still go all-seater if they want, Noades asserted, with perhaps a nod to his own scheme for Selhurst, 'but a lot of clubs are using the Report as an excuse to charge fans top money for seats, although the front rows are often soaking wet.' In a final *coup de grâce* to his fellow administrators, Noades concluded: 'It's time somebody started talking for football on the Taylor Report.'

The Palace chairman finished the year as he believed he had started it: talking for football. He presented a December meeting of Premier League chairmen with the proposal that the league should be expanded to include a second division, claiming that 'the domestic game is divided, and I don't think anyone is looking after the interests of the game as a whole.' Noades added: 'We are overexposing soccer on television, carving up the potential sponsorship market and, in general, doing the game as a whole a disservice.' His belief was that a second division would bring the top forty-four clubs together, 'sitting down to address and debate the problems of the game and the needs of the clubs and the national team'. Was Noades in fact making contingency plans to keep his club and his own voice to the fore should Palace be relegated? Whatever his motivation, England manager Graham Taylor must certainly have been impressed at this rare display of concern for the difficulties he faced at international level. The Football League, predictably enough, was in equal measure unimpressed. 'The reason the big clubs left in the first place was to be able to share the money they generated among themselves,' said a nonplussed assistant secretary, Andy Williamson. 'Now they're talking about letting in others.' However, it emerged that the current Premier League clubs would retain their own voting power, while the cut on offer to the lower tier from the TV income could have been as low as 10 per cent – bringing many clubs less money than they already earned from the Football League's central pool. 'Most will look at the figures and realise where they are best off,' Williamson reasoned.

The talking went no further. Noades's plan for a second division was rejected as premature, a decision which clearly irked the Palace chairman. 'At this moment, there is a lot wrong with football,' he wailed. 'There is no one looking at the problems and discussing how to eradicate them. Everyone is fighting their own corner on the commercial side, everyone is looking at self-interest.' If Ron Noades was setting himself up as the saviour of English football, then plenty of heads were shaking in disbelief.

FIVE

The Building of Barnet

Flashman, Fry, and soccer strife in suburbia

As the Tube clanks and creaks its way towards the very last stop on the Northern Line, you can see right into Barnet FC's Underhill Stadium. But you have to know where to look. At most of the capital's other football grounds, four spindly floodlight pylons point the way. If not the floodlights, then there is always a stand or two rearing above the rooftops to signal the site. Yet, as the train edges alongside a platform at bucolic High Barnet, the view through the window is only of terraced houses in neat ranks and acres of open fields.

The mystery of the missing football ground continues once you have left the station and climbed up a steep path to Barnet Hill. Turn right, and you are soon mingling with the shoppers along one of outer London's most affluent high streets. Straight ahead, the very names of the roads betray their suburban location: Fitzjohn Avenue, Ellesmere Grove, Mays Lane. Not a common-or-garden Street in sight. And even when you bear left towards what the A-Z describes as Barnet Vale, it is still hard to believe that you are no more than a goalkeeper's punt away from the home of a professional soccer club.

Then, suddenly, you catch sight of the squat floodlight columns, peeking almost ashamedly from just above the houses. This slightly surreal air continues once you have found your way into the stadium, through one of the gates which lead directly on to the terraces. The pitch, like everything else in this sedate corner of North-West London, is on a slope. Around it stands a fence no higher than you would see in any self-respecting public park. At the top of the hill, there is netting rigged up on poles to stop the ball disappearing through any ill-placed conservatory windows; at the bottom, though, there is nothing to prevent a wayward shot skimming the roof of the tin shed behind the goal and hurtling on into rural Hertfordshire. The main stand – in fact, the only stand – runs along one side, two doors set into a lobby just off-centre. One leads into the boardroom – 'Jackets and ties must be worn,' states a notice on the outside – and the other into a 12ft by 12ft space containing two desks, one electric fire, three people and mountains of clutter. In early-season 1992–93, this was where you would find manager Barry Fry and club secretary Bryan Ayres. So cramped is the room that, whenever Fry was on the telephone giving an interview, its other occupants were forced to halt what they were doing and sit, button-lipped, until he had finished.

It was against this homely, unassuming backdrop that Barnet – like Brentford, nicknamed the Bees – pursued their second season in the Football League after winning promotion from the GM Vauxhall Conference. It seems almost inconceivable that, for most of 1992, events at humble Underhill jostled with those taking place at far more exalted stadia round the country for blanket coverage on the back pages of the papers. If a capacity for bizarre happenings had been one of the criteria for admission, then Barnet would have strolled into the Premier League.

Only the peculiar kick-off time should have made Barnet's late-November clash with Cardiff City different from any other Barclays League third-division fixture during the 1992–93 season. Sunday at 1 p.m. was an hour chosen not by the schedulers of BSkyB or ITV, but on police advice due to the unsavoury reputation of some of Cardiff's travelling fans. And there were more than a few sleepy faces among the visiting supporters as they emerged from the Tube station and scanned the skyline for sight of the ground. The contingent from Wales, a few neutrals freed from the conflicting pull of Arsenal or Spurs, Barnet's second place in the division, and a bracing autumn day all helped to swell the gate to nearly 4,000, then the club's biggest of the season. It was, however, a remarkable attendance for another reason. This was Barnet's first home fixture since the chairman had told his own supporters that he wasn't bothered whether they turned up to watch or not. On the morning of the Bees' top-of-the-table match at York City two weeks before, Stan Flashman had claimed that Barnet did not actually need their fans. 'The supporters don't matter as far as I am concerned,' he had blasted. 'They just pay their entrance fee. I don't care whether they come to Barnet or not. We play good football whether they are there or not.'

Given that the chairman's appalling words had been heard by millions on the radio, the visible loyalty of Barnet fans to the team they followed was extraordinary. When Dave Barnett pulled the game against Cardiff level in the seventieth minute, voices were united, not in protest against Flashman's outburst but in backing for their boys. Relentless pressure finally told when, with four minutes remaining, Derek Payne – at 5ft 4in the smallest player in the Football League – rifled home the winning goal. Manager Barry Fry celebrated with his trademark jig along the touchline and, at the final whistle, dozens of followers mobbed their heroes in an expression of unconfined joy and relief. Maybe there was a reason for the apparent lack of concern at Stan Flashman's embarrassing public utterance; maybe the Barnet regulars had heard it all before?

From the mid-1980s, there was no football club in the country – though Chelsea and Crystal Palace might run it close – where the personality of the club as a whole was so entirely a reflection of the personalities of its manager and chairman. Quite simply, Barry Fry and Stan Flashman *were* Barnet. Fry arrived as manager during the 1978–79 season, having first sat in the dug-out at Southern League Dunstable Town following a playing career that earned him six England schoolboy caps and a spell at Manchester United as one of the less celebrated Busby Babes. But Underhill was a different matter altogether from Old Trafford. Barnet were languishing in the Southern League, watched by crowds that did not need many fingers to count up. 'We were fourth from bottom when I came here,' he remembered, 'and we needed to finish in the top half of the table to get into the Alliance Premier League, the forerunner of the Vauxhall Conference, which was being formed the next season. We weren't doing very well and, in early 1979, I said to then chairman Dave Underwood that we lacked team spirit. I'd had to change a lot of players when I took over, and they were coming from so many different directions and just going home after games. We had the chance to go to Italy and play in a tournament. Dave was fearful that we'd get beaten out of sight, but I said it would be great for morale. Thankfully, he took my advice and, although we lost 0–1 and drew 1–1 and didn't reach the final, we had a lot of laughs together and went the next seventeen games undefeated, which was enough to get us into the new league.'

Fry had quickly revealed his uncanny ability to motivate a set of players. But, miracle number one achieved, his next challenge was even tougher: to keep Barnet among the élite of semi-professional clubs despite a chronic lack of money. 'We fought off relegation five years on the trot,' he recalled. 'If it was two down, we'd finish third from bottom. If it was three down, we'd finish fourth from last. Our gates still weren't very good, and we always had to sell players to survive. I was manager, groundsman, secretary, treasurer, barman, the lot in those days. We were in such a financial mess that the clubhouse, which was our main source of income, was closed down. I took out a second mortgage of £12,500 on my own home to pay up the covenant to the brewers so we could keep it open.'

All of which begs the question, why? Fry's capabilities were not in doubt, so why stick around at a club which appeared to be on a fast track to insolvency? Sitting in the spartan boardroom, Fry had no problem providing an answer. 'Because it's a lovely club, full of lovely people,' he declared, his eyes suddenly sparkling from beneath the peak of the chequered flat cap which seems to perch permanently on his head. 'We had some good players, but we were always two or three short of a team to push for honours. The directors were forever saying, it'd be better if we got relegated to the Southern League and did well there, but I said no. If that had happened, we wouldn't have had the resources to climb back into the Conference, which is the best competition outside the Football League. It's the same situation as the Premier League now; I'm sure Wimbledon would rather be near the bottom of that than somewhere near the top of the first division. You always want to play at the highest level you can.'

Fry might have added 'fund-raiser' to the list of job titles he held at that time. 'By 1984, there was a writ coming into the club almost every day, and the directors just couldn't handle it. I went round all the local businesses trying to get them interested, but none were. The players suffered, and went without their money several times. The club gave me a testimonial against Spurs; I got George Best to turn out for me, and handed all the proceeds to the players.' One of the businessmen Fry turned to was a resident of nearby Totteridge called Stan Flashman. 'But he put my proposition to his accountant, who told him not to touch Barnet with a bargepole.'

By this time, the club had debts of £80,000 and were only weeks away from receeivership. And Barry Fry had had enough. On 5 January 1985, he went to Maidstone. But the move was not a success: Fry's tenure at the Kent club provided further evidence that he and Barnet were almost wedded together. 'I didn't really set the world on fire there,' he admitted. 'They wanted me to move upstairs when I wanted to concentrate on the football, so they sacked me.' Meanwhile, Flashman had had second thoughts about investing in Barnet. In May 1985, he stepped in with a reported £50,000, stalled the various debtors, and bought a 94 per cent stake in the club plus a long lease on the ground. But it did not take long for Flashman's impatience to manifest itself: 'Stan took over as chairman, got in Roger Thompson as manager and then sacked him, then got in Don McAllister and sacked him as well. I'd done nothing in eighteen months at Maidstone, so I returned. We've been back seven years now, Stan and me,' said Fry, switching to the plural as if to emphasise the partnership.

Flashman's timely intervention did indeed save Barnet from extinction. It is a fact which Fry was only too ready to acknowledge: 'He was my hero. If it wasn't for him, there wouldn't be a Barnet Football Club now.' The supporters felt the same way, too: 'Stan was something of a demigod,' says Doron Garfunkel, editor of the now-defunct fanzine *Buzztalk*. 'It was his money that changed Barnet from a bunch of no-hopers to a club that was pressing for promotion to the Football League. He had a cult status. People on the terraces heard the stories – that he bought the players new suits and paid for their overnight stops on away trips – and saw him as a lovable rogue, even though they didn't know too much about him.' Fry concurred with this view. 'He let me look after the players as well as Arsenal, Tottenham or anyone else would. We'd travel on Friday nights, have the best coach, best hotel, best meal. The players got Yves St Laurent blazers, and it made them feel good about themselves.'

As soon as automatic promotion to the Football League for the Conference champions was established, Flashman and Fry had a target to aim for; they achieved it after finishing second an agonising three times, and sealed the success at Fisher Athletic's Docklands ground on the last day of the 1990–91 season, when Gary Bull smashed home two title-clinching goals inside the last five minutes. At the final whistle, manager raced across the pitch to deliver a much-photographed bear-hug to chairman.

A week later, the rotund figure of Stan Flashman confronted readers of the *Observer* over their Sunday muesli. With a portrait by renowned photographer Jane Bown for accompaniment, a feature entitled 'Big man with the seating plan' explained how Flashman, a Spurs supporter, had begun his career in the ticketing business while still a salesman in a Houndsditch warehouse: 'I saw the boys selling tickets outside the ground. I bought a couple, sold them to a punter and made £10. If you go up to someone offering to sell, there's only two things he can say: "Yes" or "No". In a couple of hours, I'd made £40. I thought to myself, "When I'm earning £35 a week working from 8.30 a.m. to 5.30 p.m., that's all right." A few months later, Flashman began to deal directly with customers before, rather than at, events. He set up at an office in King's Cross, and the self-styled 'King of the Touts' was soon moving up in the world, buying a mock-Tudor mansion in affluent Totteridge.

The preferred term two decades on is 'ticket broker', but the practice is still the same: if you want to be present at a major occasion, Stan's yer man. He claims to have sold two passes for Princess Anne's wedding, and that 'a public servant in a high position' used to supply him with tickets for the Queen's garden parties. As proof of the effectiveness of his motto, 'Why sleep when you can make money?', Flashman drives a Mercedes with a personalised number plate and has a penchant for holidays in Marbella. One of his favourite stories is of the time he 'put one over' Frank Sinatra. In 1977, the American singer had asked that ticket prices for his London shows be kept to a sensible level, so Flashman bought up hundreds and made a killing. His *coup de grâce* was to present an unwitting Sinatra with a bottle of the finest bourbon from the best seats in the house, where he and his wife Helen were sitting.

As long as 'Fat Stan' restricted his interest in Barnet to providing the financial impetus for a push up the footballing pyramid, Fry and the fans were happy. However, as the anonymous editors of *Two Together* – a fanzine named after the most frequent request made to Flashman – put it, 'the season before Barnet got into the Football League was when he began to promote himself as the chairman. From then on, in our opinion, he started to get an inflated idea of where he was in football.' His first serious run-in with the supporters had

been in March 1989, when the popular Nicky Evans
was sold to Conference rivals Wycombe Wanderers,
despite Barnet being well placed to win the title. There
was a demonstration beneath the main stand where
Flashman was sitting, and he was accused of assaulting
the writer of a somewhat unsubtle one-off fanzine and
threatening a female supporter who intervened in the
dispute.

Despite abundant on-the-pitch evidence to the contrary, Flashman's programme notes for the next home
game slammed Evans's playing ability. However, the
editors of *Two Together* believe this incident simply
revealed a further facet of Flashman's character: 'If
he rubbishes a player, it doesn't mean he thinks he's
useless. It means he thinks he's useless for the minute
while he flips his lid.' In the *Observer* profile, Flashman
had himself admitted to a bad temper: 'It doesn't happen
often, but when it does, I have to get it off my chest.
And, two minutes later, I feel remorse.' More than once,
it is alleged, players have been reduced to tears by his
invective.

How Flashman must have ranted after Barnet's first
two matches as a Football League club. A crowd of 5,090
squeezed into Underhill on the opening Saturday of the
1991–92 season to see Crewe Alexandra, just relegated
from the third division, win a bizarre game 7–4. Ever
ready with a quip, Barry Fry faced the press afterwards:
'It was a carnival occasion, and Barnet were the clowns.
My defenders must have thought tackle is what they went
fishing with.' Within the week, his team were in action
against Brentford in the first round of the Rumbelows
Cup and, having found themselves 5–3 up with the final
whistle approaching, promptly conceded two soft goals to
draw 5–5. By the time Barnet had travelled to Lincoln
City at the beginning of September and won 6–0, the five

games played by the Bees had produced the incredible tally of thirty-one goals. The papers loved it, dubbing Barnet 'Football's Keystone Cops'. Fry wasn't so happy, worrying publicly that his team might score 200 goals during the season but concede 201.

In the end, they netted eighty-one in the league, almost half that number bagged by Gary Bull and Mark Carter with performances which had several big clubs looking on enviously and itching to ink in six-figure cheques. It was the equal-largest tally of all ninety-two clubs, and enough to earn the Bees a fully-deserved place in the play-offs during their debut campaign. But just when the entire club needed to pull together in pursuit of promotion, Barnet were riven apart by the first in a series of distressingly public confrontations between chairman, manager and players, the opening episode in a tragi-comedy of epic proportions including megalomania, violence and the humiliation of an outfit that otherwise had much to be proud of.

MAY 10: Barry Fry has never hidden the fact that he and Flashman have indulged in the occasional spat during their time at Barnet: 'The sparks fly when Stan and I get together,' he had admitted the year before. But no sooner has Fry guided his team to within ninety minutes of a Wembley play-off final by beating Blackpool 1–0 in the first leg of the semi-final than he announces: 'I've just been sacked by Stan Flashman.' Following the game, Fry claims that, 'We could have won 5–0 or 6–0, but Flashman came in afterwards and said we were crap and that the entire team should be up for transfer. If he wants, he can be manager, chairman and centre-forward next season. We'll all sit on the sidelines and have a good laugh. I will turn up for the second leg in an unpaid capacity and, if Flashman tries to stop me, we'll have a fight on the centre line and sell tickets for that.' The response from Flashman is also very much in character: 'He hasn't had the sack from me. If he's given himself the sack, then that's a different matter. As far as I'm concerned, he will be travelling with the team to Blackpool.'

MAY 13: Fry takes Barnet up to Blackpool, having been reinstated as manager two days earlier. The team lose 0–2, and the chairman is not there to see the game. However, Flashman is kept in touch with play by his son, Mark, a reserve goalkeeper at the club, who sits on the bench with a mobile phone. Like Barnet, the phone eventually runs out of power, so Mark keeps his dad updated from the press box. After the match, the players have already started drowning their sorrows in the Tangerine Club, the nightspot next to Blackpool's ground, when Fry joins Mark in the press box to phone their travel arrangements through to Stan. Ken Dyer and Mick Dennis of the *Evening Standard* overhear the conversation. 'We'll stay here until the club closes at 2 a.m.,' says Mark, 'then come home. I'll be home about 6.30 a.m.'. But this apparently does not meet with Stan's approval, and Mark tells Fry: 'We've got to go home now, and he wants to see you tomorrow.' Stan's recollection of the conversation is somewhat different: 'Mark told me the team had been unlucky and wanted to stay and have a few drinks. I told him there was no problem, and that they could stay as long as they wanted.' In fact, the players leave the Tangerine Club at 11 p.m. moving elsewhere until 2 a.m. before taking the coach back to London. 'The lads sang "Please don't go",' adds Fry. 'It was a great gesture. Then they poured beer over me, and I sat in wet clothes for four hours before going home.'

MAY 14: 'Supporters of Barnet don't realise what goes on behind the scenes at this club,' blasts Fry. 'I can assure you the players are unified behind Baz,' declares assistant manager Edwin Stein in support. 'Baz is at his wits' end, and there is a real chance he will go. If that happens, then many of the players will follow him. That is not an idle boast, that is reality. His job has enough pressures without the kind of thing which occurred after the first leg on Sunday. Fortunately, for the first time, the players witnessed it. There are times when, whatever you do, you just cannot please the chairman. It can't go on. We must talk to him and make him realise this is a marvellous opportunity to ensure this club goes forward.'

MAY 16: Barnet had reached the play-offs with a squad still largely comprised of part-time players, but Fry is convinced that the key to promotion is a full-time operation. Flashman, for financial reasons, objects. Indeed, he wants *more* semi-pros on the staff, not fewer. Before going into a crisis meeting with his chairman, Fry states: 'I don't mind a couple of part-timers, but not eleven. This club is a large part of my life, but it is at the crossroads. It can go on to be a big club but, if the insistence is to make even more players part-time, it will go the other way.'

MAY 17: Fry announces that he is staying. 'All this trouble after six successful years. God knows what will happen if we have a bad year – he'll probably shoot my kneecaps off.'

JUNE 4: Edwin Stein is sacked by Flashman. 'I intend to fight this,' he fumes. 'It seems I have been sacked because the club has been too successful.' Club captain Gary Poole is released on a free transfer because he fails to agree new terms: 'I don't want to leave Barnet,' he complains. Fry, predictably, is not impressed: 'It's a ridiculous situation, absolutely idiotic. Lots of clubs have been after him, and now they can get him on a free transfer. Normally, I would want £250,000.' Poole joins Plymouth Argyle.

'Stan is just undermining my authority yet again,' says Fry. 'He's making it impossible for me to manage the club.'

JULY 13: All twenty members of the first-team squad slap in a communal transfer request after discovering shortfalls in their pay packets. Player-of-the-year David Howell, who has just resigned from his job in the BBC's personnel department after verbally agreeing a new contract with Flashman, states: 'I had been promised a decent rise, but I end up getting £75 less than usual.' The whole squad drives to Flashman's house, but his wife Helen tells them he is ill in bed, and she will sort the matter out. PFA representative and goalkeeper Gary Phillips declares: 'The players are incensed, and I know we will all stick together on this one. We were going to take strike action, but the manager talked us out of that. None of us wants to play for Stan Flashman because of his treatment of the players and staff alike.' Fry describes it as the worst day of his life.

JULY 18: The Football League announces an investigation into alleged 'financial irregularities' concerning payments and unorthodox accounting procedures at the club. A ban on buying new players is imposed.

JULY 20: David Howell is again underpaid, despite promises from Flashman that it was a misunderstanding and the matter would be sorted out. Barry Fry praises the attitude of the players as the pre-season build-up starts: 'They were livid but they still went out there and beat Knebworth 11–0.' Striker Mark Carter is the latest subject of transfer talk and looks set to join Blackpool.

JULY 30: Barry Fry is in ebullient mood at the Barnet Supporters' Club AGM, which Stan Flashman does not attend. He reveals how he prevented Mark Carter being transferred: 'For the first time I got one over the chairman. He sent Spike [Carter] up to Blackpool to sign, but a friend of mine gave me a few bob to send Spike to Spain for a week. Spike Carter does not want to leave Barnet. This time last year I had eight offers for him, so I asked him what he wanted to do. He said, "You bought me last season, and I just want to show my faith in you." The fact that he travels from Liverpool to play, and wants to keep doing that rather than go forty minutes down the road to Blackpool, speaks volumes for everybody at Barnet Football Club.' Fry also reflects on the Blackpool play-off fiasco: 'I must admit, I felt I couldn't take any more. He [Flashman] took the piss out of me same as he's taken the piss out of the players and taken the piss out of you. But I feel if I go, it leaves a lot of players out on a limb, a lot of supporters out on a limb. I feel the club is too big to let go without a fight [applause].' Fry then widens his complaint, pointing out that he has brought in £1.5 million over the last three years through selling players: 'The annoying thing is, we should be one of the richest clubs in the country with the amount of money coming in. What's happened to it? Your guess is as good as mine'. But he is still incapable of outright hostility towards his chairman: 'Stan was my hero, to be fair. Seven years ago he came in and saved this club, when I went round stealing and borrowing to try and keep things going and no one wanted to know. He saved the club, but it frightens me to death that he's going to take it down with him.'

SEPTEMBER 19: The FA reveals that two FA Cup final tickets issued to Barnet were offered for sale by touts at Wembley in May. Club captain Duncan Horton makes a statement on behalf of the playing squad, saying: 'None of the forty-seven tickets supplied to the club for the final was made available to us or the staff.' Kenny Lowe tells the *People* that Flashman had *sold* him tickets; what's more, they were from the allocation to Kettering FC.

Secretary Bryan Ayres explains that, when he received the club's batch of tickets, he 'passed them on to the chairman, but I have no knowledge of what happened to them after that.'

SEPTEMBER 22: Horton and Lowe are suspended, transfer-listed and fined two weeks' wages for speaking out about the touted tickets. A players' rep announces that the following Saturday's match could be in jeopardy if Flashman refuses to withdraw his action: 'We shall be contacting the PFA in the morning after we have held a meeting. If the chairman refuses to back-track on the issue, then there will be no game against Wrexham.'

SEPTEMBER 23: The PFA orders Flashman to reinstate Horton and Lowe.

SEPTEMBER 25: Flashman states on the Clubcall phone line that he is placing 'terrace spies' around the ground to weed out critics of his policies. Anyone who protests runs the risk of a life ban from Underhill. 'The club has done brilliantly since I took over,' he says, 'and the time has come to root out these sarcastic people.' Later, he claims that the message was the work of an impostor.

OCTOBER 19: The players again threaten to strike after Flashman says pay cuts are necessary because the club is losing £2,000 a week.

OCTOBER 26: The players sign new contracts, under Football League and PFA supervision.

NOVEMBER 4: The players are allegedly short-changed in their pay packets by up to £60. 'Hopefully, the accountants can clear matters up once and for all,' says Fry.

NOVEMBER 5: Flashman bans Fry and the players from speaking to the press.

NOVEMBER 6: Several expletives are bleeped from an interview given by Flashman to BBC Radio 5, in which he explains the media ban imposed the previous day.

He then makes his dramatic claim that the club's fans are unimportant: 'The supporters don't matter as far as I'm concerned. They just pay their entrance fee. I don't care whether they come to Barnet or not. We play good football whether they are there or not.' Later in the day, Flashman calls the Beeb back to state that he believes Barnet fans are 'the best in the country'.

NOVEMBER 8: An anonymous representative of the Barnet Supporters' Club condemns the chairman: 'I think what he deserves is for no one to come to the games. Basically, I want to see him go. He is hurting the club.'

NOVEMBER 11: Barry Fry reaches Underhill to be told that Manchester United chairman Martin Edwards has been on the phone. 'He rang back, came straight to the point, said he wanted Gary Bull, and asked how much. I said £500,000. I gave him the chairman's number because I thought all that was left to agree was the matter of payment and the bits and pieces. He then asked me if I would pull Gary Bull out of the FA Cup game with Bournemouth on Saturday, as United didn't want him cup-tied. I told Bully that he was on his way to United. He was over the moon. I got back to Barnet after being out for the afternoon; the chairman said he'd been on the phone with Martin Edwards, the deal was OK, and that I was to ring Old Trafford to arrange when Bull was going there to sign.' An hour later, Alex Ferguson, Manchester United's manager, is on the phone and sounding very concerned. 'He said Martin Edwards couldn't have talked to me or Stan because he'd been with his chairman all day, and he definitely hadn't made the phone calls. Obviously, from Gary Bull's point of view, it was a sick joke, but he took it very well. Gary said it must have been a Bournemouth supporter trying to wind us up and get him pulled out of the match. But the gentleman who phoned me and phoned Stan knew too much about football, too much about wheeling and dealing, for it just to be an ordinary fan.' Another impostor on the line?

NOVEMBER 15: After being transferred to Watford, winger Roger Willis claims he is still owed his final week's wages by the Bees. Flashman states on radio that all staff have been paid every penny they are owed since he came to the club in 1985.

NOVEMBER 22: Barnet pull in their biggest gate of the season for the Sunday lunchtime visit of Cardiff City, maintaining their push for promotion by winning 2-1.

NOVEMBER 23: In a Football League hearing at the Metropole Hotel, a three-man commission imposes a fine of £50,000 on the club for breaching league regulations by failing to keep proper books of accounts and players' contracts. It is a fine second only in severity to the £105,000 Chelsea were levied in 1991 for contract irregularities. The official statement says, 'There are a number of mitigating factors, not least the fact that Barnet are relative newcomers to the league. Nevertheless, these are serious breaches of regulations.' Stanley Beller, Barnet's solicitor, retorts that the fine is excessive and that the club will appeal. 'There have been a number of technical offences but no question of any impropriety whatsoever,' he says. The club also have to pay the cost of the investigation, and must have their books audited again in April 1993. The embargo on buying new players is not lifted. Before the hearing, Flashman loses his temper with *Daily Mirror* photographer Dale Cherry, shouting: 'If you take a picture, I will smash that camera over your head,' before grappling with the snapper and ripping his coat. 'He just came at me like a man possessed,' says Cherry. On the way out from the six-and-a-half-hour hearing, Flashman attacks *Sun* lensman Paul Welford, pinning him against the wall of the hotel's underground car park. 'He wrapped his hands around my throat as his wife was trying to drag him off,' recalls Welford. 'What made Flashman's behaviour all the more bizarre was that he immediately calmed down and was willing to pose for pictures.'

NOVEMBER 24: In a three-page feature headlined 'The Ugly Face of Football', the *Sun* declares: 'Stan Flashman is the unacceptable face of soccer. He is a fat, ugly brute who would shame even the toughest soccer terrace. The Football League should not just have fined his club £50,000 yesterday. They should have shown Fat Stan the red card. He has turned poor little Barnet into a disgrace, where the fans are held in contempt and the players claim they have not been paid. Stan Flashman is not fit to clean the toilets at Wembley. Even though he would be among his own kind there.'

NOVEMBER 25: On the morning of the club's first-round FA Cup replay against Bournemouth, Flashman phones Barnet's training ground at Edgware and criticises the players for the previous day's events. One squad member says: 'Before training, Barry called a meeting and said the chairman had accused us of being greedy bastards and blamed us for the fine. He seems to hold David Howell, who's still owed three weeks' money, particularly responsible and wants him out of the club. We said that if David was out then we were all out, and wouldn't play against Bournemouth because we were sticking with the players still owed money. Barry then telephoned Stan, and they had a screaming match. Stan told him we could all go and, what's more, he'd give us all free transfers to go quickly.' Another adds: 'Barry was on the verge of walking out. The name of the club was being dragged down, lower and lower. We all have to stick together at this time.' In conditions deemed unplayable by both managers but acceptable to the referee, Barnet lose 1–2 to Bournemouth. Flashman does not turn up to watch, but tells Capital Radio that Gary Bull will not be sold to pay off the £50,000 fine 'as long as I'm chairman of this club, and that will be a long time yet'. Fry, meanwhile, implores Flashman to quit: 'What he has done this week has totally humiliated everyone at this club, and for his sake, football's sake and the sake of Barnet he should go. I feel sorry for the fans. They hate going to work all week and they look forward to Saturday. It's a big part in their lives. But Stan snubs those sort of people, and I find it very difficult to work with a man whose basic principles are not the same as mine.'

NOVEMBER 27: Stan Flashman is not the most fluent of interviewees. His sentences are painstakingly constructed, yet they run into each other with few breaks. On Clubcall, he answers the presenter's question on whether he is optimistic about the club's future: 'Yes, I am optimistic for the future success of Barnet Football Club. As soon as the press stop *[sic]* leaving us alone, as I've said in the past, I've been there for seven years, we've had seven years of success, and I don't see why we shouldn't have another seven years of success.' That he considers his next statement important is clear from the even more tortured syntax: 'Although people say I should resign, but unfortunately there will be a few changes at the ground in the next couple of weeks and, although people might not enjoy the people that won't be there, unfortunately, by the precise way they are talking, they don't deserve to be there.'

NOVEMBER 29: A consortium fronted by former Spurs defender Paul Miller announces a £1 million bid for Flashman's controlling interest in Barnet.

DECEMBER 1: Fry has been verbally 'sacked' by Flashman at least three times before but, on this occasion, his dismissal – as intimated on Clubcall four days earlier – is in writing. Fry is steaming: 'Flashman is a complete and utter shit. To say I am gutted is a total understatement. When I arrived for training this morning, my wife had been on the phone three times. She told me there was this letter from Stan, questioning my loyalty to Barnet and my commitment to the club. Anyone who knows me will tell you those are the last things I'm lacking.' Gary Phillips and David Howell prepare a statement on behalf of the players: 'Barry Fry is responsible for bringing every player to the club, and we all feel very confused and angry by this action. Anyone connected to Barnet would know how much Barry Fry loves the club and is the one person who has kept it together. The reason that Barnet are currently second in the league and playing attractive and entertaining football must be credited to Barry Fry's dedication, enthusiasm, loyalty and commitment. It has been increasingly difficult against a background of constant interruption, disgraceful behaviour and turmoil created by Stan Flashman, who seems intent on destroying everything that has been achieved by Barry Fry at Barnet FC.'

DECEMBER 2: Flashman is unrepentant. Again on Clubcall, again in his own peculiar phraseology, he offers an explanation for his manager's sacking: 'Unfortunately, Barry started talking too much and went, to my mind, to silly positions in what he was saying, and one cannot put up with that. How can a manager, who is a worker, tell the owner of the club to resign? Barry is no longer manager of Barnet Football Club, and unfortunately it's a sad day for me to say that, but you can only let people have their heads for so long and then, when you find that they're saying things which you couldn't believe a manager of a club would say, then it's time to call it a day for him.' To make things worse, Inland Revenue officials take away documents relating to Barnet from Flashman's house – despite being asked by his wife to call back later 'as my husband has a temperature' – and interview the entire first-team squad at their Prince Edward playing-fields training-ground. 'It was unbelievable,' says an eye-witness. 'Enough of them turned up to stage their own game.'

DECEMBER 3: At a packed Supporters' Club meeting, 49-year-old financier George Maxwell stands up to reveal that he is at the head of a ten-man consortium willing to buy Flashman out. Maxwell earns a standing ovation when he promises to reinstate Fry as manager. Despite having agreed to do so, Flashman fails to attend. His wife Helen phones two hours before the start to say that her husband has a sick note from the doctor which prevents him leaving the house.

DECEMBER 5: Fry turns up at Halifax Town and stands on the terraces as Barnet win 2–1. 'I feel bitterness and anger, but at the same time I am immensely proud of the players and supporters for the way they have put up with everything,' he announces. 'These are the people it is all about,' indicating the fans around him. 'It leaves me all choked up, and that man [Flashman] says these people don't matter. It's a disgrace.'

DECEMBER 6: Flashman insists he is ready to sell the club, but not to a consortium that includes Barry Fry: 'There will never, ever be a reconciliation.' He also expresses remorse for his comments about Barnet's fans: 'I regret saying those things because it was the heat-of-the-moment situation,' he tells Tony Delahunty on LBC's *Sunday Sport*. 'They are our bread and butter. But when you are angered by what people say who don't know the full facts, you hit out.'

DECEMBER 8: The *Sun*, milking the publicity gained when its photographer was assaulted by Flashman, starts a 'Ban Fat Stan' campaign. The paper supports the action planned by fans to boycott the next home game against

Rochdale. 'It might hurt supporters in the short term, but in the long run it could persuade Stan his time is well and truly up,' says Russell Delaney, joint-chairman of the Barnet Shares Action Group.

DECEMBER 9: As several dozen supporters announce that they intend to dress for the Rochdale match in Fry's usual gear – dark glasses, anorak pulled up round the ears, and cheese-cutter cap – to try to confuse their chairman, the ex-manager pleads with them to turn up as usual: 'I don't want people boycotting games and depriving themselves of seeing their team,' he says. 'I'm a Barnet fan as well, and I want to see them play.' Striker Mark Carter is convinced that Fry's days at Barnet are far from over: 'I think we all expect Barry to come back sooner or later, despite the comments to the contrary.' Fry drives to Northampton Town to see his former team lose 1–2 in an Autoglass Trophy tie. 'This is murder, sitting up here,' he tells *Evening Standard* reporter Ken Dyer. 'I just feel so helpless.' The home fans taunt him with chants of 'There's only one Stan Flashman'.

DECEMBER 10: Fry claims that he was sacked because he refused to dismiss any players who believed they were still due money from Flashman: 'On the morning after Barnet had been fined £50,000 by the League for financial irregularities, Stan rang me and told me to get down to the training-ground. I was to find out if any players were saying they were owed money by him – and sack them. Stan said the players had cost him £50,000. I felt sick, disgusted and ashamed. Certain players told me they were owed money. I just lost my rag. It was then I told Stan, "Look in the mirror – there's the person to blame." I told him he was making us an embarrassment, and that he should sell up and get out.'

DECEMBER 11: Banned from the ground, Fry plans to follow the Rochdale game from the bedroom window of a supporter's house which overlooks the ground. 'It's the only way I can watch the match,' he says. 'The police wouldn't be too happy if I turned up at the ground, so I hope to watch it from one of the houses behind the goal. I'm hoping he doesn't charge me admission!'

DECEMBER 12: The *Sun*'s anti-Flashman campaign continues when the paper parks a lorry outside his house carrying the hoarding, 'Ban This Fat Bully Today'. Flashman is quoted saying: 'I know I've done nothing wrong. I can hold my head up. It doesn't affect me personally, I just ignore it all. They won't make me change my mind. It shows who has got the needle over all this, and it's not me.' However, the back page of the *Daily Mail* tells a rather different story: beneath the headline 'Back in a flash', it reports that Fry has in fact been reinstated as manager after a heart-to-heart at the chairman's house. 'Stan called me and said we ought to have a chat,' Fry explains, 'and I've been down at his house all day. We talked it through. We agreed we'd had seven great years together, and why shouldn't we get it back together again. All I want now is to concentrate on football and work for the success of a great little club.' The *Mail* also runs an interview with George Maxwell, the man who wants to buy the club. His ambition is clear when he states: 'I mean to put Barnet into the 21st century, on and off the pitch. In the meantime, it would be logical to share with Arsenal or Tottenham. I'm sure they wouldn't turn up their noses at extra revenue. After that, finding the site and getting permission for a new ground is a matter of political will. All the political people say the same: "Get promotion into the first division, and then we'll get excited".'

Programme editor Tony Holmes leaves the 'Barry Fry Comments' page for the Rochdale game blank except for the line, 'This page is reserved'. Fry guides his team to a 2–0 win, which takes Barnet to the top of the table. Afterwards, he tells reporters: 'We're a bit of a joke in football at the moment because people don't know whether to take us seriously.' He also reveals his reasons for returning: 'My wife was worried that I'd make myself a complete laughing stock by going back, that I'd lose all credibility and never be offered another job in football. But if I'd said no, it would have been sticking two fingers up at the players and the fans who had supported me. I respect her views, but I feel for the place.' Flashman again misses the match due to a cold, and reserves his only public statement for Clubcall: 'This business just got out of all proportion.'

As 1992 drew to a close, Barnet consolidated their position at the top of division three. However, Fry's reinstatement was not the end of Barnet's year-long spell on every investigative sportswriter's agenda. Early January 1993 saw Flashman's son Mark signed on a full-time contract. 'I regard him as a Premier League goalkeeper of the future,' said dad. 'I didn't know anything about this, it's come as a great surprise,' stated Fry. 'The chairman told me to sign his league registration, so I did,' explained secretary Bryan Ayres. Six weeks later, Fry announced that every player on the books was up for sale: 'The chairman told me to list them all,' he said, after watching his squad extend their lead to seven points with a 2–0 win over Doncaster Rovers. 'Players' cheques had bounced, and he had to send cash to square things up before today's game.'

'The amount of paranoia that man [Flashman] generates is incredible,' says Doron Garfunkel, editor of the now-defunct *Buzztalk*. 'I think he would *like* to be liked, but is not prepared to make any effort to be liked. At the end of the day, he doesn't give a toss what people think about him. Stan rules with an iron fist, and what he says goes.' This was the reason why Flashman banned *Buzztalk* from being sold on club property after it had included, for the first time, mildly critical comments about a player's form. It also explains why Garfunkel decided to cease publication one issue later. 'It plays on my conscience that we have a chairman who makes it very difficult for me to say what I actually feel,' he wrote in his final editorial. 'The silent form of censorship that exists within the club stretches from me to the manager and the local press and leaves a sour taste in my mouth.'

Almost all of Barnet's fans, however, remained 100 per cent behind Fry as manager, and the feeling on the terraces persisted that there was very little that could not be achieved so long as 'Baz' was at the helm. If he were to get his way and was able to make all his players full-time – Mark Carter, Kenny Lowe and Paul Showler continued to live in the north and train independently throughout the 1992–93 season – then Fry was convinced that Barnet could be playing top-flight football at the turn of the century: 'By the year 2000,' he declared grandly, 'it's my aim to see this club playing in the Premier League. It's been done before and it'll be done again. Provided we get our house in order, we are capable of making the progress required, just like Wimbledon did.' Fry believed that the need at many clubs to divert financial resources into off-the-pitch activities would actually work to the advantage of smaller clubs like Barnet: 'The majority of clubs can't spend money on their grounds *and* spend money on their team. This limits the number of clubs which might be in contention. I see the next few years as the ideal opportunity for a club with the financial clout and the right ambition to go forward.' Obviously, that would mean moving to a new ground, but even this prospect did not alarm the ever-optimistic Fry: 'There's no way we could stage Premier League football here,' he said, wafting a tracksuited arm round the draughty, woodchip-papered boardroom to delineate the sloping pitch and tiny terraces beyond. 'There's no way we could do that without spending £15 million. And that'd be stupid. We'd be better off spending £15 million two miles down the road, but still in the borough of Barnet. There's a bigger potential audience for football round here, no question about it.'

Finally, as the green shoots of spring began to match the verdant nature of Fry's optimism, the eight-year Barnet saga took yet another dramatic turn. Just two days after Flashman had threatened to fine his players two weeks' wages for complaining that they had not been paid for two weeks, it was announced that the chairman – who, at the time, was supposed to be meeting the PFA chief executive to iron out those very problems – had quit, reportedly due to ill health. A new board took over immediately, headed by Robert Wolfson, a 44-year-old chartered accountant and Tottenham supporter. The new chairman's first job was to reinstate Fry, who had been sacked for old times' sake by Flashman just before he left. Twenty-four hours later, however, Fry had also departed the scene to take up the manager's job at first-division strugglers Southend United, citing as his reason his lack of trust in the new regime: 'They're just papering over the cracks,' he said. So was that it? Was it finally all over? You could never be sure with Barnet – especially since the newspapers which reported the first of these happenings were datelined 1 April.

SIX

Forward with the People

Millwall, Brentford, and a sense of community

A winter-chill Tuesday morning in South-East London. Commuter trains from suburban Kent chug out of New Cross Gate station, soon to unpack their contents at Waterloo East a couple of miles up the line. In the other direction, there is the usual snarl of buses and lorries inching through the traffic lights on the Old Kent Road towards Elephant and Castle. Between railway and road, as if marooned on an island where progress has passed it by, stands the Den – home to Millwall Football Club for the last eighty-three years. If you cut through to the ground from Surrey Docks – or Surrey Quays, as the property developers renamed that little swathe of Rotherhithe – then head down Trundleys Road and Sanford Street, you finally turn right into Cold Blow Lane. Never was a street more aptly named. Through its graffiti-strewn tunnels, past the scrapyards full of clapped-out cars and down to the Den blew the wind of malevolence that provided the public preconceptions of English football in the late 1970s and early 1980s. No ground has been closed down by the FA because of crowd trouble more often than the Den.

This, however, is a new decade. And the Den, once

the most feared soccer ground in England, is no more, its less-than-leafy acres sold to house-builders Fairview for £5 million. Most people at the club and the majority of fans were – after a few nostalgic tears – glad to get away, to leave the drab, low-slung stands, higgledy-piggledy terraces, cramped offices and a notorious reputation borne out by a spontaneous demolition derby after the final fixture. Half a mile down the road at Senegal Fields is the Lions' new lair, a spruce contrast to the confined barracks on Cold Blow Lane. Not since 1937, when Orient shunted from Lea Bridge Road to their present site at Leyton Stadium, has a London club moved grounds simply to better itself. The New Den is a symbol of a new Millwall, the result of what chairman Reg Burr, the city financier who took over the reins in 1986, describes as 'nothing less than a revolution'.

But first, back to the old Den this particular freezing February day. Three dozen footballers are limbering up for six-a-side matches on the pitch. A couple, swathed in tracksuits and bobble hats, lope a gentle lap of the playing area; other hack a ball around in an effort to keep the blood flowing while goals are set up and referees' whistles sought. It could be a typical scene at any professional club on a midweek morning, the first-team squad half-heartedly loosening limbs before training starts in earnest. But it's not: this *is* Millwall, after all, a club where very little is what it seems at first glance. Out on the turf are youngsters with learning difficulties, who have been bussed in from schools around Lewisham, Greenwich and Southwark to play in their annual tournament. This is the unexpected face of Millwall: a club once shunned by the local community has turned into a caring, upstanding pillar of it. But there is more to the Lions than their willingness to welcome mentally disadvantaged kids into the ground for a kick-about. The transformation from a club whose fans sang, 'No one likes us, we don't care', into a true 'community club' is at the heart of Millwall's whole strategy for survival.

Reg Burr may describe the move to Senegal Fields as 'nothing less than a revolution', but the real revolution in SE14 actually took place half a decade earlier. That was when the Lions signed Gary Stempel. Born in Panama but brought to England by his parents at the age of 10, Stempel wasn't another goal-scoring sensation from the local amateur ranks come to seek his fortune in the big time. He was a business studies graduate and qualified teacher who had spent his years after college bumming around South America trying to avoid work and, instead, playing a lot of sport. He came back to Britain in 1981 to find the inner-cities convulsed by riots, and used his teaching experience to land jobs as a 'sports motivator' in Ladbroke Grove and Camden, working on Action Sport schemes set up by the government-funded Sports Council in response to the turmoil.

Stempel was a football fan, but he was a self-confessed North London boy. He had hardly been south of the river, let alone ventured to the Den to see a game. Like all supporters, though, he watched appalled when, in March 1985, Millwall fans systematically dismantled Luton Town's Kenilworth Road ground and the ensuing riot was shown on the TV news that night. Six months later, Stempel was on the staff at the Den, having been appointed as a 'community development officer' with the vague brief of 'forging close links with the community'. 'I simply arrived one day,' he recalls, a faint tang to his voice betraying a birthplace far more exotic than Deptford or Docklands. 'Only one person knew I was coming. No one introduced me to anyone, I was just left to get on with whatever it was I was meant to be doing. I'd worked in some pretty difficult areas, but I'd never come across anything like this before.'

The job Stempel had taken was one of the last to be created by the much-maligned Greater London Council before its abolition in 1986. Although the GLC had no track record in promoting sport, it had spotted that London's football clubs needed to stop being seen as undesirable neighbours and present a more appealing face to the people who lived near their grounds. The GLC wrote to every club in the capital offering 100 per cent funding for a development worker who would open up their facilities to the locals and help improve their image. For their part, all the clubs had to provide was an office – but only three even bothered to reply: Arsenal, Charlton Athletic and Millwall. 'I'm sure there was so much apathy because this idea had come from the GLC, which had such a loony-left image,' says Stempel. 'Football clubs are the most conservative of organisations; they tend to react to events only when they have to rather than go out and start things up themselves. I'd like to think that Millwall responded to the GLC's offer because it was a pioneering idea and no other club had a community development officer. In all honesty, though, I think the Luton riot had a lot to do with it. They probably saw me as a bit of good PR.'

At the outset, Stempel's role was unclear. Players would walk past him a few times, and eventually grunt in his direction, 'Well, what're you here for?' His reply was obviously unconvincing: 'I'd tell them I was trying to build links with local schools and the community, but they'd just look blank. It didn't mean anything. The club didn't know what to do, the GLC didn't know what to do, I didn't know what to do. I was suspicious of Millwall, and Millwall were suspicious of me.'

Stempel at least knew how to make contact with local schools and youth groups through his previous jobs, but he found the response to an initial burst of letter-writing highly discouraging. Out of thirty schools he contacted, just one replied. Only when he met Fred Nind, the Inner London Education Authority's schools inspector, did classroom doors start to open. 'There was incredible suspicion,' Stempel remembers. 'Some of the schools thought it was just a talent-spotting exercise. Others were against us because it was Millwall. Teachers read in the papers that Millwall represented everything that was bad in life, and they not only had it next door, but now it wanted to come into their schools. We had to convince them that we were sincere. We told schools that it wasn't just an anti-hooliganism campaign or a way of getting more bums on seats at games. We explained that coaching classes were for boys and girls together, that we'd basically do anything they wanted us to do – talk to the kids, help with projects, whatever.' Six schools agreed to let him in.

The priority for Stempel then was to convince people, especially at the club itself, that community work was important and could benefit Millwall in the long term. He was given a hut by the main entrance for an office: 'That was crucial. I wanted to be at the centre of what was going on, not stuck out of harm's way.' And when the axe finally came down on the GLC, both Lewisham and Southwark councils, and the Sports Council, put up the cash to sustain Stempel's job. But it was not until the arrival of Reg Burr as chairman and Graham Hortop as chief executive in July 1986 that, Stempel believes, the scheme began to flourish. 'They gave us money but, more important, they gave us commitment. For the first time, Millwall was saying that there was more to football than ninety minutes on a Saturday afternoon. It was the first club in the country to try and change its culture.'

Coaching courses were the easiest activities to set up. And to prove the demand for what Stempel was organising, more than 250 kids attended the first one, held in Southwark Park. 'I'd struck up a good relationship with some of the youth-team players, and they came along to help. When a couple became full pros, they'd grown up with the scheme and became part and parcel of it. Ask lads of 16 to go into a school or youth club and receive all this adulation, and of course they'll do it. In fact, they love it. They like mucking around with kids, and it's good preparation for the coaching award that they take in their second year as YTS players.'

But community development is about much more than children kicking footballs and each other in the local park, supervised by teenagers in smart Millwall tracksuits. Having broken down the barriers of suspicion, Stempel set about opening up the club's under-used facilities themselves. He booked the executive lounge for people aged over 50 to play short-mat bowls. He launched a sports journalism competition, with youngsters invited to sit in on the then manager John Docherty's post-match interviews. Students were given a peek behind the scenes for business studies courses, coaching classes staged for women teachers, training sessions arranged at the Elephant and Castle Sports Centre for young offenders, a Job Club formed. And, of course, regular tournaments on the pitch were arranged for youngsters with learning difficulties. The Millwall Lionesses, one of the most successful women's football teams in Britain, have also come under the wing of Stempel and Lou Waller, the England international who is the club's second full-time women's development officer.

When, in 1987, Lewisham council, by now impressed at the efforts being made by the club to reach out and embrace its local community, became the country's first civic soccer sponsors in a £280,000 four-year deal, many of the conditions of the contract – such as providing free tickets for community groups and a crèche for parents to drop off their toddlers when going to games – were already in place. Yet, after three years of solid achievement, the creation of the Millwall Minders, football's first-ever match-day crèche, appealed only to the baser instincts in certain sections of the press. 'They wanted a picture of a little girl,' Stempel recalls, 'decked out in all the Millwall gear – hat, rosette, scarf – but with a rubber brick in her hand. There was the story: a Millwall hooligan at the age of two. I was so angry with that. We'd done so much, yet the publicity hadn't improved. Reports still began, "Millwall, the most notorious club in the country . . ." Torquay could have been doing exactly the same, but that wouldn't have been news.'

It is only in the last year that the scheme has had to make a charge to kids attending coaching schemes, something which concerns Stempel as he fears losing the children he most wants to attract, in a part of London where the recession has bitten hard and money is scarce: 'There's a lot of inner-city kids out there who don't visit leisure centres. They certainly don't belong to tennis clubs. They maybe go from school to the youth club or just hang around, yet they've got a tremendous passion for the game. Our philosophy has always been, go to the estates – and they're tough places, you're talking Peckham here – set up a course, and just let the kids come and get a taste for the sport. You can't go to some areas and set up formal structures, because these kids don't live formal types of lives. That's the problem with much of what the FA does: they've got all these flashy coaching courses with smart little certificates, but they just want to see the nice kids from Bucks and Berks coming out of the trees in their England tracksuits. Go on the course, buy the merchandise.'

Stempel believes that, in an area of the capital where

people's attitudes can be very polarised – 'They either love you or they hate you, there's not much middle ground' – a club not only has to accept its responsibility to its community, but must be completely genuine about it. 'If you aren't honest in what you do, people round here will suss you out dead quick,' he warns. It is for this reason that he is particularly keen on the club's Education Through Football project, a part of which has players talking to schoolchildren and tackling important social issues. 'I think clubs should deal with sensitive subjects. Players should deal with racism and violence smack on. One black player we had, Wesley Reid – he's at Airdrie now – was brilliant. He was only low-profile at the club, but he'd go into these Old Kent Road-type schools and tell them what it was like to be black and grow up on an estate in Peckham. Because he was from Millwall – their team – they listened. I'd like to see more black players doing this – you know, "I'm Ian Wright, and do you know what it was like for me to be black when I was 14?" In Bermondsey, just before the 1992 general election, the BNP [the right-wing British National Party] was going crazy, there was a lot of racial tension. Millwall should have addressed this issue years ago.'

Nevertheless, Stempel believes that the club has learned a great deal about its supporters and neighbours in the eight years that the community scheme has been up and running. And it is this conviction that Millwall, both as a team and as a club, matters to people far beyond the perimeter wall of the ground that has been at the heart of the club's ambitious relocation to Senegal Fields.

* * *

A 'ground-breaking ceremony' is one of the building industry's most abiding traditions. When a major new project gets off the drawing board and on to site, its developers pull in a clutch of civic dignitaries and a famous name to 'turn the first sod', wish the scheme well, and retire to a well-upholstered lounge with a healthily stocked drinks cabinet. As Millwall embarked on their final season at Cold Blow Lane, who better to heave up the first clod of earth half a mile away at Senegal Fields than the Secretary of State for National Heritage, that well-known face around London football grounds, David Mellor MP? Unfortunately for Millwall, however, Mellor – the self-styled Minister for Fun – had that week become dubbed the Minister for Fun and Frolics after tabloid revelations about his affair with Spanish actress Antonia de Sancha and bedtime activities conducted while wearing the kit of his beloved Chelsea. At the last minute, Mellor cried off from his engagement at the New Den, forcing chairman Reg Burr to turn to the mayor of Lewisham, John O'Shea, to make the main speech. Fortunately, Councillor O'Shea was willing to oblige. 'I'm only too happy to wear the No. 12 shirt at Millwall,' he declared, leaving Mellor well and truly relegated to the substitutes' bench.

Millwall always knew they would have to quit their old ground if the club was to realise its aspirations for regular Premier League football played in a stadium that complied with the requirements of the Taylor Report. But crucial to the plan was the fact that it had the support of the local authority. When, in the spring of 1987, Lewisham signed up to be the sponsor's name on the team's blue shirts, then council leader Dave Sullivan became a non-voting director of the club. And so, when faced with a £15.5 million bill for building a new Den, Millwall naturally turned to their loyal backers for help. The council came up with £2.65 million, a sum which delighted Reg Burr: 'Lewisham has always been supportive, progressive and interested,' he purred. 'The council sees the importance of having a successful football team in the borough.' Fans of Wimbledon, whose club was embroiled in protracted debate with an intransigent Merton council over a site to which the Dons could relocate, must have looked on with envy.

However, Lewisham wanted something for its money – namely, a community sports hall built alongside the ground. No problem, said Burr: his club had learned from the achievements of Gary Stempel's operation how important it was to provide facilities for local people. Even better, Deptford City Challenge and the Sports Council also put up money towards the £1.5 million centre, and both these bodies would have a say in its management and pricing arrangements.

The same policy was to apply to the stadium itself: the needs of the supporters came first. Having inspected the final plans for the new ground, Burr was confident that they would like what they found. 'I think they are going to be pleasantly surprised,' he chimed. 'It will be different to anything that has gone on before, because we will have the customer in mind.' As Burr saw it, the era of fans being treated as turnstile fodder was over. 'We want them to come early and leave late, instead of the other way round. We want them to arrive at 11 a.m. and watch last week's game on the video screen, have something to eat, watch the match and then stay for recorded highlights until six or seven o'clock in the evening. We want them to be able to stand in the stadium concourse and watch the match on TV if they so desire.' Burr's major wish was for his punters – and that meant all of them – to feel wanted.

One group in particular had been busy letting the chairman know their demands on that score. The Independent Millwall Supporters' Association (IMSA) was founded in 1989 and, after the initial plans for relocation were drawn up, produced in response 'The IMSA Blueprint', a forty-page document subtitled 'Putting Safety, Sanity and Supporters into British Football Stadium Design'. If supporters' associations had previously been derided for doing little more than complain about poor stewarding and long queues at the tea bars, here was evidence that fans could make a worthwhile and informed contribution to their club. The introduction set out IMSA's demands: 'The blueprint's primary function is to identify, record and propose items for adoption into the official scheme from a supporters' point of view, thereby allowing Millwall supporters a say in the proceedings and placing Millwall supporters on the agenda.' It went on: 'This will bring the 21st century not only to the forthcoming major programme of football stadia design, but also in terms of the new relationship that a collaborative effort would symbolise between a football club and its supporters.'

Maybe the phrasing was clumsy, but the sentiments rang through loud and clear. Contained in the document were detailed proposals for the design of the new stadium, crowd safety, the need to balance money-making commercial enterprises with the traditions of a football ground, and even a line on the colour of the goal nets. It ended with a section on funding the new ground. Top of the agenda was the fear that Millwall would follow West Ham and Arsenal and launch a bond scheme to raise the last couple of million needed. This simply wouldn't do, rapped IMSA. The club had written in match-day programmes of the fans' need to 'do their bit as well' to get the stadium built, but the association was determined to get in a pre-emptive strike on this point. 'Bond schemes are generally seen as an enormous rip-off by fans,' the Blueprint stated. 'Reg Burr has said that, "We will not be asking our supporters for something for nothing." This can be interpreted in any way the reader chooses.' And with that comment, the ball was booted firmly down Millwall's end of the pitch.

'The Lions share', ran a headline in the *Evening Standard* in April 1992. 'Millwall launch scheme to help fund £15.5 million move'. The story went on to explain that 'Millwall are to become the fourth London football club to launch a bond scheme.' Then came the crucial line: 'But they will be careful not to call it one.' Well aware of the disasters that had beset West Ham and Arsenal since both those clubs had sought financial help from the fans to redevelop their grounds, Millwall named their innovation 'The Lions Card'. The dreaded word 'bond' was nowhere to be seen. On the cover of the explanatory blue and yellow leaflet was a sketch of a comatose lion and the text, 'If You're 100% Behind Millwall . . .'; inside, the lion had awoken and, alongside tub-thumping messages from terrace favourite Keith 'Rhino' Stevens, former Den hero Barry Kitchener and manager Mick McCarthy, was roaring encouragement to supporters to 'Become a Lions Card holder and you'll be quids in.'

At West Ham, fans had rebelled against being asked to pay for nothing more than the right to buy a season ticket, with a few meaningless fripperies shoved in as a supposed bonus. Millwall had learned that the only way to enlist the backing of supporters was to offer financial incentives. And so, in return for £250 – which could be paid in ten monthly interest-free instalments – Lions Card holders were offered at least £250-worth of reduced admissions over seven seasons. The discounts did not only apply if you bought a season ticket, either: there was £1 off the turnstile price during the final campaign at the old Den, and a total of £50-worth of reduced-price admissions following the move. Writing in the *Independent*'s 'Fan's

Eye View' column in October, Dominic Egan couldn't help but brag: 'Next season we're moving to a new 20,000 all-seater stadium, which is being financed in part by the fans under a scheme drafted in consultation with the fans. Are you watching, West Ham?'

Millwall's 'open door' policy went one stage further in February 1993. Manager Mick McCarthy and chairman Reg Burr hosted two evening presentations at Lewisham Theatre, when supporters could ask questions either about the move to Senegal Fields or about the team's performance. Hosted by Capital Radio DJ Mick Brown, the nights were boisterous but good-natured. An auditorium that would be occupied later in the month by fans of American singer Howard Keel and hamster-eating comedian Freddie Starr was two-thirds filled by Lions fans of all ages, from youngsters eager for the autographs of their heroes to old boys who had supported the team for decades. 'Here's a question for Reg,' belted out one unmistakably South London voice. 'Why did we sell Jack Cobb to Plymouth in 1937?' A broad grin creased the lips of Millwall's normally reserved chairman. 'Mick's having him watched tomorrow,' he retorted.

There were few searching enquiries on the playing front: after all, the Lions were at this time third in the first division, unbeaten at home, and playing a brand of entertaining, attacking football utterly different from the style many fans had anticipated when McCarthy – who, as a player, was a craggy, no-nonsense central defender – took over the managerial chair. But there was a rumble of discontent when Burr revealed that admission prices in the East and West Stands at Senegal Fields would be £15 and £20, a considerable increase from the £10 or £13 fans were paying during the last season at the Den. The chairman, however, quickly explained that purchasing a Lions Card would bring these new figures down, and into line with current prices. 'We want to make the transition from a standing stadium to a seated stadium as painless as possible,' he said, and then reiterated: 'You must do something for yourself to help us achieve that.' But it was the call to club loyalty that saw Burr win over any dissenters. 'If you are a real Millwall fan,' he announced, 'and buy a Lions Card, then you won't be affected by these increases. It is the casual fan who only wants to come and see the glamour matches who will have to pay accordingly.' As Mick Brown brought four Millwall players and two members of the audience on to the stage to play 'A Question of Sport', the jocular mood of the evening soon returned.

★ ★ ★

Encouraging clubs to take more interest in their followers and local communities was on football's agenda many years before Gary Stempel and the Independent Millwall Supporters' Association arrived on the scene. The phrase 'Football in the Community' was actually invented by Denis Howell MP, the avuncular ex-referee who became the first and, so far, only Labour Minister for Sport. In 1978, Howell took the view that building more sports facilities might help to combat hooliganism – then at its height – by giving disaffected youngsters something better to do than wander the streets looking for a punch-up. With hindsight, Howell's belief seems naïve in the extreme; yet, to back it up, he provided the Sports Council with an extra £2.5 million. Many of the projects that the money helped to create, such as the Aston Villa Sports and Leisure Centre near Villa Park, are still running.

By 1986, though, the Sports Council had changed its priorities and begun to put people before premises. Action Sport initiatives such as those on which Gary

1 One of the Sky Strikers, disproving the notion that it's 'A Whole New Ball Game'.

2 Chelsea chairman Ken Bates looks optimistically to the future.

3 Crystal Palace chairman Ron Noades points the way forward for football.

4 Charlton Athletic fans celebrate their club's return to the Valley.

5 Clive 'King of Goals' Allen, who netted an astonishing forty-nine times for Spurs in 1986–87.

6 Arsenal manager George Graham with the heavy weight of history just above his head.

7 West Ham v Everton, February 29, 1992: a one-man protest which even Julian Dicks can't prevent heralds a mass pitch invasion.

8 Self-styled 'King of the Touts', former Barnet chairman Stan Flashman.

9 The then manager Barry Fry looks on anxiously as Barnet come from behind to beat Cardiff in November 1992.

10 John 'Fash the Bash' Fashanu, star striker for the 'raggy-arsed rovers', Wimbledon.

11 Peter Storrie, West Ham's managing director, has big plans for the club's future.

12 Gerry Francis of Queen's Park Rangers, not yet grey-haired despite the pressures of management.

13 Former managing director Frank Clark believes the only way is up for Leyton Orient.

14 Milwall community officer Ron Bell coaching at a school in Bermondsey.

15 Mike, Norma and Chris (sadly beheaded in the photograph) Dench, Upton Park 'refuseniks' demonstrate thier love of West Ham.

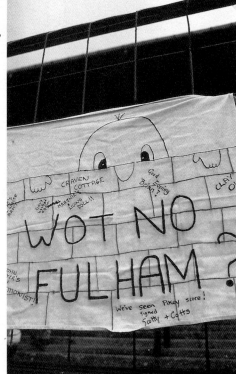

16 The Craven Cottage faithful have their say.

Stempel worked in Ladbroke Grove and Camden were proving effective in motivating kids to think about giving sport a chance. The Sports Council believed that the idea of fostering a sense of 'belonging' to a local football club might not only do something to reduce hooliganism and wanton vandalism, but it might also encourage clubs to make better use of facilities which, for most of the week, lay empty, and create temporary jobs and training opportunities for the unemployed. It sounded promising, and the Sports Council persuaded the PFA and the Football League to run a pilot operation in the north-west using six clubs. Their hopes were fully justified. Within a year, clubs in neighbouring Cheshire and Merseyside were eagerly setting up projects of their own. By 1990, there were some fifty clubs backing the principle of 'Football in the Community', and now it is easier to count the ones which don't have schemes. When Chelsea became involved in 1992, they made it a full complement of thirteen out of thirteen London clubs.

Joe Patton is a senior development officer with the Sports Council, and has been involved with 'Football in the Community' since its early days. He is convinced not only that every club should run a community programme, but that decisions affecting it should be taken within the club at board level. Patton applauds the successes Millwall have had, and the close interest vice-chairman David Dein and manager George Graham take in Arsenal's scheme; however, he is less enthusiastic about progress elsewhere. 'There's a need for a change in attitude among the directors at some clubs,' he states. 'They're happy with the schemes as long as there is no financial drain and they don't impinge too much on what they see as the club's main aim – which is to play football. But I'd like to see every club have a designated director responsible for community affairs. What's more, this should be seen as the most, not the least, important of all the directors' portfolios.'

With Arsenal as London's notable exception, Patton finds that lower-division clubs often put more emphasis on community work than their more illustrious neighbours. He mentions the oft-quoted maxim that the best thing a club such as Liverpool can do for the people of their city is to be successful on the pitch, and accepts that 'there may well be a strong argument in favour of that'. But he points to Leyton Orient at the other extreme: 'A club of that size needs to work hard at establishing its market and its loyalty, because it's a minnow in North London.'

When Brentford set up its 'Football in the Community' project six years ago, the Bees were – at the risk of mixing metaphors – a minnow in West London. Until the club won promotion to the top flight of the reconstituted Barclays League two seasons ago, loyal fans had had to endure an unremitting diet of lower-division fare for thirty-eight years. However, Griffin Park has an altogether more prosperous air about it these days, brought about not only by improvements on the park. Seven years ago, Brentford's chairman Martin Lange appointed Keith Loring as chief executive with the specific brief of finding new sources of income for the club. The two men shared similar business philosophies. Lange had inherited a debt of £1 million when he had taken over two years before but, using the expertise which made him a fortune in property development, he wiped that out by building and selling forty-eight flats on the old car park and training area at the Brook Road end of the ground. Loring, for his part, is now at the helm of a commercial department which made a profit of around £400,000 during the promotion season. It needed to: Brentford's wages bill was in excess of £800,000, around

£100,000 more than the club brought in through the turnstiles.

However, Loring has two aces to call on when conceiving his commercial card-tricks. First, Brentford's Clubcall phone line averages some 600 calls every day and, in the third week of January 1992, had more people surreptitiously ringing from their offices than any other club's information line. Fans may moan at the premium rates such lines charge simply to hear tongue-tied players stuttering out their clichés, but the service that February netted Brentford a very tidy £7,600.

Second, Brentford have been sponsored by the Dutch airline, KLM, since 1984 – the longest partnership involving any league club. Griffin Park lies directly beneath the flight path into Heathrow, and the airline's advert on the roof of the New Road Stand, 'Next Time ... Fly KLM', is reputedly the largest hoarding in the world. As the 1991–92 season opened, KLM announced that they had signed an unprecedented five-year extension to their contract with the Bees. A couple of years earlier, Lange and Loring had shown that they never missed a trick: when inflatable club mascots were all the rage, the duo not only ensured that the club shop had a good stock of inflatable bees, they even got KLM to endorse them. Little wonder, then, that when Brentford announced their financial results for the year to 31 May 1992, the club had turned a £43,000 deficit into a £46,000 profit.

Sponsorship deals are usually signed for business purposes: plenty of advertising boards round the edge of the pitch, fulsome credits in the programme, and a decent pre-match lunch for VIPs. However, KLM cited a rather different reason for wanting to continue their relationship with Brentford. As Barry Evans, the airline executive lumbered with the unwieldy title of 'Passenger Sales and Marketing Manager UK/Ireland', put it at the time: 'The club's recent success in the "Football in the Community" awards was instrumental in helping the company decide to renew.' Commerce and the community clearly can be married together: Evans was referring to the accolade of Brentford, along with Sunderland, being jointly voted community-club-of-the-year for 1991 by the Football Trust – an award which also carried the not inconsiderable prize of a cheque for £20,000.

When Fulham made the short trip over from Craven Cottage for the penultimate league game of 1991–92, it was make-or-break for both sides. Under manager Don Mackay, the Cottagers had emerged from the mid-table morass with a late burst for the play-offs. Brentford, however, were hoping to reach what was to become division one without recourse to the agonies of a two-legged semi-final and one-off showdown at Wembley for the last promotion place. Victory would see them into the crucial second spot, with only a visit to Peterborough on the first Saturday in May still to come.

In every respect, it was a filthy day for such a vital local derby. Not only was it Sunday, but the kick-off was set for 11.30 a.m. – an hour when most self-respecting football fans were either still in bed dreaming of banging home the winner in the Cup final, or poring over the match reports on the back pages of the papers. Even worse, it was pouring down, the rain lashing the fans jammed into the streets outside Griffin Park from a louring, leaden sky. There would be no respite once inside for supporters on the open Ealing Road terrace either: the game was strictly all-ticket and, instead of being able to switch to one of the covered sides, they would simply have to cheer on the Bees drenched through.

Clubs usually try to make the last home game of a

campaign into a special event. Often, however, their imagination goes no further than encouraging the players to form a circle in the middle of the pitch and wave sheepishly at the fans who have laid out so much money and emotion over the previous nine months. Brentford did far better. The atmosphere leading up to kick-off was crackling with anticipation, but any hint of tension was quickly defused when, a few minutes before the teams appeared, out on to the turf sploshed all the boys and girls who had been mascots during the season, resplendent in full Bees kit. It was an amusing, light-hearted touch and, if the sight of so many miniature red-and-white striped shirts pouring on to the pitch didn't put the wind up Fulham, then the whirlwind start made by the real red-and-whites certainly did. In front of a capacity crowd of 12,071, the biggest at Griffin Park for a decade, Brentford rattled home four goals inside the first forty-two minutes to secure an emphatic win. The die-hards at the Ealing Road end were steaming even before they had eased through the throng to grab a much-needed half-time cuppa.

Sitting in his office underneath the main stand a few days later, Martyn Spong looked back on the Fulham game with enormous pleasure. 'Fantastic atmosphere, absolutely superb.' He was pleased, too, with the reception given to the mascots, and disappointed only that he had not been able to put on more pre-match entertainment. General wariness at having a full house – something, after all, that was a new experience for most of the staff – had prevented him.

'For the Darlington game a week ago,' he added, 'we had 250 kids in on a coaching day and they made a hell of a noise. But it's satisfying to sit back and think, if I was a supporter coming in who hadn't been to many games, I'd see all this activity and be pretty impressed. It gives a warm feeling.'

Shorter than Gary Stempel, bearded, but equally athletic-looking, Spong heads Brentford's four-strong 'Football in the Community' team. He was a teacher, too, at the pioneering Cranford Community School, near Hounslow. He is also a good footballer, having been on the books at Diadora Leaguers Enfield until a year ago. Spong is well aware of Brentford's reputation for running a tight financial ship, but he does not believe that this precludes the club investing in its local community. Indeed, the numbers speak for themselves. Before he started work in January 1987, the club's average home gate was 3,918. Five years later, it was around 7,000. This can partly be explained by the team's better performances and free tickets dished out to deserving causes, but not entirely: 'We've run coaching projects in parts of London where you wouldn't expect kids to know much about the club. Some of them had never heard of us. Now they have, now they talk about us. It might only be, "Oh, Arsenal are my favourite team, but Brentford are my second favourite", but we consider that a success. Some of these kids have since been to a game here, they've experienced the atmosphere, and they're coming back again. They don't support Arsenal any longer, because they've never seen them play and maybe never will.'

Like Stempel and Joe Patten, Spong believes that community schemes can only work if support comes from the top of the club down. The chairman, chief executive and manager all sit on Brentford's 'Football in the Community' project committee, along with representatives from co-funders Hounslow and Ealing councils, while the players are regularly involved in coaching, teaching and making presentations. 'I don't think there are any players at Brentford – and players are usually the last to hear about such things – who don't know that, over the last two or three years, we've had one of the best community schemes in the country. Since I've been at the club,' Spong adds, 'we've had no more than three or four players who didn't want to get involved. There's nobody like that at the moment, and some of the lads are exceptionally good at it.'

It is this enthusiasm from top to bottom that has smoothed the transition from Brentford being, like Millwall, a club simply running a community scheme into a fully fledged 'community club'. Spong believes it is all down to attitude. 'We're certainly fortunate in that Brentford has always been seen as a friendly set-up, whereas Millwall's transition has been harder because of the club's reputation, right or wrong, for trouble. What matters is getting everyone from chairman to tea lady to see that working with the community isn't just a token or a way to boost the attendance figures, that it has a worth.'

At the Sports Council, which still makes grants to projects all round the country, Joe Patton believes the way is clear for the concept of football in the community to move even closer to the hearts of clubs. 'I don't think it's too idealistic to believe that this might happen,' he says. 'Look at the big clubs on the Continent. Barcelona and Real Madrid, for example, are multi-sport clubs. They're famous for football, of course, but they're just as well known for the other activities they provide for people of all ages from their cities. It's not incompatible for clubs in Britain to develop by setting up separate sections in this way. If they use the club name – call it the Millwall Community Sports Club, for example – then they can keep the strong association with the football club. After all, in soccer, there's nothing more powerful than a name.'

Or, more certainly, than a good name. For proof, just ask anyone living in Lewisham or Hounslow.

SEVEN

Young, Gifted – and Free!

Leyton Orient and the search for schoolboy stars

Not for Leyton Orient the marble entrance halls and sleek office suites that characterise London's more affluent clubs. The way into Leyton Stadium is via a buzzer in the ticket office; announce your presence, and through an unassuming pair of stained-wood doors you are ushered into a 1970s time-warp. Pine-effect hardboard panelling lines the walls, and the main reception lounge is upholstered in crimson velveteen with a low-slung artexed ceiling. There is a bar along one side, an old TV perched precariously on top of a fridge and, taking pride of place on the walls, a framed photo of the Orient team who, in 1962, won promotion to division one for the only time in the club's history – and dropped back down again the very next year. Alongside it is a pennant from the England v Turkey Under-21 international staged at the ground in November 1992 – a game which provided official recognition that, even if Leyton Orient cannot field the best team in the country, they have certainly got one of the best pitches.

The manager's office, at the end of a maze of narrow hardboarded corridors, is equally nondescript. It is no bigger than a single bedroom, and an MFI-style desk spans almost its entire width. It could be the office of a junior executive in a company strapped for cash. There is very little that signifies it as the heart of a football club, still less that identifies the club as Leyton Orient. Indeed, the most prominent item on the wall is, bizarrely, a pennant for rivals West Ham United.

Until May 1991, the occupant of the office was Frank Clark. His Geordie tones unsoftened by years away from his Durham birthplace, Clark is the model of affability. He was with the O's for eleven years, initially as team manager and, from 1991, as managing director with Peter Eustace in charge of the playing side. One of the game's hoariest old chestnuts, based on a single throwaway comment made several years ago, was that he was earmarked for Brian Clough's job when Ol' Big 'Ead finally decided to vacate the green sweat-top at Nottingham Forest. But it seemed that he had missed his chance of a prestige post when, attending a club managers' meeting at a West End hotel in the summer of 1990, he opened the wrong door and found himself facing the interview panel for the vacant England boss's job. In a cartoon showing FA chief executive Graham Kelly holding a newspaper report suggesting the appointment of Graham Taylor would cost the FA £2 million, the *Leyton Orientear* fanzine pictured Clark pointing out, 'Hold on, Mr Kelly, I'm available for only two pints of Newky Brown.' Happily for Clark, Clough's prediction finally came true with his appointment as Forest's manager in May 1993.

Clark's own football career, which was to lead to two European Cup medals with Notts Forest, began in that traditional school of hard knocks, the northern back street. There, young lads honed the skills that they hoped would take them into the professional game through soccer's equivalent of legal indentures, the apprentice system. 'If you were playing in a street game,' Clark recalls, 'whether it was one against one or twenty-three against twenty-three, you had to learn to manipulate the ball. If you didn't, you never got a kick.' The back streets of 1950s folklore are long gone; and with their passing, Clark believes, went an era when the opportunity to play football was available to any boy in the land, even though the goals might be no more than a pile of jackets and the ball a bundle of newspaper tied up with string. Forty-odd years on, there is such an array of sport and leisure activities available to youngsters that, for many, the dream of being a footballer has diminished. 'When I was a boy, we could play football any day almost anywhere we wanted to,' Clark adds. 'Now, unless someone gives kids an opportunity to play, it's less likely that they'll go out and do it themselves. And this means that, by the time they're 14 or 15, fewer boys have the desire and perhaps the skills to go on and play professionally.'

His answer to the first problem is to encourage eight-, nine- and ten-year-olds simply to enjoy kicking a ball around on one of Leyton Orient's 'Football in the Community' projects. The club's community development officer, Neil Watson, operates in largely the same way as Gary Stempel at Millwall and Martyn Spong at Brentford. 'The community scheme,' says Clark, 'is for many kids their first real contact with football. We want them to play in a fun, unstructured, non-competitive way. No parents, no coaches.' So convinced is Clark that boys and girls now need to have 'the football habit' instilled at a young age that he was happy to run courses which barely broke even. 'Orient's "Football in the Community" work doesn't make money,' he says, describing how Waltham Forest is a borough split socially and economically across the middle, while neighbouring Hackney is one of the most deprived in the whole country. 'The club could put on a scheme in Chingford, charge what they liked, and parents would pay it. If they tried that in Leyton or Clapton, even if they charged an economic rate, kids wouldn't come because their families couldn't afford it. Orient would rather have boys and girls there and paying less than not there at all.'

However, Clark's interest in the sporting welfare of North-East London was not entirely altruistic. For it is on youth that the former managing director pinned the very future of Leyton Orient. His policy was simple, and born of necessity: for a club of Orient's size and precarious financial position, dipping in and out of the transfer market at will was impossible. Developing home-grown talent, to play in the first team and then maybe to sell on, was the only way to survive.

Orient's youth scheme began in earnest seven years ago, when a Ruandan coffee plantation owner, Tony Wood, bought the club and took over as chairman. Wood had been an O's supporter all his life, and looked back with pleasure on the exuberant young team created by the then manager George Petchey in the 1970s. Orient were division-two stalwarts in those days but, since that decade, the club had slipped back down the divisions and crowds had dwindled to a meagre 2,000. When money is scarce, the axe inevitably falls first on the youth set-up – and Orient wound theirs down through the first half of the 1980s. 'The club still had a team,' Clark adds, 'but they were only paying lip-service to it. My first five years there, from 1981 to 1986, were solely about the survival of the club. There were no resources to think about a proper youth policy. It was a case of taking everyone else's cast-offs: we'd have a trial among that lot, and pick the best of what there was.' It was a system that paid dividends in one notable case: hard-tackling midfielder and captain Steve Castle, who departed to Plymouth Argyle for £195,000 in the summer of 1992. But it was not a case of Castle being the first saleable product off the conveyor belt; he was the only one.

The turning-point for Clark and his vision of an Orient

side crammed with local lads came with the arrival of the new chairman. For Tony Wood had the same dream. However, here was a chairman prepared to put his hand in his pocket. 'You ask any football club director if they want a youth policy,' says Clark, 'and they'll all nod their heads and say yes. When it comes to financing it, though, it's a different matter.' But Wood's decision was not to be the indulgence of a football fan turned millionaire. The policy was to be developed on sound commercial lines – or at least those applicable to a club that, in 1985, had dropped down to the depths of the fourth division. 'However unpalatable it may have been for the fans,' Clark states, 'the policy was that, at certain times, we had to sell players to balance the books. It's the only way we could have run the club that gave us hope of achieving progress on the field while still making ends meet.'

Bernie Dixson is the man charged with the task of building the first blocks of Orient's future. Indeed, Frank Clark describes this amiable, down-to-earth East Londoner as the most important individual at the club. Dixson arrived at Brisbane Road in 1987 initially as youth-team coach, having spent fifteen years as a manager in non-league football. But he soon found himself devoting more and more time to setting up the organisational structure that had previously been lacking, and narrowed his roles down to those of youth development officer and chief scout. Until the end of the 1992–93 season, the coaching work was carried out by Geoff Pike, the former West Ham battler who ended his playing career at Orient in 1991. Dixson has just five scouts spotting new talent for him, each operating on an expenses-only basis. He does not believe in using too many, as they all want to bring boys in, 'and you end up not seeing the wood for the trees'. Rather than being responsible for a particular part of the country, each of Dixson's scouts is in charge of a different age group, which enables them to make comparisons between players more easily. Orient's quest for stars of the future has broadened out from the traditional East London and Essex areas, and the scouts are often up in East Anglia and Cambridgeshire watching games.

If a scout spots a promising player he will find out his name and where he plays on Sundays, and go to have another look. For Orient, the next step is to invite the boy along for weekly coaching at the club's Centre of Excellence, based at the Douglas Eyre Sports Centre in Walthamstow. 'We take them from the age of 11 upwards,' explains Dixson, 'but we do keep an eye on boys slightly younger, too. At nine or ten, though, if I said to a boy do you want to come down to the Orient, he'd think it was a Chinese takeaway round the corner. At that age, we simply try and make kids aware that the club exists.'

Standing on the touchline in a park in Barking or Basildon is not, however, the exclusive preserve of a Leyton Orient scout. Schools and Sunday league matches are the haunts of scouts from every club, each trying to bring the cream of the talent into their own youth set-up. The task facing Dixson is to encourage a boy to choose Orient rather than one of the more famous names that might be interested in him, both for coaching at the Centre of Excellence and then at the age of 14, when he can sign on associate schoolboy terms. Why choose little Leyton Orient when Arsenal or Tottenham might be clamouring for a boy's signature?

Dixson recognises the dilemma, but believes Orient are equipped to counter it on several fronts. 'I describe a football club as like a bottle,' he explains. 'The base can be as big as you want, but the neck – which represents the first team – is always the same size. Only thirteen players can be in that neck each week. At a club like Arsenal, for example, the movement through the neck is going to be relatively small, because you don't constantly disturb a successful team. At Orient, there's going to be a lot more movement, as the best young players are sold on and others come up from the base to take their place. Arsenal can lure kids along with the promise of being in the first team at 19 or 20 and playing in the Premier League. We *have* to get ours in the first team by that age so we can sell them to Premier League clubs. Sure, it must be wonderful to take a kid to Highbury or White Hart Lane. You walk in, and you're in awe of the ground, in awe of the place and its history. You can understand why kids are starstruck by the big clubs. But isn't it better to be starstruck at the age of 21, when you've just been bought by Arsenal and are picked to play for them, than to be starstruck at 14, taken on at Highbury, but never reach the first team?'

Orient have long been regarded as the capital's 'friendly club', the team which every London football fan has a soft spot for but rarely comes along to see play. In a sense, this is the kind of patronising tag that is always attached to perpetual losers, but Dixson considers it another useful tool in bringing boys in. 'The management team here is very small, and it's easy to get to know the people in the senior positions. Peter Eustace wants to be involved as much as possible with the kids, assistant manager Chris Turner [the former Manchester United and Sheffield Wednesday goalkeeper] works at the Centre of Excellence. Frank Clark has a wonderful memory for names, and as soon as he'd been introduced to a boy he'd remember him. Next time he saw the lad, Frank would greet him by his Christian name. The boy must have thought, "Wow, the managing director knows who I am".' But Clark and Dixson both see Orient's reputation for friendliness stemming directly from chairman Tony Wood. 'He's been a fan all his life and never misses a game whenever he's in the country,' says Dixson. 'It doesn't matter what age-group it is, the chairman will be there to watch.'

Tony Wood's ambition is to see an entire O's first team comprising players brought through the youth set-up. As Orient's 1991–92 season drew to a frustrating close, with hopes of making the play-offs dashed by successive home defeats to Fulham and Peterborough United, the club's reserves took the field for a routine Capital League match against Wealdstone. The O's had performed creditably in this competition, obtaining an upper-table place against the second strings of rivals such as Crystal Palace, Brentford and Cambridge United and fielding the usual mixture of first-teamers recovering from injury and squad players hoping to catch the manager's eye. What distinguished the Orient side that lined up this pleasant April evening from those which had turned out earlier in the campaign was its average age: apart from triallist Sam Kitchen in defence and novice striker Paul Cobb, both in their early 20s, every other member of the eleven was still eligible to play for the youth team.

Reserve games have an atmosphere – or, to be more exact, lack of atmosphere – all of their own. About 100 spectators clustered in the centre part of the main stand, with another fifty choosing their usual spot on the terrace beneath. These are football's hard-core fanatics: the season ticket holders determined to wring every last penn'orth of value from their annual investment, the addicts greedy for another fix as summer's soccer-free months drew close, and the players' friends and family come along to cheer on a mate. There was good-natured ribbing for referee Philip Don, whose whistle-blowing c.v. now ranged from Liverpool against Sunderland in front of 80,000 people at a Wembley Stadium FA Cup final, to Orient Reserves v Wealdstone Reserves in front of 150 people at a Leyton Stadium Capital League clash. And, of course, there were the inane comments which are lost in the general hubbub at a first-team game but here, in an almost silent stadium, ring out loud and excruciatingly clear: 'You're using your weight again, Barry,' as slender midfielder Barry Lakin is hustled off the ball by an opponent almost twice his size; 'Jump, Cobby!' as the diminutive striker fails to win a challenge with a Wealdstone defender nearly a foot taller. This, after all, is literally a game of boys against men: Orient are playing a team with limited technical ability, but far stronger physical presence. And three of Wealdstone's goals in their 4–3 win come directly from superior strength in the home team's penalty area.

One of the Orient youngsters, however, made hardly a mistake all night. Steve Okai was born in Ghana in December 1973 and came to England with his family ten years later. He had been spotted by Orient scout Ron Cook while playing for Villa Court Under-14s in Lewisham, and won a place in the London Schools Under-15 side. Okai first appeared in an Orient shirt in 1990, when he played thirty-three games for the youth team and four times for the reserves. He then clocked up a similar record of appearances in 1991–92. Frank Clark had immediately liked what he saw: 'Steve is one of those players you can really enjoy watching, and there aren't many individuals around who would make you go to a game to see them on their own. He's very graceful, has great skill and, although he looks frail, there's quite a bit of mental toughness about him.'

Just before the Wealdstone game, Okai had signed a two-year full-time contract with Orient. However, the winger from whom great things were expected had spent the rest of the week very differently from his youth-team colleagues. At the age of sixteen, boys whom a club wants to sign are taken on for two years as YTS trainees. They are paid £29.50 a week in the first year, £35 a week in the second, and combine football training and odd jobs around the ground with compulsory study for a BTec or City and Guilds qualification, usually in a leisure-related subject.

Okai, however, had passed his time at the St Francis Xavier sixth-form college in Clapham, with his nose in geography and politics A-level textbooks. His parents had insisted he finish his education before making a career in football. 'There's no way someone could come into the club and combine A-levels with being a YTS trainee,' says Bernie Dixson. 'We'd rather they stayed on at school and came in to train as much as possible. We know that, when he's at college, a boy can't devote as much energy to football as a full-time YTS trainee. But he can catch up afterwards. We knew Okai would be a few months behind the others in terms of physical development, but it was more important to get his A-levels done.'

It is an attitude which not all clubs adopt, preferring to get youngsters on board first and think about their studies second. Dominic Ludden, who won a place at full-back in the Orient first team in 1992 after starring for his home-town team Billericay at the age of 16, turned down a week's trial at Tottenham because he was concerned about missing work for his A-levels. Orient proved more flexible: like Okai, Ludden stayed on at school and ended up with two grade Bs and two Cs in his A-levels, enough to give him a place at Loughborough University. But after winning five England schoolboy caps, he decided to opt for Orient rather than academe: 'When I played for England Under-18s, that made my mind up. The A-levels will give me something to fall back on, and if I find the time I might try and take a part-time degree.' That prospect is not something which worries Dixson unduly: 'Your education is with you all your life. So is football – but only as memories.'

As gifted at passing exams as passing the ball, Okai and Ludden are the latest products of Orient's youth policy to establish themselves in Peter Eustace's first-team squad. Indeed, when the O's met Chester City on the last day of the 1991–92 campaign, they finished the game with seven former youth-team players on the pitch. However, it was the progress of the first player to emerge from the set-up which convinced Clark and Tony Wood that their emphasis on the youngsters would pay dividends in the long term.

Chris Bart-Williams was born in Sierra Leone, came to Britain when he was four, and began playing football six years later for the Grasshoppers Sunday side in North London. His skill and composure on the ball quickly highlighted him as an outstanding talent, and Orient's former chief scout Jimmy Hallibone moved in to invite Bart-Williams along to the club's Centre of Excellence for extra training on Monday evenings. The shy, slightly-built boy first wore an Orient shirt when he began to turn out for the Under-12s and, while still in his fifth year at St Catherine's School in Hornsey, he was picked for the reserves – playing alongside one of the game's renowned old stagers, Justin Fashanu. He signed on YTS terms just after his 16th birthday and, remarkably, was propelled into first-team action a mere four months later, as substitute against Grimsby. In an interview with the *Leyton Orientear*, Bart-Williams revealed that, once he had got over the shock of getting on to the pitch, he 'didn't find it that much different from the reserves'. His home debut followed three months later, when what the *Orientear* described as 'that perfect goal scored by Christopher Bart-Williams – what a way to warm the heart' set his team on the way to a 4–0 rout of Tranmere. He was the club's youngest-ever goal-scorer. Now settled in midfield after first being used as a right-winger, he finished the 1990–91 season 'all set for a bright-lights future', as the fanzine put it.

They were right, too. A week before his 17th birthday, Bart-Williams was the youngest player called into the England Under-19 squad for the World Youth Championship in Portugal. And, on 24 September 1991, he was part of the Orient side which gave Sheffield Wednesday the fright of their lives in the second round of the Rumbelows League Cup, outplaying the top-flight team at Brisbane Road but failing to score before going down 1–4 in the return leg. Wednesday boss Trevor Francis was highly impressed by the right-midfielder in Orient's zebra-crossing strip: when the O's suffered a goalkeeping crisis, with Paul Heald and stand-in Paul Newell both sidelined with long-term injuries, he agreed to loan them the experienced Chris Turner on condition that Bart-Williams would travel up to Yorkshire on trial. The loan arrangement was soon made into a permanent deal. Orient's star-in-the-making played only six more games for the club, ending his lower-division career in the inauspicious surroundings of Plainmoor as the O's stumbled to a 0–1 defeat by Torquay United. He had played just thirty-five games, and gone from Hackney Marshes to Hillsborough in only eighteen months. No sooner had the *Orientear* pictured Bart-Williams facing the opposite way to his team-mates in a defensive wall with the speech bubble, 'Sometimes I just don't know where I am any more', than the very next issue of the fanzine featured a cover shot of the youngster in a blue-and-white striped Wednesday shirt. 'Well, the inevitable happened sooner than we expected,' began the downbeat editorial. 'The consensus seems to be that Wednesday got a bargain for a player with great potential, and at the time of writing he has already made three first-division appearances.' However, the article then took on a more accusatory tone: 'Peter Eustace both played for and managed the Sheffield club, but that's just coincidence, of course.'

Frank Clark sympathises with the fans' disappointment at losing one of the most exciting players seen at Brisbane Road in many years, but scotches any suspicion that Orient's manager was instrumental in swinging the deal. The £275,000 transfer, Clark insists, was necessary both financially and as a vindication of his former club's own investment in youth. 'It was a day of conflicting emotions – we were all sad to see him go. But it was a marvellous deal for us and a marvellous opportunity for Chris,' Clark stated in the programme for the England v Turkey Under-21 clash, when Bart-Williams returned wearing international colours to the club with which he had started out. Sitting in his office, Orient's former managing director was willing to elaborate further: 'Yes, of course we were sad to see Bart-Williams go,' Clark reiterates. 'But selling him was in another respect the best thing that could have happened to the club. The fact that Wednesday came in for him proved that our system worked. We needed to sell someone to a big club and for him to establish himself in the Premier League. We could then say to the next batch of talented kids and their parents, "Look what happened to him. He was in our first team at 16, and now he's playing in the UEFA Cup".'

Leyton Orientear editor Steve Harris accepts Clark's argument on this point: 'From the moment any of us saw Bart-Williams play,' he says, 'it was obvious that he'd be sold as soon as a decent offer came in.' Harris's mood of resigned disappointment turned to apoplexy, however, as events in late March 1992 unfolded. Nor was he alone in feeling almost betrayed by the club he supported. Having watched the team pull themselves into a third-division play-off position with only seven games remaining, Orient fans turning to the *Ilford Recorder* for their weekly round-up of club news found two wildly contrasting items. At the top of one page ran the screamer, 'Orient to go up predicts their Spurs loanee', as Ian Hendon, the midfielder borrowed from White Hart Lane, praised the 1–0 midweek victory at Darlington in glowing terms. Beneath that article, however, was a more sombre item, its cumbersome headline appropriately printed on a black background: 'Nugent sale a sequel to £500,000 loss and cash flow fear'. The story began: 'Their accounts showing a £500,000 loss on the last financial year, and a hoped-for major sponsorship deal having failed to materialise, Leyton Orient last week transferred leading scorer Kevin Nugent to Plymouth for £275,000 to meet a short-term cash flow problem.' It read like the announcement of a death in the family.

To the club, the striker's transfer was a fair deal at a time when, as Clark explained, there was 'quite a big hole in our projected finances. Things were getting very tight at the bank.' At first, it seemed that Nugent's departure might even go unnoticed as Orient walloped Hartlepool 4–0 in their very next match. But then the bubble was pricked. With alternative strikers Danny Carter and Mark Cooper both injured, Orient lost every one of their last six games. From apparent play-off certainties and outsiders even for automatic promotion, they tumbled into mid-table. 'What were we expected to think?' retorts Steve Harris. 'We're in with a good chance of reaching the play-offs at least, and we sell the top scorer. Nugent wasn't a brilliant player by any means, but he was still good for fifteen goals a season. In the six games we then lost, we had all the possession yet couldn't score.' But, with that streak of cold objectivity which is vital when supporting any team of seemingly boundless ambition but seriously limited resources, Harris adds: 'I suppose if we'd got the fifty grand Nugent is actually worth, it would have been a really bum deal. As it was, we made £275,000, so it wasn't a bad bit of business.' For Frank Clark, no doubt then breathing a sigh of relief at paying off some of the club's overdraft, there was another important factor in the transfer: Kevin Nugent had joined Orient when he was 13, and was another graduate from youth team to first team. He had not cost the club a penny.

The view from the terraces was predictably more vitriolic when the new campaign got underway with Orient having off-loaded three more first-teamers, including Steve Castle. In its first issue of the 1992–93 season, the *Leyton Orientear* blasted: 'Hope you've had a better summer than Leyton Orient have. The club couldn't have been more unsubtle about its lack of ambition if it had built a huge neon sign in Brisbane Road saying, "We didn't want promotion anyway". Let's sell as many players as possible to ensure this doesn't happen and, if gates fall as a result of poor performances, we blame the fans for being disloyal. Brilliant.'

Frank Clark is scathing of this view, believing that supporters do not understand – nor do they really want to understand – the precarious financial knife-edge on which his former club is balanced. 'The fans don't comprehend the economics of Orient. They say they do, but they don't. I accept that; they're concerned with what goes on out on the field, and the money problems are for the management to sort out.' But Clark, who in his efforts to pare running costs to the bone had been known to man the office telephone from time to time, will not accept that Orient's straitened circumstances are a sign of lack of ambition. The fact that chairman Tony Wood has invested so much of his own money in the club is, Clark asserts, proof of that: 'You cannot accuse a chairman who has put more than £1 million into Leyton Orient of lacking ambition.' However, sound financial housekeeping comes first: 'Orient have to maintain *realistic* ambition. I spent eleven years there, and the first five were just about survival. Results were immaterial. I was there too long to get to a position where I would have threatened the future of the club for a short-term gain. I reckon it cost us half a million pounds not getting promoted in 1992. If someone could have lent me the money we got for Kevin

Nugent and said pay me back when you go up, I'd have taken it. Now that is the answer to people who say Orient lack ambition.'

* * *

In contrast to Bernie Dixson's 'office' at Leyton Stadium, which is little more than a few square metres of kit-strewn corridor, Terry Murphy operates from enviably spacious surroundings. Murphy is Dixson's direct counterpart, the youth development officer for Arsenal. He shares a quiet, soothing room with chief scout Steve Burtenshaw, next door to George Graham's own bolt-hole on the first floor at Highbury. A drinks cabinet stands in the corner, bottles of spirits and soft drinks set out in regimented formation. Underneath, there are pull-out drawers full of neatly-organised files. It is from this disciplined base that Arsenal plan their own campaign to draw the country's finest young players into what is widely regarded as the best youth development set-up among top-flight clubs. Certainly Frank Clark is quick to praise its success: 'Arsenal have never been afraid to buy players,' he states, 'but they've also been one of the best clubs in the country at bringing through their own players from the youth team.'

The Christmas holiday has left Murphy facing a mountain of letters, all saying very much the same thing: 'Dear Sir, I want to be a professional footballer and play for Arsenal. Please can I have a trial?' He smiles when he explains that this is still a popular method of seeking recognition, but that it rarely produces leads worth following up. 'We have three standard letters. The first is for boys under 14, and we explain that our scouts might have missed them, so could they send us details of their forthcoming fixtures to let us have a look. The next is for the 14- to 18-year-olds, and is basically the same, only stronger – if you're any good, then we really should know who you are by now. The third is for the 18-and-overs, and is what I call my "too old" letter – unless a boy is playing in good-class non-league football, in which case we might be interested.' Murphy painstakingly answers every request on official Arsenal headed notepaper, but very few of these exchanges progress any further: 'Not many bother to send me their fixtures,' he says. 'I think they're delighted just to get a reply.'

Murphy has been at Arsenal for ten years. Before that, he was a PE teacher at one of inner London's most famous sporting state schools, Holloway, from whose playground emerged one of the capital's most maverick soccer talents this century, Charlie George. Murphy chuckles when he reveals that he taught the fathers of some of the boys now coming to prominence at Arsenal's two Centres of Excellence, one at Highbury itself and the other at Grays in Essex. Arsenal employ twenty-six scouts, all on an expenses-only basis. They are looking for boys of exceptional all-round skill aged nine upwards – not, contrary to popular belief, boys of limited ability who can be moulded into the 'Arsenal way' of unswerving devotion to the club and rigorous application of inflexible tactics. The best are passed on for training at one of the Centres of Excellence, although Murphy personally disagrees with the lower age limit: 'I think it's too young, but I have to fall in line with the club. Someone else might take a boy at that age, which makes it very hard for us to get hold of him later.' Nevertheless, Arsenal are extremely choosy about whom they accept at a tender age; while other clubs may have up to thirty boys in each year from nine to twelve, there are barely a dozen Under-12s in total at Highbury.

Nor are the Gunners any less selective when it comes to picking players to sign on associate schoolboy and then

YTS terms, even though money is no problem. Arsenal could take up to thirty boys aged between 14 and 16, but accept nowhere near that number. Nor do they offer incentives to the cream: 'We want boys who want to come here, not because we have to dangle carrots in front of them.' Once they have been brought into Highbury's close-knit community, however, Arsenal's associate schoolboys are well provided for. 'We look after them in lots of little ways,' says Murphy. 'If they need a new pair of boots or want tickets for a match, we take care of that.' The same rigour is applied at 16. 'Arsenal are not interested in the numbers game. We would never take twelve YTS trainees one year and twelve the next. If we had a big intake one year, such as when Ray Parlour became a trainee in 1990, we would be very selective the next to keep numbers down.' As Orient's Bernie Dixson puts it, what's the point of being starstruck at 14 if you never get to play in the first team? Arsenal, it seems, are in the business of ruthless refinement, each year separating the probables from the impossibles until Parlour, Mark Flatts, David Hillier, Kevin Campbell and Ian Selley are the distilled product at the end – ready-made Arsenal footballers, in other words.

Yet the history of the game is littered with stories of 'the ones who got away'. Leyton Orient passed over Wimbledon's £3million-rated defender Warren Barton when he was 16, preferring to offer Kevin Nugent their last professional contract. The England defender Des Walker was rejected by Tottenham at 16. And even Arsenal have made mistakes in their time. 'Kids develop at different rates,' says Terry Murphy, 'and there was one year when we had two 14-year-old left-backs we thought were of about equal ability. In the end, Robbie Johnson got the nod. We thought he was the most likely of the pair to make it into the first team. He didn't do as well as we'd hoped, but still went on to captain the reserves. As for the other lad, well, no one else was interested in him, so he drifted into non-league football with Wealdstone.'

Robbie Johnson: not a name that ever hit the headlines. That of Stuart Pearce is a touch more familiar, though.

EIGHT

From the Pitch and the Dugout

George Graham, Terry Howard, Clive Allen, Julian Dicks, John Fashanu and Gerry Francis

GEORGE GRAHAM

The Arsenal manager was born in Bargeddie, near Glasgow, in 1944. Nicknamed 'Stroller' for his languidly elegant contributions to the Gunners' midfield between 1966 and 1972, he was a member of the double-winning side of 1971 and collected thirteen caps for Scotland. In May 1986, after four seasons as manager at Millwall, Graham took charge at the club he had once played for. Since then, Arsenal have won two League Championships and the League Cup. Here, he recalls his childhood days playing football in Scottish back streets, and worries that youngsters today are no longer brought up with the same all-consuming fervour for the game – with what he calls 'the football habit'. He also bemoans the deterioration in the quality of football since he was a player, and explains why skill and flair are being sacrificed for work rate and athleticism.

'We had automatic floodlights when I was a boy – they were the lamps in the streets. We didn't have any problems with cars, because no one where I was brought up could afford them. The ball we played with was usually stuffed with newspaper, as we kept bursting the bladder. There was no distraction like television, and we certainly couldn't afford to play tennis or golf. They were middle and upper-class sports.

'Now, life has changed – for the better overall, but not for the better for football. The working-class boy has a lot more avenues into a lot more sports. That is good for society, but it means we don't get boys wanting to play football in the abundance we did before. And if we don't get the numbers, then it's unlikely we'll produce as many top-quality players as we did in the past. I am concerned that "the football habit" is disappearing for many youngsters. I was lucky: I learned to play on the streets. Football was my whole life as a boy – there was nothing else to do.

'I believe that I played in the last "golden age" of football. And I don't think it's romantic to look back and remember that era when players could master the ball, make it do what they wanted. It's not romantic, it's practical: Continental players can still do this, so why can't ours? Football was more enjoyable then. It was rewarding to play, there were more characters, there was less pressure. I'm not knocking the modern game, because I believe it is a reflection of the way society has changed. Now, everyone demands instant success. We have instant television, and if people don't like it they turn it off. People go to football matches, and if they don't like what they see they instantly react – by booing. I used to play against smaller clubs and, win or lose, the fans would cheer their team off the pitch. They don't any more. That's why managers have such a hard time.

'Now, we've got what you might call lowest-common-denominator football. We condense the play so much that, with coaching, the poorer players can be turned into productive players and make a valuable contribution. However, the best players haven't gone on improving. The average players are catching them up, and the gap between the best and the rest is narrowing. That's why Paul Gascoigne stands out. In my day, there was Best, Law and Charlton – and that was just at Manchester United. Then you could take Leeds; they had Eddie Gray and Johnny Giles. Because there are so few genuinely outstanding individuals around now, we put pressure on them to perform brilliantly all the time.

'There are quite a few old players who could probably still play today, if you gave them time and space. But the aim of modern-day football is to deny the best players the time and space they need to operate. Not that there's anything wrong with this technique. Look at AC Milan: they've had enormous success with what is basically an English style – pressing up, condensing, playing offsides. But they're doing it with world-class players, who have all the skills to boot. And they still regularly score four or five goals a match.

'Compared to twenty years ago, the game today is far faster, the players are fitter, there's much better organisation. And, most important, the coaching has improved. I'm a great believer in coaching, and it upsets me when I hear ex-players saying on TV that we're coaching the talent out of youngsters. That's a load of rubbish. What they're saying is, why don't we let the youngsters progress naturally? Nonsense. Coaching is a form of teaching. In life, there are good teachers, average teachers and bad teachers. Same with coaches. Just because you get one bad coach, it doesn't follow that all coaching is bad.

'Although I believe that the overall quality of football was higher when I was playing, I don't think I'd get picked in my own Arsenal side now. So many good midfield players have been at Highbury in recent years – David

Rocastle and Paul Davis, for example, they're better players than I was. I needed time and space – I was slow, don't forget! But I was good on the ball, and I could think quickly. I wouldn't hold down a regular place in a decent Arsenal team now, though. If you're in central midfield and you're slow, then you've got to be exceptional. Liam Brady? He was exceptional. Glenn Hoddle was exceptional.

'The British game is famed throughout the world for its athleticism and its commitment. British teams are well-organised, work very hard, and have a never-say-die attitude. These are all good qualities, and they're widely admired. What we'd like to borrow from the Continentals is their skill factor. But because we put such physical effort into the game, we're the ones who should be playing fewer matches; in fact, the Continentals, because they don't value work rate so highly, could even play more. The problem that keeps arising here is the chairmen of clubs saying that they can't survive without playing so many games. I personally think that the fewer matches you have, the more money people would have in their pockets and so the greater the number that would come to watch.

'I firmly believe that we must encourage quality in our football, not quantity. Managers want to get players back in the afternoons to brush up on their skills, so we can't just keep sticking games on them. I'm denied the quality time I want with my players to improve them. There are so many matches, and they're all physically demanding – even against the bottom teams. There's no such thing as an easy game now. Managers are forced to rest players so they can recharge their batteries before they face the next gruelling battle. This is the way the game is going. Sadly, I believe a lot of people are burying their heads in the sand.'

TERRY HOWARD

Known to Leyton Orient fans as 'Oooh Terry' for his surging runs from defence and powerful shot at free-kicks around the penalty box, Terry Howard was born in Stepney in 1966. He began his career at Chelsea, the club he had supported as a boy, but faded after a bright start. Following unsuccessful loan spells at Crystal Palace and Chester City, he felt he might have to quit professional football. Then Orient signed him on a free transfer in March 1987. Below, the popular full-back tells how Chelsea let him down when, as a struggling young player, he needed support and encouragement; and he contrasts life at one of the capital's glamour clubs with his humbler but far more fulfilling existence at Brisbane Road. He also explains why so many London supporters name Leyton Orient as their 'second team'.

'I was an ardent Chelsea fan when I was a kid. I would have been happy to play for any professional side, but when I signed for the team I'd dreamed of playing for, then it really was the biggest thrill in the world. When I was playing schoolboy football and training twice a week over at Stamford Bridge I wasn't sure I had it in me to make the grade, so I treated the whole thing as a bit of an adventure. It was only when I reached 17 and was still doing well that I thought my dream might become reality. It helped that I was part of a very successful youth set-up at Chelsea, and playing in a team that had a lot of admirers.

'I made my first-team debut in April 1985, when I was 19. We played Aston Villa, and I was marking Mark Walters. We won 3–1, and I thought I did OK. Then I played against Spurs – a big London derby that was on *Match of the Day* – and at Anfield, where we lost 3–4. It all happened incredibly fast, and they rested me. I knew they were just giving me a little taster, checking how I coped, so that I might possibly get a more regular place the next season.

'But then John Hollins moved up from coach to manager, and I didn't see eye-to-eye with the bloke he brought in as the new coach, Ernie Walley. He was very sergeant-majorish, and didn't think I was aggressive enough. Players respond to criticism in different ways, and I just went into my shell. I look back at it now as character-building, but at the time I let it affect me in a bad way. I put on a bit of weight, and lost my fitness. In the end, I only played one more game for Chelsea, when we got beaten 2–6 at home by Nottingham Forest in September 1986.

'Chelsea is such a huge club, and I felt like the proverbial small fish in a big pond. I couldn't get any feeling for what was going on around me. It didn't help not living in the area; being based out in Essex, there weren't that many Chelsea supporters around, whereas now I talk to Orient fans almost every day. Away from the club there wasn't any contact with people who were interested in me and in what was going on; now, if I go to the dogs at Walthamstow or to a nightclub, I see Orient supporters all the time. It's as if there's an invisible cord attached; I didn't feel that at Chelsea at all. Although I was a committed Chelsea supporter, I never felt close to the club itself when I was a player there.

'I was put out to Crystal Palace on loan, but I was confused as to why I'd gone there. I didn't know whether it was to find some fitness and form or with a view to a permanent deal. There was no communication. John Hollins is a terrific coach, but I never felt he was a good man-manager. When you're young you need a bit of guidance, someone to put you in the picture, and there was never any help when he was in charge. I had a good debut for Palace – it was against Charlton, the first time the two had met at Selhurst Park while they were ground-sharing – but after that it was a struggle. When you've played in the reserves for a long time you get stale, you lack that edge of fitness. There's no substitute for first-team football. I knew Steve Coppell had been a fan of mine when I was in the Chelsea youth team but, at the end of my month at Palace, he was perfectly honest and I appreciated that. He said I hadn't done well enough. It was then that I learned Chelsea would have offloaded me for a small fee.

'So Chelsea put me out to Chester. Again I made a good start – we won 5–0 at Fulham on my debut – but we played Sheffield Wednesday in the FA Cup in midweek, when the boss [Orient manager Peter Eustace] was assistant there. I had Brian Marwood running past me at regular intervals. Then I played at Bournemouth, and got pulled off. I was knackered, I just wasn't fit enough. I came back from Chester despondent. I'd been doing really well at 19 and seen it all evaporate by the time I was 21.

'Chelsea's reserve-team manager at the time was Martin Hinshelwood. He had Gareth Hall coming through and he said, "I don't want to have to do this, Tel, but I've had orders from on high to drop you." I went in to see John Hollins to ask what they were going to do with me. But it was Ernie Walley who said, "Go on, tell him" – he had to prompt the manager to say, "Well, actually, we're going to give you a free." I asked why they hadn't told me that two months ago, instead of wasting my time.

'It crossed my mind that this could be the end of my career, that I might drift out of the game. Although I feel I was treated shoddily at Chelsea, I have to accept some of the blame as well. I simply felt sorry for myself. But the experience has helped me a lot since. You learn far more about yourself when things are going badly.

'Luckily, Frank Clark had also been an admirer of the youth team I'd played in at Chelsea, and he took me to Orient on the free. People think I came to Orient for a small fee, but it was actually a free transfer. If money had been involved, I don't think he'd have taken the chance. It was an ideal move for me. I'm a local lad, and I used to come and watch the O's occasionally when I was a boy as well as go to Chelsea. I had a soft spot for them in the way that a lot of London fans do. It's strange that the two teams I watched are the ones I've played for.

'I settled in very quickly. I liked the fact that people knew each other, and got on with each other. There have been arguments, of course, but over the six years I've been here we've always pulled together when we've needed to. That's the main strength of a small club – you've got to work for each other.

'There was no social life among the players at Chelsea. You'd get two or three going off together, two or three going somewhere else, but it was always in little cliques. For most of the players, as soon as training or the match was over, it'd be: "See you tomorrow." At Orient, it's "What are we doing tonight?" Some players want to get away from football at times, but I think it's important that we all go out together now and again. I'm sure this helps on Saturdays. It doesn't stop players dishing out rollickings, even to their mates, but part of our success has been due to the fact that we stick together.

'Everyone at Brisbane Road is well aware of how supporters of other clubs view Orient. They adopt a slightly patronising tone – "Ah, look at little Orient; we want them to do well." The reason is that we're not seen as a threat, never have been. True, we've not had much to celebrate over the last ten years, but it was the same when I used to watch as a kid, and we were in the old second division then. It's only when we're playing the likes of West Ham and Millwall regularly – and beating them – that this might change. I think people who have never been to a game at Leyton Stadium imagine Orient supporters to be blokes of 50 or 60 – you know, all turning up in their caps, overcoats and mufflers and waving rattles.

I could have made a few quid in the summer by leaving the O's. Cambridge came in for me, and I had a couple of offers from other first-division clubs. But none of them were actually worth leaving here for. I was a devoted Chelsea supporter, but when I was a player there I never got a feel for the place in the same way that I have here. I didn't want to leave for the sake of money. I tried to explain all this to the Cambridge manager, John Beck, but he just thought I was mad. As it is, Cambridge have struggled, John Beck got the sack, and we're doing well. I think it was the right decision.'

CLIVE ALLEN

Clive Allen is the ultimate 'Mr London Football'. He is the best-known member of the most talented footballing dynasty London has ever produced, and has played for six of the capital's biggest clubs: QPR (twice), Arsenal, Crystal Palace, Spurs, Chelsea and, currently, West Ham. His father, Les, played in the Spurs side that won the double in 1960–61, and both his younger brother and two cousins are with London clubs too. Clive was nicknamed the 'King of Goals' after scoring an astonishing forty-nine times for Spurs in 1986–87, smashing Jimmy Greaves's long-standing club record. His phenomenal average of a goal every two games in a long career has prompted clubs – also including Bordeaux and Manchester City – to splash out a total of £6,175,000 to capture his skills. He is 'a better finisher than Lineker', according to Tommy Docherty, his first manager at QPR. Below, he describes the special attraction of London derby games and explains his view that the sheer number of fiercely competitive matches between clubs in the capital every season is 'an inbuilt disadvantage' to a London club winning the Premier League.

'Football has been in the Allen family's blood for a long time. All four of us playing now – myself, my younger brother Bradley at QPR, and my cousins, Paul at Spurs and Martin here with me at West Ham – were brought up with professional football from the day we were born. I got an early insight into football because, when I was four or five, I used to go and watch my father, Les, playing at QPR, and he later became the manager there. Dennis, Martin's father, was a player too, with Charlton, Bournemouth and Reading. Paul's father was called Ron Allen but he wasn't the WBA footballer Ron Allen. So football has been a way of life for the four of us from a very early age. A football club has never held any fears for us. I remember when we were kids, we would meet up every Saturday morning at my grandmother's and then go our various ways: to watch my dad playing or managing, or watch Martin's dad playing, or go to a game we wanted to see.

'Having three brothers and four sons involved professionally in football is very unusual. Sometimes in one family you get two brothers involved, like Bobby and Jack Charlton, but here you've got seven members of the same family, which is possibly unique. I suppose it's like a dynasty in a way. Mind you, the Allen name isn't always the help that people think it is. It does bring an added pressure, and that can be difficult. Martin has had to come through it, and it's especially hard for someone like my brother Bradley now. As well as having a famous father, he's also got an older brother who's had a career, and to follow in two people's footsteps is very difficult. There are always comparisons – "Oh, he's not quite as good as his brother," that type of thing – so it's not easy for him.

'It *is* just an incredible coincidence that six of the eight clubs I've played for have been in London. People wonder if I've not wanted to leave London because my family and friends are here, but that's not the case. I nearly left QPR when I was still only 19 to go and play in America, where things were starting to happen with the North American Football League. However, QPR didn't want me to leave; but if they hadn't turned down a big offer for me from a team in Seattle, I would have gone, even at that early stage of my career. Although moving away from London didn't hold any fears for me, it wasn't until eight years later that I finally left and signed for Bordeaux. I really felt that, at that stage of my career – I was 27 – I had to take the opportunity to play abroad; it was probably the last chance I'd ever get.

'I don't think moving to Bordeaux was a mistake but, yes, I was relieved to come back to England. Everybody thought I would come back to London again but I went north to Manchester, which was just as big a change as leaving London and going to France. I enjoyed my two and a half years in Manchester and [despite a well-publicised fall-out with incoming manager Peter Reid] all that was associated with playing for a big-city club like Manchester City. The City-United rivalry is similar to the rivalry in North London between Arsenal and Tottenham, but in some ways it's even more intense because, in Manchester, the focus is on just two teams, whereas in London there's so many. You can have a derby game in London every few weeks but, in Manchester, there are just two a season, and they're so, so important.

'People talk about any game between London teams being "a London derby". I don't agree. I think a match can only be called a real London derby when it's between a club and the nearest club to them, because of the rivalry that closeness creates. Tottenham-Arsenal, Chelsea-QPR and West Ham-Millwall or West Ham-Charlton would be considered true London derby games – not a game like West Ham-Watford. The thing is, with so many derby matches of one sort or another each season, I think that makes it very, very difficult for a London club to win the Championship. You see, whichever division you're in, there's always a few London derbies, and those are such difficult games: your opponents try harder, and form goes out the window. Take the 1991-92 season: there were seven London clubs in the then first division – West Ham, Arsenal, Tottenham, Chelsea, Crystal Palace, Wimbledon and QPR – which meant that each club played twelve derbies. That's a serious handicap to a London club with its eyes on winning the Championship; it's an inbuilt disadvantage of being a London club.

'Games between London teams always have that extra edge, at least from the players' point of view. A lot of the players know each other, so you obviously want to win, and that adds spice to the game. I think supporters feel that as well: they've got a friend or relative or somebody at work who supports the side that their team is playing on Saturday, so there's always a bit of extra rivalry attached to the game for them because of that.

'Players appreciate how much it means for their

supporters and themselves to beat other London teams. You don't want to let anyone down. You want to be the winners, because it takes a little bit of pressure off: you know that when you walk down the high street the next week, you're not going to get any jeers or taunts that you've just been beaten by a team considered to be your arch-rivals. In the run-up to, say, a West Ham-Millwall game, you get plenty of people who emphasise the importance of that one game – who say, "I don't care what you do all season, just so long as you beat Millwall this Saturday." In footballing terms that's crazy, because a game against any other team is just as important in the league campaign. But having said that, I have to admit that there *is* an added significance about winning against Millwall or Charlton rather than Barnsley or Peterborough. Not that it means more – you still get three points – but there is something special about winning a London game, definitely.

'The trouble with London derby matches is that they're rarely very good games to watch – or to play in. There's two sorts. You get the odd one where it's end-to-end stuff with a lot of action and a few goals. But the majority are stalemates, close games where there's not a lot between the teams and the sides just cancel one another out. Those games tend to be dull, very fast and furious, and form doesn't matter because neither side wants to lose. The pattern of a London derby game rarely reflects how you play week in and week out, because of its frantic pace. Take our game against Millwall at the Den early last season, for example. Before that match we'd both been playing a controlled, possession type of game, but we never got the opportunity to show it in that clash because it was so fast and furious. The papers afterwards said it was a kicking match; it wasn't, but the ball was never in either team's possession for a very long time, so it did become a disjointed and unattractive game.

'That said, I have played in some great London derbies. I remember a couple of QPR-Chelsea matches: they have always been good games, because you get 24,000 people packed into Loftus Road, which is a small ground, and that creates an exceptional atmosphere. The most difficult derbies I played in were the Tottenham-Arsenal League Cup semi-finals in 1987, when I was at Spurs. There were three games in all: we won 1–0 at Arsenal, where I scored; they won 2–1, at Spurs; and then we eventually lost – again by 2–1, and again after we'd been 1–0 up – in a replay at Spurs. Those were really big games, and I enjoyed playing in them.

'People say to me they think it's strange that, with my scoring record, I've almost always been transferred against my will – I've only ever actually *asked* for a transfer once, at Crystal Palace – and I suppose it is. But football, like anything else, is about supply and demand. Being a manager is a precarious and difficult job, and they take calculated risks: some are prepared to buy you because they think they can get better players. That hasn't bothered me. I feel that each time I've moved I have justified what has been paid for me. I have maintained my scoring record throughout.

'And yes, I can see why some of the moves I've had have left the fans mystified about why I was leaving. The move from Arsenal was baffling, I admit. I still don't know to this day why they sold me on again so quickly, before I could kick a ball for them. I went to Highbury at the end of one season on a long contract to play for Arsenal. Yet, within two months, Terry Neill came to me and said, "We need a left-back, we want Kenny Sansom, and the only way we can bring him in is to in October 1990, I saw a different side to the club. They weren't interested in me and didn't do anything for me, which really annoyed me.

'I had been in hospital for a major operation and, when I came out, I wanted to get straight to the Chadwell Heath training ground again. I couldn't do any training, but I wanted to talk to the players. So I asked the club for an automatic car, just to get me to training and back. I needed an automatic because the injury was to my left leg, so I could only drive with my right. But the club said, "We can't do it. If we've got to do it for you we've got to do it for everybody." I knew people who would have given me a car if West Ham had contacted them, but they didn't contact anybody. That really annoyed me. It was such a small thing. I don't know why they wouldn't do it; all I asked for was a car. I mean, I worked my balls off for this club, but they just said no straightaway. It's a strange way to treat one of your star players, but it's also not very nice to treat anybody like that.

'Things were very tense for me for a long time because of the injury. I didn't know if I was ever going to play again; it was fifty-fifty. And then, when the club turned round and said, "No, we're not giving you a car", I was down. When they said that, I couldn't get to the training ground. My wife Kay had to drive me in from Billericay, where we live, to Chadwell Heath, which takes half an hour, and then go back home. She did that week in week out, but the club still wouldn't give me a car; she had to drive me in. Every morning we had to get our twin little girls, Jessica and Katie, up and then Kay would drive me in to work. That was probably the lowest point of my career: it was fifty-fifty if I'd ever play again, and then the club turned round and said, "Oh no, we can't do that". That really put the top on it.

'A couple of times, the strain of it all – the injury, not

knowing if I would play again, my treatment by the club – nearly broke my marriage up. I just couldn't handle it. I would stay at home with my leg up, and that was it. But the club weren't interested. The rest of the players were great for me; I went out with them. They didn't ignore me because I couldn't walk properly or anything else, and they would always speak to me. But I was shunned by quite a few other people at the club, top people, and that was amazing to me. It really annoyed me badly. The top people at the club just blanked me. People just walked straight past me at this club – literally put their head down and walked straight past me. I really don't know why. Peter Storrie, the managing director, always spoke to me every time I saw him while I was injured, but he was the only one of the directors who did.

'That said, the medical treatment I received when I was injured was excellent. John Green, the West Ham physio, was great to me. John used to take me up to the Devonshire Hospital in London two or three times a week, out of his own time, and I think that if it wasn't for him I wouldn't have got back playing again. The reasons I'm still here at the club and still playing football are John Green, Billy Bonds, the supporters and John King, the surgeon at the London Independent Hospital, who did a great job on my knee.

'I felt like quitting the club because I was so annoyed at the way I'd been treated. While I was injured, Billy and the players and the supporters were interested in whether or not I was coming back, but the top people just blanked me. The reason I signed a new contract was for the supporters. They're the best I have ever played in front of, and they're the major reason I signed again. The other reason I signed again was Billy Bonds, who's a great bloke.

'West Ham might be a "big happy family" between

the supporters and the players, but it's not from the other people at the club towards the players. Don't get me wrong, it is a great club; but I wouldn't have found out the other side to it unless I'd been injured. It's hard to explain why they behaved like that to me, really: you work your balls off for the club, and then they just totally blank you. Everyone I talked to about it thought their treatment of me was bizarre.'

JOHN FASHANU

Nicknamed 'Fash the Bash' by the *Sun* for his all-action style, John Fashanu is the ideal centre-forward for Wimbledon FC, the club everyone loves to hate. Abused by fans, feared by opposing defenders, Fash personifies the combative never-say-die spirit which has underpinned the Dons' legendary climb from non-league obscurity to Premier League status. Since signing from Millwall in 1986 for £125,000, his consistent goal-scoring has helped Wimbledon win both promotion to the first division (1986) and the FA Cup (1988) and, perhaps more remarkably, stay in the top flight against huge odds. A successful businessman and accomplished TV presenter, too, Fash is one of the most articulate footballers around. Below, he defends Wimbledon against their many critics, talks about the pleasure and pain – mainly pleasure, he insists – of playing for English football's 'raggy-arsed rovers', and explains how sticking with the Crazy Gang has denied him the chance of adding to his two international caps.

'Since joining Wimbledon I've been part of an incredible success story. Success has mainly meant staying up in the first division and now the Premier League, despite the critics on our backs all the time and by defying the odds

– that's been a hell of a success. With the supporters we get, we've done amazingly well. We've also won the FA Cup, played in the Charity Shield, and we got to the quarter-finals the year after too. Now in 1993–94 we might get into Europe which would be really great for us. Wimbledon in Europe? Why not? We should have been in Europe when we won the FA Cup. In the last few years, we've been the second best team in London after Arsenal, in terms of our final league position. So where's Tottenham? Where's Chelsea? Compare Chelsea's wage bill to ours, and tell me which club you'd rather be running.

'The funny thing is, everybody says "Wimbledon can't play", yet everybody's buying our players! It's incredible how many ex-Wimbledon players now at other clubs are internationals: Terry Phelan and Keith Curle, the two most expensive defenders in the country, went to Manchester City for £2.5 million each. Then there's Dave Beasant, Eric Young, Glyn Hodges. And Vinnie Jones. He's had nearly £3 million in moves, yet everybody says he can't play, and the managers who have bought him have been soccer purists like Howard Wilkinson and Ian Porterfield. Everybody shouts and screams and hurls abuse at Vinnie Jones but, when it comes to picking the team, every manager wants him on their side. Isn't it strange that, when Vinnie was at Leeds and Chelsea, people said, "Oh, he can play a bit", but when he came back to Wimbledon, suddenly it was "No, he can't play"? You ask players who they respect, and they'll all say Vinnie Jones.

'The fan-mail Vinnie gets is incredible. He gets sacks of it, far more than people like Lineker – and it's all nice stuff too! Tell me, why does Vinnie get so much fan-mail? Why has he been so successful financially? Why does Jackie Charlton want him to play for Ireland? When

Vinnie was fined £20,000 by the FA [for presenting the infamous *Soccer's Hard Men* video], ordinary people sent him cash to pay it. People like building workers were offering to give *their* wages to pay *his* fine. But Vinnie donated the money they sent in to a children's home and paid the £20,000 himself. That tells you that the layman, the working-class person, respects him. I know other successful players who have been fined, and no one has bothered to send any money in. They say, "Rich bastards, why should we?" Vinnie's off the building site, he works hard, he can play well, he has generated £3 million in moves, he's made himself a lot of money, he's famous not just in this country but in Europe. Everyone has their niche in life.

'For the last four years, I've been one of the top three highest goal-scorers in the first division or Premier League. Gary Lineker was asked on TV who he'd most like to play up front with. And who did he say? He said *me*. That's Gary Lineker, one of soccer's purists. Spurs have tried to buy me several times, but I've turned them down. What would I want to go there for? To win more trophies? I've already got medals in the cabinet – the FA Cup, the Charity Shield. What would I do there, make more money? I'm the third highest-paid player in the country at the moment. So what would I move for? I run companies; I do what I want to do here. My attitude is: "I play football, but there are other things in life apart from football." Yet, every season, I still score twenty-odd goals.

'The whole mythology of the club is based on the underdog syndrome, like David and Goliath. But we *thrive* on being the underdog. I *like* the fact that it's the world against us. I admit that the players and the manager and the chairman do all encourage our monster image, but that's because that's what we've got going for us. We love that. We don't want to go into a game where people are saying, "Oh, Wimbledon, they're great players"; we want people to be scared of us, and they are.

'Take the 1988 Cup final against Liverpool: we already had the match won before we started, because we out-psyched them in the tunnel before kick-off. Liverpool said afterwards that their biggest mistake was to let their boys line up against ours for ten minutes beforehand in the tunnel. For the first five minutes, we just stood there staring each one of them in the face, not wanting to shake hands or talk. None of us had shaved or washed; we were stinking, looking like animals. Then Jonesy started up the "yidaho!" shout, which spread right the way down the line. When I looked into John Barnes's face I could see he was nearly crying before he went out. The only one who stood up to it was Steve McMahon, as we knew he would. So, five minutes into the game, he went in for a tackle with Vinnie, whose tackle started at his neck and finished at his ankle, and that put him out. We knew after that, because everybody had seen what a tackle it was, that they didn't want to play.

'People say it's amazing we won the Cup. Bollocks. It was always going to happen because we're a one-off team. We're a very, very strong side, not just physically but mentally too. People say we're just a bunch of hard men, but we've got a lot more than that. Psychologically, we're tough, we're very resilient; you have to be when you're being slagged off all the time. If you want to play for Wimbledon you have to be able to come in, join the camaraderie with the rest of the boys, close everything else off and think, "right, let's go for it!"

'Is that monster image in danger of becoming a millstone around our necks? No, not at all. In the middle of last season we were second from bottom; then we were thirteenth from top. If we could have got a few more wins we could have got into Europe. Now what team has the balls to come through as strongly as that? We're playing three games a week, with a small squad, yet we're still doing the business. We're not Liverpool, where we can put one big-name player in for another. How do we keep doing it? Nobody can understand. We are an enigma. People ask, "How can you afford to pay players such vast wages on the crowds you get? How can you only get 4,000 fans in and still beat Everton? How come every season you manage to stay in the Premier League?" I don't know. If I knew the formula I'd be making millions by selling it to all the other clubs. Nobody knows.

'All we know is, there's no jealousy among the players, every year we sell one of our players, and everybody has that "don't give a damn" attitude. When people say, "I don't know how you guys cope with all the abuse you get", I say: we're honest, we work hard, all the boys graft. We've done a league double this season over Arsenal and Liverpool, we beat Manchester United away when they were on form, and we've done Aston Villa in the Cup. Give us some credit. Give us some credit! People who know about football know we haven't just done that by running around and being thugs; that's come from football.

'All people see is the low gates we get. They forget that we've only been in the Football League since 1978. We haven't celebrated our centenary yet, for God's sake! We haven't even handed down season-tickets to our kids yet. Why don't people understand that instead of saying, "Oh, you're only getting 3,000 crowds, that must piss you off." If you know about football you'll know that Wimbledon's catchment area isn't very good, and that we're a new club, a baby club that's growing up. Give us another century, and I'll say, "Hey, look at the number of season-ticket holders we've got." At the moment, we haven't even got our own stadium – though we will have soon. We're slowly starting to get the infrastructure we need by actually *buying* players, not just selling them. We've brought in our first million-pound player, Dean Holdsworth: six months after we bought him we had a bid from Chelsea for him of £1.6 million, and even though we could have made a profit of six hundred grand in just six months we said no. We had a bid of £1.2 million from Liverpool for John Scales. Not from Shamrock Rovers or Hereford United, but from *Liverpool*, arguably one of the greatest teams in the world. Now why is it that Liverpool want to buy our defender? Why did Everton want to buy Warren Barton? Is it because we've got bad players and everybody hates us? I think not. How then can we be the raggy-arsed rovers?

'Success for me has also meant winning two England caps, one against Chile at Wembley and the other against Scotland at Hampden Park. But what's stopped me playing more times for England is what Don Howe calls my "outside activities". He had been here at the club and seen me coming and going, doing my business, and he didn't like that. He told me that I had to cut down on my interests outside the game and concentrate on my football. But I do a lot of things, all of the time. I'm a workaholic: I run four companies, I present two TV shows, I'm a director of Kiss FM radio station. My argument is that, if you look at my track record at the end of every season, it's better than most people's. Don's reply to that was, "There's more to playing for England than just scoring goals." I think that, if anybody should be playing for England, it's me, because I'm a good ambassador for football.

'Don Howe wanted me to cut back on my "outside activities", and I wasn't prepared to do that. Players like Lineker, Barnes, Gazza and myself have proved that there's more to life than just football, that you *can* do other things off the pitch and still be successful when you play.

'Playing for Wimbledon has definitely held me back too. Keith Curle moved from Wimbledon to Manchester City and, suddenly, he was straight in the England side. Dave Beasant moved from Wimbledon to Newcastle United and got straight into the England team, too, even though he was playing terribly with Newcastle! The same with Dennis Wise: moved to Chelsea, straight into the England side. But I don't feel bitter about it. Look at it this way: I can name you loads of players and managers who've got over sixty England caps – but they haven't got enough money to pay the mortgage.

'I don't feel hard done by. I know that, while I'm playing football and enjoying life so much, I don't really give a damn. I've got two England caps. What difference is there between two and ten? Football is my priority: if they select me, I'd be there. I'd be a loyal servant. But if they don't call me, I won't lose any sleep over it. It's fine if they want to pick me: I'll work my heart out and do the best I can. But sometimes, as we have seen before, the best is not always good enough.'

GERRY FRANCIS

Gerry Francis was born in Chiswick, West London, in December 1951, the son of the former Brentford player Roy Francis. He made his debut for Queen's Park Rangers, the team he had supported since boyhood, at 16. Under his captaincy, Rangers finished second, just behind Liverpool, in the first division in 1976, their highest ever end-of-season position. Don Revie made Francis, then aged 23, captain of England after only four appearances; sadly, however, a back problem restricted him to just twelve internationals. In all, Francis spent twelve years with QPR as a player; at 27, he became player-coach at Crystal Palace under Malcolm Allison, and he also had spells with Coventry, Exeter, Cardiff, Swansea, Portsmouth and Bristol Rovers. His managerial career kicked off at Exeter City in 1983 and, after subsequently taking over at Bristol Rovers, he began to acquire a reputation as a miracle-worker and talent-spotter *extraordinaire*. His success in leading Rovers – heavily in debt, with no home ground and a team costing less than £100,000 – to the third-division championship and their first ever Wembley appearance, the 1990 Leyland DAF Cup final, prompted an over-the-top nickname from the fans: 'God'. He even lent Rovers his own money to buy players. In May 1991, Francis 'went home' to become manager of QPR, bringing rapid and unaccustomed consistency in the league. He has been called 'the best manager in the country'. Below, he describes how the manager's lot can be a 'seven-day-a-week hell'; admits that, statistically, Rangers are unlikely ever to win the Premier League because of their habit of losing their best players; and discusses what it would be like to try out his undoubted inspirational skills as a coach with a bigger club.

'I would go back to playing straightaway if I had the opportunity – tomorrow, if possible. Playing is the easy side of things. Management can be a seven-day-a-week hell, where nobody seems to come out any younger. Hopefully, I might be able to come out with half my hair still black! When I was a player, you'd do your training, go home and have the rest of the day off. Now, as a manager, football is a seven-day-a-week job throughout the year. Your work starts in the summer when the season's finished. New contracts, new kit, new sponsors, end-of-season tours, pre-season tours, dealing with football agents every day. It just doesn't stop. Your life's not your own by a long way. You can't go off and have a week's holiday because you need it – I think only Brian Clough could do that – because you're here all the year round.

'The pressure is immense. I saw Jock Stein in Bristol the day before he died, and that will always be a vivid picture in my mind. He looked very stressed. He had a major Scottish game coming up the next day, and the Scots were under pressure. It's the same with league managers. I can quite understand why Kenny Dalglish left management for a year, because it's not just the stresses on *you*, it's the stresses on your whole family and friends – through Easters, Christmases and New Years, you're never at home, you're never with your family. Your family probably get it worse than you in some respects, in that the first people you take the stresses of the job out on are the people you love the most or are closest to. If you can show me someone who came out of football management looking younger than when he went in, I'd like to see him.

'This isn't meant to sound like a sob story, because there's enormous pressure in all walks of life: people who are out of work have got tremendous pressure, for example, and they accept it. I mean, I lived in a pre-fab council house with my parents for eighteen years, so I know what life can be like. Football has given me a chance to earn some money and to do certain things I would never have done otherwise, so I appreciate it. But whatever you do in this game, there's always pressure from something happening. You might be successful for two years, then have five or six bad games and have a row with the chairman. You might have the situation that happened to us at Middlesbrough last season, where two players, Ray Wilkins and Gary Penrice, broke their legs in the space of a couple of hours. You never know what's going to happen, and that uncertainty is added pressure.

'As the manager, you have to make difficult decisions: about the future of YTS players, and about picking or not picking players – maybe it's a player who's been very good to you, but he's getting a bit too old. You have to deal with chairmen, deal with boards of directors, deal with the media. I mean, at Bristol, the whole community depended on me and the team, and it's the same here at Rangers. You, the manager, become the focal point. If the team wins or loses, that sends 12,000 people to work happy or sad. You become the symbol of people's happiness or frustration, people's desire for success. Like when I left Bristol Rovers, 5,000 people wrote to me on postcards asking me to stay. You've got to be a bit thick-skinned if that doesn't get to you.

'I love football, otherwise I wouldn't have spent all my life in it; but the demands for success have become greater and greater. And when you condense that pressure for success – from chairmen, managers, players and crowds – you find a lot of people getting scared because they're concerned about their jobs, about the club doing well and making a profit and being successful. People forget that only a tiny minority of clubs *can* be successful in any one season.

'That's why you get such a high turnover of managers. These days, managers are the first ones to get blamed. Management is a very fickle game, to say the least. When I was playing, managers had a bit longer to prove themselves; they normally got around three years before they had any pressure on them. Now you're lucky if you get three months. If clubs look like getting relegated from the Premier League, or any other league, they can't afford to wait; suddenly it's "bang!", the manager gets sacked and someone else comes in.

'I have served a difficult apprenticeship, learned the hard way at Exeter and Rovers, and now I'm in charge of the team I supported as a boy – I've always had blue and white blood running through my veins – and I'm very fortunate. But when I came back to Rangers as manager I knew that I had to find £2 million just to put us back in the black. I took the job knowing that, so I can't argue; I *had* to do it. So I sold Paul Parker to Manchester United. Since then I've sold nearly £4 million worth of players. In the summer before the 1992–93 season we didn't spend a penny on players, and the two players I did buy afterwards cost £100,000 and £60,000. Yet I don't think we were out of the top eight virtually all season. People ask me: what's the knack you've got of having success with limited resources? I don't know if it is a knack; I suppose you've just got to be good at what you do, or just lucky. I'd say it was probably a bit of both. I think a manager's record has to speak for itself, taking into consideration the resources of his club.

'But having said that, what is the future? I find it very difficult that when I discover players, I lose them. I have spent most of my time as a manager getting players from the lower levels or on free transfers from somewhere else and trying to make them into the finished article. That's the side of football management I do enjoy: trying to make players better through coaching. I get great satisfaction from seeing players I've worked with, or helped discover, going places – like Nigel Martyn, the first million-pound goalkeeper, who was sold against my wishes from Bristol Rovers to Crystal Palace. Gary Penrice was never a striker until I made him a striker at Rovers; he went on to Watford for £500,000 and then to

Aston Villa and now he's here at Rangers. Those are the things you enjoy.

'Unfortunately, if you are successful at spotting talent, and you do bring those players along to become the finished article, then you lose them and that can be very frustrating. QPR simply cannot afford to compete with the likes of Blackburn, Leeds, Manchester United and Liverpool in finance or in wages. Plus players' agents are there to make sure that their clients – my players – do the best for themselves, their families and their children, which is understandable. So it does make it very difficult indeed to hang onto your best players.

'It's very hard to say what the future holds for Queen's Park Rangers. QPR have never won the first division. In fact, QPR haven't won a major trophy since the League Cup in 1967. QPR have once only finished in the top three in the first division when we were second in 1975–76, when I was captain. If you put all that together in a computer and ask it to say realistically what QPR's chances are, I would imagine it would suggest that our chances of winning the Championship were slim.

'Look at the clubs who have won the first division in the last twenty years: Liverpool, Arsenal, Leeds, Derby when Cloughie was there, and Forest – they've virtually all been big clubs. With rich clubs getting richer and poor clubs getting poorer in terms of not being able to buy million-pound players, you wonder if it's impossible for QPR to win the Championship. History shows it's not very likely. To be honest, in the future, success for QPR would be making sure they stay in the Premier League, particularly if it's going to get smaller, which it undoubtedly is. To stay in there takes some doing, especially if you're losing your better players.

'Would I fancy having a go at managing a bigger club than QPR? Well, if you're asking me would I like to be able to spend money, the answer is yes because that way I can be successful quicker. If you're saying to me, "Here's £5 million, Gerry, go and buy Alan Shearer", I'd go and buy him tomorrow because I know that Alan Shearer would quickly make my team better and that's what some of the bigger clubs can do. If a manager doesn't win anything after spending a lot of money then you understand that you're not going to be around very long – but that happens at any level of football anyway. There's no difference in the pressure involved in running a smaller Premier League club to a bigger Premier League club except that expectations might be higher at a bigger club. But with those expectations comes the finance to buy players: I wouldn't be worried about losing my top players at Manchester United.

'I'm not saying whether or not I'd fancy a crack at managing a bigger Premier League club like Manchester United. What I'm saying is that if QPR were a big club, I wouldn't have to worry about Les Ferdinand or Andy Sinton leaving, or what I read in the papers every day about other clubs coming in for my players, because I would know that my players would be as well-paid and as well-looked-after as anywhere else. And I could go and get Alan Shearer or anybody I wanted. I would know that my job would depend on whether I won anything or not, but at the same time I would know that I had the best possible resources. Then the question would be: how good are you in actually making these players win the Championship? That's the side of it that would really appeal to me.

'To be perfectly honest, I don't see myself staying in the game into my later years. I mean that, hand on heart. I want to be able to enjoy other aspects of my life while I'm still fairly young, and football gets in the way because management is a seven-day-a-week job. During my playing career, I invested the money I made from football in three limited companies hopefully to look after myself financially in the future. Those companies really are my future. I don't regard football management as something you can base any future on, so those companies are very important to me.

'I never set myself targets. I never look further ahead than the next day. I'll see out my contract at Rangers until the summer of 1994, and then I'll decide what I want to do. But I certainly don't see football being my life to the sort of ages that some managers have done. Once I feel I've had enough, I'll call it a day. Lots of things in life are just as important as football.'

NINE

Perverse Passion

*London fans who even sing
when they're losing*

'Palace fans are an odd assortment, to say the least. The club, located in the nethermost suburbs of South London, has never provoked the kind of passion found in our neck of the woods or the big northern cities.' Arsenal fan Mike Collins, writing in the Gunners' fanzine *One-Nil Down, Two-One Up*, summed up the view of most London football supporters towards those whose blue-and-red loyalty is directed, apparently inexplicably, towards Selhurst Park, SE25. A Monday-night, mid-season visit for a league match convinced Collins that, for Palace followers, 'soccer is an adjunct to shopping and waxing the Astra GLS, the big time across the river an unknown territory. Some of the local fans walking down Holmesdale Road really imagined they would win, muttering optimistic mantras into their Hewitt's anoraks. Hey, boyz, wise up,' Collins concluded. 'You're on the downward slide to Hull and beyond.'

If Crystal Palace was the starting-point in a game of word association, enthusiasts would struggle to keep the sequence going for long. Third division. Malcolm Allison. Terry Venables. 'The Team of the Eighties'. Relegated, again. Steve Coppell. That 4–3 win against Liverpool. Er . . .

For a club whose history began in 1905, it is an undistinguished list. Even John Ellis, editor of 4,000-selling fanzine *Eagle Eye*, admits that following Palace is a 'fairly masochistic and thankless activity. But people enjoy it. I don't know why. I know the team is useless, so you set your sights very low because you know they're absolutely crap, and if they rise above it that's great. But certainly there's no legacy of success; there's not even a mythology of success like you get with the two big North London clubs. Crystal Palace are traditionally a third-division club, really, so simply being in the Premier League meant that those were halcyon days for us. But there's no glamour, no glory to speak of – except one defeat in a Cup final replay and winning the Zenith Data Systems Cup. But that's it, you see: Palace win Mickey Mouse things because they're a Mickey Mouse club. Everybody would like to think that the success of the last few years hasn't been a freak, a blip in the club's history, but I think it probably is. I know Ron Noades has this great masterplan to turn Palace into South London's first superclub, a club to compare with the great powers of North and East London. But I don't think it's going to happen.'

By day a computer programmer with British Gas, it is hardly surprising that Ellis confesses to Crystal Palace being a kind of personal hall of dreams. But as an escape route from the humdrum, there must surely be easier options. After all, the Eagles' pedigree is more chump than champ. 'They've always had good players, but then lost them,' admits Ellis ruefully. 'Johnny Byrne played for the club in the late 1950s, but it wasn't until he signed for West Ham that he became an England international and a household name. Although they finally got into the first division in 1970, they only spent four years there and quickly slid back into the third. Even then, Malcolm

Allison still steered them to the semi-finals of the FA Cup as a third-division team, beating Chelsea, Leeds and Sunderland away from home on the way. When they finally got back into the top flight in 1980, some journalist coined the phrase, "The Team of the Eighties". They were meant to be this great young team who were going to clean up in English football for the next decade. They topped the first division for one week – which is always remembered at Palace – but then it all fell apart. Terry Venables went to QPR, took seven players with him, and soon we were a laughing stock. We returned to the second division as real nothings again.

'I reckon the revival in our fortunes started in a game against Oldham in 1985, when our centre-forward, Trevor Aylott – a donkey footballer who was the epitome of Crystal Palace ordinariness – was substituted and Ian Wright, who had just been signed from Greenwich Borough, came on. We were 1–2 down at that stage. But Wright created one goal and scored another, so Palace won 3–2. That, for me, was the turning-point; it seemed a case of "usher out the old, bring in the new". I remember his first goal: after scoring it he ran round like mad for about ten minutes. He was so fast, like a whippet. We were used to seeing absolutely atrocious, slow, old footballers who had come to the end of their careers at Chelsea or Arsenal. Steve Coppell began to build a team round Ian Wright. We knew then he was special. We always suspected he'd leave one day, but it still hurts now he's gone. And when Mark Bright came from Leicester City, the two of them clicked. Suddenly, we had this brilliant pair of strikers who started scoring loads of goals. They netted over fifty between them every season they were together, and the club's fortunes rose with them. They were the key. Things got better and better every year, like in 1990, when we finished third in the league and got to the Cup final.

'But that run of success was ended with the sale of Ian Wright to Arsenal in 1991. Everything till that point had been on the up and up. I suppose the club's fortunes depended to an unhealthy extent on Ian Wright and, by losing that one player, it means that the spell has been broken. Other players have got pissed off: Bright and Andy Gray have gone, and Geoff Thomas tried to leave. The trouble is, people now *expect* success. A lot of our fans have grown up with the idea of Palace as a big Premier League club with international players. But I'm worried that, if we start to struggle again, the fans will melt away as they did in the 1980s, when gates dropped from 30,000 to a hard core of just 6,000.

'Now that Palace have been relegated, I fear that they'll turn into a Luton Town or something horrible like that. They'll have their nine or ten thousand fans, and probably still sell out for the odd big game or if they draw Liverpool in the Cup. But the fans are a fickle lot. I suppose they don't believe Palace are going to be a sustained force in football over the next few years. And if the supporters don't really believe that's going to happen, it's no wonder players don't want to sign for the club. Despite their recent success, Palace have a credibility problem. They got £2.5 million for Ian Wright, but they still couldn't go into the transfer market and say, "I've got £2.5 million, I want you at Selhurst Park," because they had the difficulty of getting any decent player to come.

'Why do I support Palace? That's a good question. I started watching them regularly when they were really atrocious, when they were in the second division in the early 1980s. I started going *despite* how bad they were. Why do I keep going? I don't know why. It's irrational, I suppose. I'll really have to think about that . . .'

Comedian Ronnie Corbett's support for Palace began for one very practical reason: he lived five minutes' walk from Selhurst Park in Church Road, Upper Norwood. 'It seemed silly not to support the community team. You find Manchester United and Liverpool fans in London, and you hear of Arsenal and Chelsea fans coming from all over the country to see them, but Crystal Palace fans tend to be from South London. I suppose I am the exception that proves the rule.

'The first thing I remember from when I started going in 1966 was how nice the walk was, because the crowd was so friendly. Back in those days, I was still an unknown, I was doing shows in nightclubs and just starting to appear on *Crackerjack*. When I moved to Addington Park in Surrey a few years later, my friend Brian Huggett, the former Ryder Cup captain, used to come and collect me on Saturdays in his car with two of Colin Cowdrey's sons, Graham and Jeremy, who were then schoolboys. I liked going with some mates, because if you're a face you can be a bit vulnerable going to football on your own. But it's always been a very homely club. Certainly the boardroom was always nice, where Brian and I used to have a cup of tea and where we were always very well looked after by the ladies. We had seats, of course. I mean, with my height, if I stood on the terraces I wouldn't see much anyway!'

Born in Edinburgh in 1930, the diminutive funnyman spent childhood Saturdays at Tynecastle Park, supporting Heart of Midlothian FC. The character-forming experience of watching Hearts trying to compete with Celtic and Rangers in Scotland left him with an ingrained mistrust of football's glamour clubs. To Corbett, football and showbiz are united by the fickleness of their audience; both, he says, often have a 'here today, gone tomorrow' quality about them. 'Clubs such as Arsenal and Manchester United retain great charisma, but it is possible to enjoy supporting a club that had never been regarded as glamorous before I started watching them, like Palace. Although they were decidedly average in every way, I fastened myself to them. When you've been brought up with the wooden stands and pies at half-time at Tynecastle, you can see that the marble halls at Highbury are lovely – but they don't mean any more about football than Tynecastle did.'

According to Corbett, the only time Palace could be accused of being even vaguely glamorous was in the Malcolm Allison-Terry Venables era in the 1970s. 'Between them, they dragged the club into the limelight. Malcolm had tremendous charisma, probably even more than Terry had, but he was his own worst enemy really. He had that great Cup run in 1976, but then he got the bullet after the "communal bath" incident [when a naked Big Mal was photographed enjoying the company of actress Fiona Richmond in the tub at Selhurst Park], which upset the high moral stance of the board at the time.'

With that infamous episode, the larger-than-life Allison showed that acting the comedian probably is not the ideal way to hold on to your job as a football manager. Ronnie Corbett proves that you don't have to be a comedian to support Crystal Palace – but it does seem to help.

★ ★ ★

When the legendary devotion of football fans to apparently hopeless causes is finally captured between hard covers, as it surely should, a chapter must certainly be reserved for the antics of Billy Grant and the Official Unofficial travel posse. Once, their loyalty to Brentford FC even compelled them to drive 600 miles north to Aberdeen one Saturday – despite the fact that their heroes had no plans whatsoever to play there. It sounds like a bizarre idea. It *is* a bizarre idea. But to Grant and his fellow adventurers, it was the most natural thing in the world to do.

'I'm absolutely knackered . . . but it was a wicked trip!' Standing in the pouring rain on the open Ealing Road terrace at Griffin Park, before Brentford's crucial Sunday-morning third-division promotion clash with Fulham in April 1992, Grant is not letting the deluge dampen his enthusiasm for telling and retelling the story of his last forty-eight hours. The previous Friday afternoon, he and twenty other Bees fans had set off in a chartered minibus on a 'pilgrimage' to see two former Griffin Park favourites, Richard Cadette and Eddie May, in action for their new club, Falkirk. The venue: Pittodrie. The game: Aberdeen v Falkirk in the Scottish Premier League. The purpose: well, none really, except a glimpse at two former stalwarts. But to Grant & Co., the rationale was simple: if you're going to see Brentford v Fulham on Sunday morning, why not take in a match in Scotland en route?

This arduous and expensive undertaking had its own rewards for the Official Unofficial posse. On the Friday night, they were welcomed by hospitable Falkirk fans, who put them up in their homes. Next morning, everyone rose early and travelled the 200 miles north-east together up to the granite city. Game over, they met Cadette and May in the players' lounge. And when the time came for the minibus to start the all-night trip back to London, the driver counted on board four extra passengers – Bairns' supporters, somehow persuaded that a noon kick-off at Griffin Park would be an equally good laugh.

This trip across the border was not an isolated outbreak of lunacy, though. Since January 1989, Grant and his fellow Bees devotees have organised similarly enterprising trips to promote fun and friendship between fans of different clubs. 'It all started during Brentford's run to the quarter-finals of the Cup,' Grant recalls. 'A group of us wanted to travel to the fifth-round tie at Blackburn, but in a vehicle that showed we were from London. We tried to hire a Hoppa bus from London Transport, but they warned us that its top speed was only 50 m.p.h., so it would have taken us all day to get there. In the end, twenty of us went on a rickety old coach. There was no hassle on the way up, we won 2–0, and on the return journey everyone danced to Abba and David Essex tapes in the bus. We wanted our day out to be as different as possible from the traditional football away-day, so we made a point of avoiding motorway service stations. Instead, I did a bit of research beforehand so we could stop off at a quaint old Egon Ronay-type pub out in the country.'

Almost inevitably, fancy dress was introduced to Official Unofficial outings. In early 1992, a trip to the top-of-the-table Stoke City v Brentford game was turned into an eighteen-hour 'Magical Mystery Tour'. The Bees fans who had signed up for this escapade were divided into teams – based on the themes of *The Three Amigos*, *Captain Pugwash*, *Grange Hill* and *The Magic Roundabout* – and asked to dress accordingly; then they were given a mystery pack whose contents revealed the day's very individual pre-match entertainment. Instead of suffering penalty shoot-outs and marching bands, Grant's posse enjoyed a cruise up the River Trent and a VIP reception at a lunchtime ice-hockey game.

The Amigos theme resurfaced three months later at the last game of the season, when the Bees clinched the third-division championship at Peterborough. It was the first time they had won anything in living memory, so it was definitely a time for celebration. Wearing Mexican-style ponchos and sombreros, the Official Unofficial squad pressed home their message of encouraging peaceful relations between rival supporters.

Proof that other fans were receptive had come early in their wacky career, when a trip dubbed 'The Bee-Brum-Brom Experience' brought together fifty supporters of Brentford and West Bromwich Albion at the 400-year-old Stag's Head in rural Warwickshire. The link-up had come about because the Bees were playing Birmingham City, whose great rivals West Brom were hosting Oldham. 'I remember when we walked in, the bar staff looked really nervous. I heard someone whisper, "I told you they were football fans",' Grant recounts. 'But by the time we had to leave, the whole village was in the pub. I was playing the organ, and we had all the Brentford and West Brom boys and girls singing along.'

Billy Grant is a symbol of the changed atmosphere among fans since the dark days of Heysel and Hillsborough, an indication that friendly rivalry is, happily, back in fashion. But why does he spend so much time organising such elaborately public statements of faith, both in Brentford and in football itself? He's already got a full-time day job; he doesn't get rich on the back of the Official Unofficial posse; and he doesn't get any awards from the club or the FA. So what's in it for him? 'I suppose I just think that watching football – even Brentford – should be a great day out. People call the things we do "alternative", but they're only alternative because we aren't doing things football supporters are expected to do, just travelling to the game and then heading back home again. We're going out of our way to be a bit more creative.'

* * *

Dave Thomas is unlikely ever to be accused of committing the football fan's worst offence: being a 'Part-Time

Percy' – the insult hurled at a team's less-devoted supporters by their much more committed mates. Each season, Thomas clocks up around 20,000 miles following Queen's Park Rangers, the club he has supported since the mid-1960s when he 'fell in love with this third-division team who seemed to win 6–0 every week, and who had a very unusual name, which I liked'. At the time he was an eleven-year-old growing up on the Isle of Wight. 'Everybody there supported Southampton or Portsmouth, but I always had this streak in me that likes to be different', he recalls. 'So when kids in the school playground asked "who do you support?", I said "Queen's Park Rangers".'

Now, every fortnight Thomas undertakes a 400-mile round trip from his home in Shropshire to see Rangers play – and that's just for home games in London, W12. Away matches in places like Southampton and Ipswich require an even earlier start. He's been following that same punishing schedule week in, week out since the 1986–87 season. Usually he takes his car, which he ditches at a service station on the M6 near Keele and hitches a lift with two fellow QPR nuts, Martin and Liz from Warrington. 'It may seem like madness, but we love it; to us it's perfectly sane. The people who think we're mad, what do they do? They sit in their armchairs in front of the TV. They never experience all the ups and downs of supporting a team – the different moods, the triumphs and the anguish, the elation and the devastation – that bring people together because they're sharing the same things. It's like a small club; the people who travel together become friends. People say "Oh, you poor thing, you must be mad doing what you do", but I think we're richer and more fulfilled for it.'

Pressed to explain why his automatic response to a Saturday-Wednesday-Saturday schedule of matches at

Loftus Road is an unhesitating readiness to travel the 1,200 miles involved, Thomas, editor of *A Kick Up The R's*, the Rangers fanzine he started in 1987, isn't quite sure. 'Why do we do it? Well it's certainly not glory-hunting! I don't know; it's just something you choose. Why do you like a certain rock group or a particular actor? With a football team, you like the way they look, or their style of play. We don't question it. We don't necessarily think it's unusual, but I suppose if you think about it, it is pretty unusual.'

He does know one thing for certain, though: that he's not alone in his devotion. 'You'd be surprised how many other QPR supporters there are who do the same as me. We've got season ticket-holders living in Blackpool, Grimsby and York who go to home games and as many away games as they can. Sometimes we run a coach from Manchester down south. It's quite bizarre when we're leaving Manchester in a coach that's got QPR flags all over it; the next thing you see is people in their cars looking in their paper to see where we're playing. If it's somewhere like Southampton, no one can accuse you of glory-hunting, but if it's Manchester United or Liverpool then people think "they're only out for a big game". But we pound up and down the motorway week in and week out. And the accents on our trips are something to behold because there's so many different ones: Brummies, people from Stoke, Wrexham, a 16-year-old lad from Rochdale who does three paper rounds a day so he can fund going down to games – he only missed three last season. I think we've only got one Londoner'.

Thomas reckons he's seen 95 per cent of all QPR's games, home and away, league and all the cups, since 1975–76, 'the season we won the Championship'. History shows, of course, that no such event ever took place, that Liverpool clinched the title – albeit on the last day of the season, and only a whisker ahead of a Rangers team captained by a young Gerry Francis. Undeterred, Thomas and some of his friends still insist on referring to 1976 as 'our championship year' in homage to what they feel should have been. No wonder they get strange looks in pubs when their conversation in praise of that 'triumph' is overheard.

Fired by the very real possibility that Rangers could actually win the championship that season, Thomas packed in his job as an able-bodied seaman with the Merchant Navy in order to attend matches. Irregular shore leave simply wasn't enough. 'It was so exciting to be top of the table, so I left the Merchant Navy so that I could see out the second half of the season', he recalls. 'I knew that if we were going to win the title I *had* to be there, not matter what'. Before then, the highlight of his week at sea was devising a way of finding out Rangers' result. 'I used to tune in to the World Service when we were in places like South Africa. And I remember once having to phone a mate in England at three o'clock in the morning from a call-box in America to find out how we had got on against West Ham, because it was the one result I couldn't find out. We lost 0–2, I think'.

A Kick Up The R's was founded after the almighty row in spring 1987 over the short-lived plan for a merger between QPR and Fulham, a move proposed by Jim Gregory, then the Rangers' chairman. Initially viewed with suspicion by the club as a voice of dissent and criticism, the fanzine has 'matured' enough for Thomas to have become a regular columnist in a more official publication – the QPR match programme. Sensitive to allegations that he has 'sold out', the editor insists that 'I write what I want. I don't hold back'. His loyalty, he points out, is the same as ever: 'We're not anti anybody. We're pro Queen's Park Rangers Football Club and we're pro Queen's Park Rangers supporters'. His audience, he says, are 'those who have to fight back a tear because of a result, those who understand what it is to go to Manchester United and win 4–1 and wake up the next morning and go "yeah!".'

Little gets Thomas's hackles up more than Rangers' image as one of football's natural underdogs. 'That's so trite. We may be seen as underdogs but we certainly don't consider ourselves to be underdogs. In my view QPR is the biggest small club in the country: big enough to succeed but small enough to care. Although we're seen as being small, we are capable of going to Manchester United and Liverpool and beating them, as we've proved. We're potentially the best side in the country . . . on our day'.

Michael Nyman was already twenty-six and the survivor of a childhood flirtation with Spurs before a friend asked him if he fancied a trip to Loftus Road. 'I must confess I had to ask him, "what or who is QPR?",' he confesses. That was in 1970, Rodney Marsh's last season at the club. 'I wasn't doing anything so I went along and became . . . passionate, stupid, obsessed, moronic, couldn't talk about anything else', recalls the contemporary composer, who is best-known for scoring the weird films of director Peter Greenaway such as *The Cook, The Thief, His Wife and Her Lover*. 'There's nothing else in my life which has that obsessive pull. It amazes me that it happened to me, and friends who aren't into football just can't understand it.

'Now my whole week is geared around the match. All the Saturday papers. Then watch the lunchtime coverage. Go to the game. Watch "Match of the Day". Sunday morning, all the reports. Sunday afternoon, ITV. Monday, read the reports again. Then you carry on reading more reports, previews, who's in, who's out, until it comes round to Saturday again'. This faithfully-observed ritual will draw a knowing smile from those similarly obsessed: the club is irrelevant, it's the helpless dedication that counts.

Mightily impressed with Rangers' performances under Gerry Francis, Nyman's got the same feeling that Dave Thomas started to have midway through the 1975-76 season: that maybe, just maybe, Rangers are soon going to break the habit of a lifetime and win something. 'In those days there were loads of characters in football – Stan Bowles, Don Givens, Gerry Francis, Alan Hudson, Duncan McKenzie, Charlie George. You could have made three fantastic England teams out of all the characters there were, players who were too good to get into an England team. My personal heroes are the players who've worn the No. 10 shirt for QPR: Marsh, Bowles, Currie, Stainrod, Wegerle. Like society as a whole, football seems to have become more standardised since the 1970s. But I haven't lost my passion.'

* * *

Gary Lineker, the exiled ultimate gentleman of English football, has rarely been accused of courting controversy. Not for him the nightclub incidents and tabloid grievances about former managers' selections so common among his fellow professionals. And during his six-month stint as a summariser on 'Match of the Day' before leaving to play in Japan, his comments reflected his style of play: clean, economic and thoroughly inoffensive. Yet, in February 1993, he found himself plastered all over the back pages of the tabloids because of one lighthearted, throwaway comment. For once, a Lineker public pronouncement – 'I'd rather watch Wimbledon on Ceefax than live' – had highlighted one of the unpalatable truths of English football: that the Dons are widely loathed for their rumbustious style of play. The nation's fans were not fooled by the papers' attempts to manufacture a row where none existed, however; everyone already knew Wimbledon were 'orrible.

Although the club's manager, Joe Kinnear, was encouraged to hit back – 'that Gary Lineker's not worth two bob,' he fumed – he could hardly have been surprised by this latest verbal assault on the Dons. Reviled for their bully-boy tactics on the pitch, ridiculed for their pitiful home attendances, and taunted for their nomadic status, the club's few fans had known for years that Wimbledon are the Most Hated Team in Britain. And, like their heroes, the fans of the self-styled Crazy Gang are the footballing equivalent of the 187 Texans who stuck it out with Davy Crockett inside the Alamo.

In the annals of football fealty, however, this long-suffering bunch deserves a special mention. Undaunted by the fear and loathing which their team inspires, they persist in making the journey from the few places which could even begin to justify the description 'Wimbledon heartland' – Cheam, Worcester Park and Sutton, out in comfortable Surrey – albeit in dwindling numbers. No one typifies this loyalty more than Laurence Lowne, editor of *Grapevine*, the supporters' club magazine produced 'for Wimbledon fans, by Wimbledon fans worldwide'. An employee of *Encyclopaedia Britannica*, Lowne began life as a West Ham supporter, but mysteriously switched his loyalty in the mid-1970s to the Dons, his local team, when they were still in the Southern League. Despite the fact that Wimbledon are now in the Premier League, Lowne believes that success has not changed the distinctively friendly atmosphere at the club. 'The reason I have stuck with them in because they're small,' he explains. 'It's very easy to talk to anyone – manager, players, chairman, officials. We're all on first-name terms.'

Despite his pride in the club's belief that 'small is beautiful', Lowne fears that this approach may eventually prove to be their downfall. He points to the baffling statistics which show that Wimbledon in the 1990s, apparently a permanent fixture in the cash-rich Premier League, attract fewer fans than they did during their famously irresistible rise. The difference now is that they never play any home games. Evicted from Plough Lane in 1991, their base for seventy-nine years and the backdrop to many of their famous exploits, 'home' means Selhurst Park, a half-hour drive across South London. 'Even though we did amazingly well to make sure we stayed in the old first division when it changed into the Premier League, our home gates still dropped,' bemoans Lowne. 'People used to go to Plough Lane regardless of the opposition. But now we're sharing with Palace, fans are becoming more selective about the games they go to because it takes more effort to get there. Early in the first Premier League season, our crowds against smaller clubs like Coventry and Southampton were down by a third. The few gates which went up were the London derbies and against the likes of Liverpool.'

In fact, the only honour Wimbledon were to win in the inaugural Premier League season was for a succession of lowest ever attendances. Just when you thought they had reached their absolute rock-bottom, they proved you wrong, prompting headlines such as 'Home Alone'. 'It's a gloomy scenario,' admits Lowne. He is concerned that, slowly but surely, even the club's bedrock support is being eroded. 'My prediction for the future? Oh, we'll be at Selhurst Park for about the next fifteen years, by which time we'll be called Womble Palace or something like that. I'd give us two more seasons at Selhurst, and then the support will really start drifting away. I mean, there's only 4,000 of us at the moment.'

In the fans' eyes, the club's only long-term salvation lies in returning to a new ground somewhere near their spiritual home in SW19. But at the moment, the finances of Wimbledon FC would induce a coronary in even the most liquidation-hardened accountant. They are haemorrhaging cash by the bucketload. Take the incomings and outgoings for the late-January 1993 league clash with Everton, which pulled in just 3,039 spectators – another Premier League low. Gate receipts came to a derisory £25,000, programme sales brought in a further £3,000, while bar receipts of £2,000 and the £1,000 match sponsorship by Ladbrokes made the total income £31,000. Yet total expenses were almost £48,000, the player's wages alone accounting for £45,000 of that sum.

So how do the Dons do it? How do they escape the financial consequences of having so few fans? Traditionally, it has been by selling players such as Keith Curle, Terry Phelan and Nigel Winterburn for huge sums. But there is surely a limit to how far you can take a policy of flogging off the family silver. As Lowne hints, the fans' main fear is of a merger with their current landlords. Supremo Sam Hammam has admitted, however, that: 'If a computer was to look at the situation, it would say that Palace and ourselves should merge to become a very strong unit. But I would rather die than merge Wimbledon. This is not to do with cold, hard logic, it's to do with human emotion – and my heart would have to stop beating before I allow anything like a merger.'

Despite this emphatic denial, Wimbledon supporters still fear the worst. They are determined to get back to South-West London to regain their identity and pride before merger or extinction becomes a better-than-evens prospect. The conspiracy-theorists among them would doubtless detect further evidence of the universal contempt in which the Dons are held in the attitude of the London Borough of Merton, the local authority which must license any return home. Councillors have already rejected a succession of proposed sites for a new ground, and seem unwilling to welcome the club back within its boundaries. 'No wonder Wimbledon can't find a new ground,' ran the headline on a poster produced by the supporters' club. 'The council keep moving the goalposts.'

Displaying the resourcefulness borne of a backs-to-the-wall desperation, Wimbledon fans surely deserve better than to see their club extinguished by town hall bureaucrats – a feat which not even the footballing free market has managed to achieve.

* * *

In spite of the devotion of Laurence Lowne and the rest of Wimbledon's faithful few, it is doubtful that the world of football would grieve too deeply if Wimbledon FC simply ceased to be. It is unlikely it would make even the last item on the 'Nine O'Clock News'. Curiously, the demise of second-division Fulham FC *would* probably merit such coverage. Even though Wimbledon have enjoyed unparalleled success over the last twenty years, during which time Fulham's only achievement was to reach the 1975 FA Cup final, the Cottagers still retain a special niche in English football folklore. Johnny Haynes. Tommy Trinder. Bobby Moore. Lovely ground on the banks of the Thames. George Best. Jimmy Hill's foot deodorant ads.

Younger fans will be bemused by the idea of Fulham ever having been successful but, for the older generation, those names evoke an era when football mythology holds that Fulham were one of the major powers of the English game. The record books tell a different story, however. During the club's supposed golden years, the 1950s and 1960s, the Cottagers never finished higher than tenth in the first division, and ended the decade being relegated in successive seasons to the second and then the third division. Since then, Fulham have established a reputation for letting players such as Paul Parker and Ray Houghton slip through their fingers, hiring and firing a procession of managers, and bestowing exorbitant appearance fees on once-glorious has-beens such as George Best, Rodney Marsh and Steve Archibald.

Success on the pitch has long ceased to be a realistic ambition at Craven Cottage; promotion, cup runs and European glory happen to other London sides, never to Fulham. In recent times, the most pressing issue has instead been the very survival of the club. Ironically, it is Fulham's crowning glory – its Thames-side ground, whose magnificent frontage is Grade II-listed – that has imperilled its very survival. Situated in tree-lined SW6 amid some of London's most desirable addresses, the site has been coveted by a variety of property developers, most notably Cabra Estates, who were keen to banish the club and construct penthouses on the pitch where Best and Marsh used to amuse themselves by refusing to pass to any Fulham team-mates except each other.

This gave rise first to a proposal of merger in 1987 with Queen's Park Rangers, a scheme quickly seen off by an early example of fan power. Rumours have also persisted that Fulham would be uprooted and forced to share Chelsea's nearby but unpopular Stamford Bridge ground. 'It wasn't the name of Chelsea that was a particular hindrance to a ground-share,' explained David Lloyd, editor of the award-winning, 1,500-selling fanzine *There's Only One F in Fulham*. 'It was Stamford Bridge itself.

Had it been QPR, we might have accepted it more easily because it's a compact stadium. But a lot of people simply didn't like the Bridge. It's got a horrible atmosphere, a bad reputation and poor views. The general feeling was that, if we did move there, many fans wouldn't have wanted the Shed opened. But with the numbers who would have turned up, we would all have been able to sit in the dug-outs!'

Fulham without Craven Cottage, as former chairman Ernie Clay once remarked, would be as ridiculous as Laurel without Hardy. And, throughout a particularly precarious period, fans couldn't help but ask each other: we want to stay, but does our chairman Jimmy Hill feel the same way? They had got too used to the doleful routine of August arriving and them wondering if that season would be their last beside the river. Amid that uncertainty, David Lloyd even went so far as to accuse the BBC TV pundit of having neglected the club. 'It appears that [Jimmy Hill] is trying to run down Fulham,' he said. 'Staff who have left are often those who have Fulham's interests at heart, while they've been replaced by people who have less of a feel for the club. Crowds are down to 3,500. And Hill won't give me a straight answer about the club's future. If he's doing his "Uncle Jimmy" act after games, his PR skills are second to none. But if you try to pin him down on hard issues, he can be very stubborn. I wonder just how aware he is of the grassroots feeling about how important it is that Fulham stay at Craven Cottage.'

Such dedication led Fulham fans to mount an ongoing campaign to keep the Cottage open. When 120 die-hards chartered a riverboat and headed east down the Thames to an away game at Leyton Orient in April 1992, the stern of the boat was covered with a banner proclaiming a simple message: 'Craven Cottage IS Fulham FC.' The club's destiny appeared to depend on the attitude, ambiguous thus far, of Jimmy Hill.

One man who certainly knew where his heart lay was Johnny Haynes, who played a phenomenal total of 657 games for Fulham and was capped fifty-six times for England during the 1950s and 1960s. When the supporters' club launched 'Fulham 2000', their latest initiative to ensure a footballing future for the Cottage, they found a willing figurehead in the club's best-loved player. At the press reception in late February 1993, he praised the 'Fulham 2000' plan – which asked supporters to donate a tenner towards the cost of redeveloping the ground as a 15,000-seater stadium – as 'a realistic way to help achieve a secure and successful future at our traditional home. I urge all fans to join me in giving it their complete support.'

Less than three weeks later, however, the six-year saga was suddenly over. Jimmy Hill took everyone by surprise, 'Fulham 2000' included, when he announced that the club would be at Craven Cottage for at least the next ten years. With Cabra's development plans for the ground scuppered by the recession, the Royal Bank of Scotland, the club's new landlords, had agreed a ten-year lease and given Fulham the right to buy the site during that time for a fixed price of £8 million. 'It is great news for us,' crowed Hill. 'But we look on it as just the beginning of something, not the end.' As Fulham's centenary at the Cottage approached in 1994, everyone associated with the club could be proud of the part they had played. Once again, they could bask in the reflection of a glory that was never really theirs.

TEN

Ten Thousand are Missing

West Ham: loyalty, betrayal, and the lessons of 1991–93

It's ten to three on a Saturday afternoon in Ken's Café on Green Street, E13, a couple of hundred yards from the claret and blue main gates of the Boleyn Ground, home of West Ham United. Norma Dench and her two sons, Chris and Mike, sit sipping tea at a formica-topped table and discussing the prospects for the game. Today it is West Ham v Barnsley, who two weeks before walloped the Hammers 4–1 in the fourth round of the FA Cup. This time it is a first-division clash. Among the Dench trio, who a fortnight ago braved a 6 a.m. start to catch a coach up to the Sunday midday Cup kick-off in Yorkshire, the talk is of revenge – and three valuable points towards promotion to the Premier League.

Curiously, though, at 2.55 p.m., Norma, Chris and Mike head for their car, not the game: they are going to watch the match – but at home, 'live' on Ceefax. They have been doing the same thing since the season kicked off last August. For the three members of the Dench family are among the thousands of Hammers fans who no longer go to Upton Park, not because they have fallen out of love with the team – far from it – but because they distrust the people who run the club. The Dench trio accuse the board of directors of slowly ruining a club that used to be, and still should be, great. They charge the powers-that-be with spending years selling off exciting, home-grown talent such as Paul Ince, Tony Cottee and Stuart Slater, then buying inferior replacements, often from the lower leagues, at inflated prices. With having unforgivably bastardised West Ham's classic claret and blue strip with a series of hideous designs, oblivious to club tradition and popular feeling. With starving successive managers of funds to buy decent players, precipitating a destructive spiral of relegation-promotion-relegation. Though discontent has been rife for years, the final straw for Norma, Chris and Mike Dench arrived early the previous season with the launch of the club's Hammers Bond scheme: they saw it as a crude attempt to blackmail loyal supporters out of between £500 and £975, only offering in return something they already possessed – *the right to attend matches*. The club insisted that there was no alternative to asking the fans to dig deep to pay for converting Upton Park to an all-seater stadium.

For the Dench family, their boycott is total. After what the club tried to do to us, they reason, giving West Ham any of our money now would be immoral, criminal. At the end of last season, they tore up their long-standing North Bank season tickets and threw the pieces on to the Upton Park turf, pledging not to return until the hated bond scheme had been scrapped and apologised for. Thousands of others did the same. Nine months on, that is no nearer, and the Denches have dug in for a long battle of wills. They still go to away games – Mike, a twenty-three-year-old foreign exchange dealer, has already spent £1,500 this season travelling to places such as Newcastle and Grimsby, and two trips to Italy in the Anglo-Italian Cup – but all three refuse point-blank to enter Upton Park. Ceefax and ITV's 'The London Match' are the closest they get to seeing home games. They also boycott all club products such as match programmes, the magazine *Hammers News* or replica shirts; they even buy official West Ham videos in HMV, not the club shop, to deny the club a pound or two. 'People might query why we spend all this money going to away games when we could stand on the North Bank for £8,' says Norma. 'But we won't pay it because we don't want it going into the wrong hands. The £8 might as well be £80.'

The boycott has not altered their Saturday routine that much: from waking up, the day's events still centre on the match involving the West Ham team. If the Hammers are playing away, Norma, Chris and Mike will be there, just like they have been regularly since the 1982-83 season. They catch a coach organised by the Hammers Independent Supporters' Association (HISA), the 1,000-strong pressure group set up to fight the bond, and head off to watch their beloved West Ham seek another three points. If it is a home game, Mike turns up at midday and stands behind HISA's fold-away table, located in a concreted-over front garden beside Ken's Café, and waits for custom. Sometimes Chris comes too. Both are now highly committed members of the organisation whose professed aim is to secure a better deal for fans. Mike dispenses tickets for HISA's coaches – 'Eleven quid return to Sunderland, cheaper than the club's own travel!', he shouts – while Chris sells HISA sweatshirts, T-shirts and copies of *On A Mission From God*, the fund-raising fanzine set up by HISA chairman Shane Barber. Towards kick-off time, Norma arrives to soak up the atmosphere, enjoy a chat, buy the latest issues of West Ham's four fanzines and have a cup of tea. Then all three go home.

'It felt strange doing it the first game of the season,

against Charlton,' recalls Mike. 'Chris and I were walking past the ground at five to three and we could hear the crowd, but we still got in the car and drove home. It was a very funny feeling. Yes, it did hurt; it still does. The trouble is, I *want* to be in there supporting the team, but my morals won't let me give in to those who run the club.' To him, his brother Chris and mother Norma, not physically supporting West Ham at Upton Park is a matter of principle.

Norma, 43, works for a local council in East London and has supported West Ham since they won the FA Cup in 1964. 'The principle of the bond scheme,' she recalls, 'was totally out of order. They were asking us to give them money and get nothing back in return; they wanted us to invest £975 in the club just to get our names on the back of a seat! If they had perhaps thrown in a free season ticket for the first year or two afterwards it might have made a difference, but they didn't . . .' Chris, 24 and unemployed, chips in: 'We weren't going to give West Ham a free gift of a lot of money for nothing in return. I was annoyed by the fact that we had no say in what the new all-seater stadium was going to look like; they already had the model drawn up. Their attitude was, "This is what we're going to build for you. You've got no say in it. All we want is your money".'

Both Chris and Mike have been active in HISA since they attended its first meeting back in January 1992 as interested observers and got caught up in the determination of those present to 'save the club for its fans'. In common with many other supporters, Mike reckons the origins of the Hammers Bond can be traced to a sunny Sunday afternoon at Villa Park, in April 1991, when the self-styled Billy Bonds's claret and blue army of supporters showed awesome devotion to their team in their FA Cup semi-final drubbing by Nottingham Forest.

First, West Ham defender Tony Gale was sent off after a harsh decision by referee Keith Hackett; then Forest scored four without reply. But, as the goals went in, the chanting of the claret and blue contingent grew louder and louder and louder, not even pausing in recognition of the fast-widening scoreline. 'That was the most phenomenal display of loyalty in the 110 years of the FA Cup,' claims Mike. 'What happened was spontaneous: all of a sudden, there was a feeling among the 19,500 West Ham fans around the ground that everything was against us and that we should get behind the team – that the team might be losing, but the fans were special. The problem, I think, was that the club looked at the passion of the fans and thought, "These people would do anything for the club. Even being 0–4 down in an FA Cup semi-final can't break their spirit".'

'But,' reminds Norma, 'they forgot that we were intelligent human beings, that we were East End, that we could spot a rip-off when we saw one. I think they genuinely thought they could pull the wool over our eyes with the bond scheme.' If that was indeed the logic of the West Ham board of directors – that fans would put up with *anything* out of a time-honoured sense of loyalty and duty – their judgement could scarcely have been wider of the mark. Instead of raising the millions needed to update the decaying stadium, it produced a movement of Upton Park 'refuseniks' – thousands strong, but united in a shared sense of having been deeply wronged – who simply stopped going to see West Ham. After all, if your best friend tries to rob you once, do you give him a second chance – or do you simply start avoiding your best friend? Some, like the Dench trio, now just go to away games. But many others lost the Hammers habit altogether, and surprised themselves by finding other ways to spend Saturday afternoons. A constant in their life has disappeared. 'I know people who have been West Ham fans for fifty years who've stopped going on principle,' says Norma. 'They will always be West Ham in their hearts, but they will never actually put a step through the gates again. I don't know if there's anything now the club can do to make amends.' Still, today, those fans blame the club for ruining the only enduring love affair they had ever known: with a team famed for nice football, having great fans and turning in gloriously unpredictable results.

The immediate effect of the Bond scheme was a season of turmoil unprecedented in the history of any English club. But its troubled legacy can still be seen today in both the crowd figures for Upton Park and the ongoing financial crisis which has engulfed a club legendary for a tradition of almost pathological parsimony. Since the Bond was launched, West Ham have lost ten thousand regular fans and, consequently, millions of pounds in revenue. In 1991, despite the team's return to the first division, the average home crowd fell by 1,500 compared to their recent stint in the second. As with previous relegations, a Hammers team on top of the second division had attracted more support than one languishing in the end-zone of the first. But no longer. That curious recent historical quirk has now been reversed. In the 1992–93 season, the bitterness lingered, the fans did not forgive, and the crowds tumbled to anything between five and twelve thousand below what would previously have been expected, despite the team spending much of the campaign in a two-horse race with Newcastle for the championship of the reconstituted first division.

'It's funny,' says Chris Dench. 'It's got to the point where I feel I'm a more loyal supporter than the people who go to every home game. I know that's a very selfish attitude, but that's the way I feel. We are trying to make the future better for West Ham ultimately, but at the moment that includes boycotting the club because of the bond scheme.' So what would make them go back? Mike Dench: 'We just want someone to treat the fans with the respect and consideration their loyalty deserves.' Mum, fittingly, has the last word: 'I'll only go back if there's a huge banner on the tallest crane at Canary Wharf which says: "The West Ham board apologises to the West Ham fans"!' She is at least half-serious, then turns completely serious: 'Without the fans, there's no club. West Ham can't exist without us, but we *can* exist without West Ham. It's hard, though. We don't *want* to live without West Ham, but we feel forced to do so for the moment. We do want to go back, but we want to go back to something better, and it's up to them to put it right.'

West Ham's recent history, then, is of neglect compounded by fatal misjudgement. Some clubs, like the former Lancashire giants, Burnley, Bolton Wanderers and Preston, lost their support gradually over decades. East London's favourite sons, however, lost 10,000 followers in the space of one close season. That story – of how a self-styled 'family club' alienated thousands of supporters renowned for their humour in adversity, of how it took a Bond to break a bond – was extraordinary then and remains extraordinary now. It deserves telling in some detail, from the beginning in August 1991:

AUGUST 17: Newly promoted from the second division, West Ham kick off the new season with an uninspiring 0–0 draw at Upton Park against Luton Town. Fan discontent is already evident. Disillusioned with the club's failure to sign some top-quality players during the close-season to ease their return to the top flight, supporters chant 'Where's the money gone?' They are questioning the use of millions of pounds generated by the 22,500-average gates recorded during the club's spell out of the first division, and by the team's appearance in the semi-final of both the FA Cup in April and the League Cup a year before.

OCTOBER 26: West Ham beat Tottenham Hotspur 2–1 in an enthralling encounter at Upton Park.

NOVEMBER 2: Hammers complete a double over their North London rivals by beating Arsenal, the league champions, 1–0 at Highbury, courtesy of a Mike Small goal and some stout defending.

NOVEMBER 8: West Ham launch the Hammers Bond scheme with a press conference at Upton Park. It is designed to raise £15.1 million towards the £15.5 million needed to turn Upton Park into a 25,500-all-seater stadium through the sale of 19,301 debentures costing £975, £750 or £500. Fans will have to buy a bond before they can purchase a season ticket in the refurbished ground.

A massive promotional campaign, using the slogan 'We Shall Not Be Moved' above a photograph of the main gates at Upton Park, follows. Advertisements appear on billboards, the sides of red London buses and at Tube stations. The slogan refers to a poll showing that 94 per cent of West Ham fans questioned in a small-sample survey said they would prefer to stay at Upton Park than move to a new ground elsewhere; the question of paying between £500 and £975 for remaining at the Boleyn Ground was not posed. The redevelopment is expected to start at the end of the season, in May 1992, and take until August 1994, the deadline for first- and second-division clubs to comply with the all-seater requirements of the Taylor Report.

West Ham launch a media offensive to promote the Bond, with new managing director Peter Storrie and former Hammers hero Trevor Brooking briefing journalists individually about its merits. Alternative fund-raising methods, such as a Stock Market flotation or a huge bank loan, have been ruled out; there is no alternative to the Bond, says Storrie. 'The debenture route offers everything that we are looking for in our fund-raising: we raise the money, the club remains under internal control, we do not take on a huge debt, and monies for the team are not affected.' West Ham's three fanzines denounce the Bond as a rip-off and an attempt to blackmail supporters into parting with money that most do not have, using the threat of being excluded from Upton Park in future.

After the launch, Hammers lose six and draw three of their next nine league games and do not win again until 18 January 1992.

NOVEMBER 14: Amid growing criticism of the Bond scheme, Storrie reassures the fans: 'At the end of the day, it's not our club, it's yours.'

NOVEMBER 17: Red cards, distributed by fanzine *Fortune's Always Hiding* and urging 'Don't buy the Bond', make their first appearance among West Ham fans. They are waved at corner-kicks and throw-ins during the televised 0–0 draw with Liverpool.

NOVEMBER 30: Fans are urged to wave red cards carrying the numbers 3 and 11 when they want to see left-back Mitchell Thomas or striker Trevor Morley substituted. West Ham lose 1–2 to Sheffield Wednesday.

DECEMBER 5 and 6: Around 1,000 fans attend open days at Upton Park to meet Storrie and Brooking; some voice what the club calls 'constructive criticism'.

JANUARY 4: As 1992 opens, the first ever chant of 'sack the board' is heard at Upton Park during West Ham's humiliating 1–1 draw in the third round of the FA Cup against Farnborough Town, part-timers in the Vauxhall Conference. The *Independent* later reports: 'West Ham suffered the indignity of being loudly booed from their own pitch by the most stoical following in the first division – the same fans who were the talk of football after supplying indomitable support throughout the 4–0 drubbing by Nottingham Forest in their semi-final last season.'

Despite taking the lead through Julian Dicks on sixty-seven minutes, West Ham are nevertheless lucky to salvage a draw. The *Independent*, again: 'Two months without a win in the league was bad enough, but to see the pride of East London clinging on, relieved to have the referee bring an end to their torment by a motley assortment of plumbers and caretakers, was more than the bubble-blowers could stomach.' The non-leaguers are applauded off the pitch by both sets of supporters.

After the game, about 3,000 fans stage a spontaneous sit-in on the Upton Park turf in front of the directors box, chant 'Sack the board' and 'Stuff the bond', and demand to meet club officials. MD Storrie invites a six-man deputation into his office for talks about the Bond, the team's appalling form and the club's 'missing millions'. He tells them that any surplus cash is needed for improvements to the ground, not the playing staff. The last protestors do not leave until around 7 p.m.

Club captain Julian Dicks comments: 'The mood is very bad. I've never known morale to be so low here – not even when we went down.'

JANUARY 11: In the match programme for the league clash with Wimbledon, Peter Storrie takes three pages to reply to questions about the Hammers Bond. He answers question 17 – 'Isn't this really blackmailing the supporters?' – thus: 'The club does not enjoy asking supporters for such a financial commitment, and we really do understand the strength of your feeling on this matter. But it really is the only viable way forward for the club.' Thousands of fans wave a new, A4-size red card urging the board: 'Resign!!!'

Hammers manage a 1–1 draw thanks to a late goal from substitute striker Morley. Disregarding a plea in the programme to stay off the pitch, thousands of fans again gather in front of the West Stand after the final whistle. Initially, the mood is of cheerful, good-natured defiance. But the atmosphere changes. Chants of 'Sack the board', 'Cearns out' and 'Resign', the fans' new anthems, give way to choruses of 'Let's all storm the boardroom'. Police reinforcements prevent fans getting down the tunnel into the West Stand; some minor scuffles occur. A massive banner is unfurled carrying the accusation: 'Lying, Thieving Cheats'. Renditions of 'I'm Forever Blowing Bubbles' and 'Billy Bonds's Claret and Blue Army' lead to an appearance by manager Billy Bonds to appeal for calm. Although he is heard to say that he understands the fans' frustrations, his message goes largely unbroadcast because his microphone is broken; 'like everything else in the club at the present time, it didn't work,' fanzine *On The Terraces* later writes of the episode.

JANUARY 12: The *Mail on Sunday* makes the two-hour protest its lead back-page story under the headline, 'Uprising!'

JANUARY 14: In the FA Cup third-round replay, Farnborough again perform admirably, another Morley goal the only difference between the sides.

JANUARY 20: The inaugural meeting of the fledgling Hammers Independent Supporters' Association takes place. Around 300 fans pack an upstairs room at the Denmark Arms, East Ham. Anger at the Hammers Bond, the ruling Cearns dynasty and the club's alarming decline are passionately articulated by North Bank Norman, a West Ham fan since 1962, a Chicken Run season ticket holder and the editor of the *Fortune's Always Hiding* fanzine.

Tony Willis, editor of the Arsenal fanzine *One-Nil Down, Two-One Up*, is applauded for a speech outlining the fight of Gunners fans against the Arsenal Bond, launched the previous May after Arsenal won the Championship. He wishes the West Ham fans success. HISA supporters resolve to step up the protests. The die of organised opposition is cast.

JANUARY 25: After a planned mass picket of the Boleyn Ground before the following Saturday's league game with Oldham is called off on police advice, fans turn Upton Park into Up-down Park by staging a wacky, Monty Pythonesque sit-down, stand-up anti-Bond, anti-board demonstration at the start of the FA Cup fourth-round tie with Wrexham, fourth-division conquerors of Arsenal in the previous round. At 3 p.m., fans in all standing areas sit down, while those in the seats take to their feet; about 95 per cent of home fans participate.

FEBRUARY 19: The second HISA meeting, again at the Denmark Arms. About 250 fans attend; HISA adopt a constitution and elect officers. Peter Storrie and the stadium manager, John Ball, run the gauntlet of deep fan hostility to address the gathering. Bravely facing his critics, Storrie admits that, like them, he favours retaining some terracing at football grounds. The government is adamant about all-seater stadia, however; so, reluctantly, he declares there is no alternative to the Hammers Bond. Fans demand a share issue to enable them to gain a stake in the club while funding the redevelopment, avoiding what they see as the 'something for nothing' principle of the Bond.

FEBRUARY 29: West Ham's league game against Everton is held up for ten minutes when a lone fan walks on to the pitch carrying a corner flag, sticks it in the turf in the centre circle and sits down, refusing even a plea by Julian Dicks to leave the field. A mass pitch invasion ensues.

MARCH 14: West Ham v Arsenal. In an unusual display of unity, twenty members of HISA and the Independent Arsenal Supporters' Association meet for breakfast in Ken's Café to plan the day's activities. Their theme: 'Bubbles against both the Bonds! A joint and co-ordinated action by fans working together against greed and loyalty abuse.' Lord Justice Taylor, architect of the all-seater proposals so vehemently opposed by most fans, has not responded to a cheeky invitation from the groups to attend Upton Park to see for himself the strength of feeling against his plans.

Before the game, thousands of claret-and-blue and red-and-white ballons are given out, and signatures collected on an anti-all-seater petition. A West Ham-appointed bailiff and two PCs arrive at the HISA merchandising stall and seize seven T-shirts for alleged breach of the club's copyright to the crossed-hammers symbol. Inside the ground, stewards spend five minutes bursting the balloons, and massive, Italian-style banners are unfurled by both sets of fans, bearing the slogans 'Stuff the Bond', 'Ban both Bonds' and 'United We Stand'. Ian Wright, in majestic form, scores two great goals after carving his way through a feeble Hammers defence. Soon after, two West Ham fans occupy David Seaman's goal, two others invade Ludek Miklosko's goal, and a fifth fan jumps out of the North Bank, uproots a corner flag, and hands it to a bemused Seaman. All five are grabbed by police and booed as they are led away.

Today reporter Rob Shepherd, on duty on the North Bank rather than the press box, writes in his match report: 'More than twenty years ago, when my father planted me on a wooden stall in the Chicken Run, there was magic in front of me. It started with Moore, Hurst and Peters, to be continued by Bonds, Brooking and Lampard. Fortunes hid, but you kept believing because you always felt the players and the club really cared. Cared about the tradition, some say the myth, of the family club and the footballing academy that made West Ham special to generations of East Enders. But it's hard for me to believe any more. Where there was always banter, even in adversity, now there is bitterness . . . the consequence of the Bond issue.'

MARCH 20: The Football Association charge West Ham over the pitch invasion during the Everton game; the deduction of points is a possible punishment.

MARCH 21: Ex-club chairman Len Cearns, father of current chairman Martin Cearns, and one of three family members on the West Ham board of directors, takes a page in the match programme for the game against Queen's Park Rangers to reply to the calls for 'Cearns out'. He writes: 'Recently, during supporters' demonstrations over the club's Bond scheme and our recent lack of success on the field, a very anti-Cearns feeling has been shown both in writing and in verbal abuse, and personal threats of violence have been made . . . Football, like most things in life, tends to have its ups and downs and would not hold our interest if it did not. At the present time, football has many serious problems and the club's current position gives cause for concern.' West Ham, four points adrift at the bottom of the first division, scrape a 2–2 draw – their first league point since 1 February.

MARCH 26: Clive Allen, the well-travelled striker who once scored forty-nine goals in one season for Spurs, signs for West Ham for £250,000 in a last-ditch bid to help them avoid relegation.

MARCH 30: The third HISA meeting attracts 600 people to the Broadway Theatre, Barking. Eamon Sheridan, an inspector from the Football Licensing Authority, explains that first- and second-division clubs have to go all-seater by August 1994 or face having their remaining terraces closed.

A leaflet advertising the meeting says: 'We've had red balloons, red cards, claret and blue balloons, pitch invasions, game stoppages and insults chanted at the board. Where has it got us? Nowhere.' Fans, frustrated at the lack of impact of the protests, reject calls to boycott a whole game but vote narrowly to stage a walk-out during the forthcoming match against Southampton. HISA spokesman Peter Cullen comments: 'The vastly-reduced empty terraces will say it all about the Hammers Bond.'

APRIL 2: Tom Duncan, editor of the *Newham Recorder*, the biggest-selling paper covering West Ham's home turf, writes: 'The saddest part of the problems facing West Ham United this season has been the way in which it has lost its special relationship with so many supporters. For some time now, many people have felt that the club has only been interested in their money. The Bond scheme has merely heightened those feelings, yet the club believes there was no alternative. Whatever the fate of the Hammers Bond, I fear irreparable damage has already been done to the special relationship which has existed between the club and its supporters for as long as any of us can remember.

'If lower-grade football returns to Upton Park next season, and that is a daunting probability, the club can no longer assume that its support will be as strong. Many fans are already saying that they will vote with their feet. And once they walk away, it is most unlikely they will ever return' – an uncannily accurate prophesy.

APRIL 14: With the score 0–0 and West Ham needing three vital points against fellow-strugglers Southampton, the planned mass walk-out by HISA members five minutes into the second half does not materialise. In the eighty-ninth minute, West Ham reject striker Iain Dowie scores for Saints.

APRIL 22: With only the remotest mathematical chance of avoiding the drop, West Ham nevertheless beat would-be league champions Manchester United 1–0 in a thrilling match, dealing a massive blow to the Red Devils' fast-faltering title ambitions. Hammers fans stream out of Upton Park chanting 'We are bottom of the league' and 'Going down, going down, going down' in ironic praise of the feat.

After seventeen issues in three seasons, *Fortune's Always Hiding*, a publication of almost legendary off-the-wall wit, publishes its last ever issue. Editor North Bank Norman explains: 'No longer will North Bank Norman, Fred Smeggins and Part-Time Percy [fictitious characters in the fanzine] find humour in the tiresome antics of the no-hopers from Green Street, as they have decided to go down with the Hammers. Even with West Ham relegated, our directors are still determined not to abandon their bastard bond. They have succeeded in the seemingly impossible task of destroying our love for our club, and many of us will not be returning to Upton Park until they have packed their bags and left. Hopefully, that day will come very soon.

'We're packing it in ultimately for this one reason: you can't be funny about something that's breaking your heart.'

APRIL 25: West Ham are officially relegated after losing 0–1 at Coventry City, whose fans applaud the travelling Hammers faithful for their good humour, raucous support and performances of the hokey-cokey. The next day, the *Independent on Sunday* match report says: 'A theory goes that West Ham are never happier than when sitting on top of the second-division table. They will not even have that to look forward to next season, as yesterday they became the first English club to be relegated from the first division to the first division.'

APRIL 30: HISA and members of West Ham's executive lounge combine to launch the Ironworks Initiative. A variation on a share issue, it seeks to inject supporters' money into the club in return for a parcel of existing shares on behalf of contributing fans, thereby giving them a partial influence.

MAY 2: West Ham thump Nottingham Forest 3–0 in the last game of the season. All three goals come in the second half from substitute striker Frank McAvennie, a £1.25 million signing recently handed a free transfer. The crowd of 20,629 brings the season's average attendance to almost 21,000. West Ham finish bottom of the league.

During and after the match, hundreds of fans rip up their season tickets and throw them in the air like confetti. At full-time, the presence of hundreds of police and stewards around the edge of the pitch cannot prevent 5,000 fans climbing on and again gathering in front of the directors box.

In a break with tradition, the West Ham players do not appear for the usual end-of-season clap by the fans, something that has always happened regardless of the team's performances during the campaign.

Despite relegation, despite the Bond, despite the traumatic season, the mood is light-hearted, almost celebratory. Chants of 'Down with the Luton/We're going down with the Luton' and the inevitable 'Sack the board' give way to a sea of fans, scarves and hands raised above their heads, belting out a highly emotional 'Bubbles'. An impromptu Cockney carnival ensues: 'Knees up Mother Brown', 'Maybe it's because I'm a Londoner' and 'The Hokey-Cokey' entice hundreds of people to join in. In the Upper West Stand, a man wears a sweatshirt which says: 'Wife, two kids and Cearns to support'.

Hundreds of fans pledge never to return to Upton Park. All three West Ham fanzines – *Fortune's Always Hiding, Over Land and Sea* and *On The Terraces* – urge supporters not to renew their season tickets. The planned demolition and rebuilding of the South Bank does not begin. Despite relegation and the recession, West Ham increase admission charges by up to 50 per cent.

MAY 28: Martin Cearns resigns as club chairman. The *Daily Mail* reports: 'Cearns has been subjected to a hate campaign ever since the row over the club's Bond issue first started. He has received abusive telephone calls, even threats, and his car has been attacked. Quiet in demeanour, he has found it hard to take.' Terence Brown, a holiday camp owner and property developer who already possesses a large stake in the club, assumes control.

JULY 7: Harry Redknapp, a West Ham flying winger in the 1960s, returns as assistant manager to Billy Bonds.

AUGUST 7: Two weeks before the start of the new season, and after a long search for a sponsor, West Ham finally announce a one-year deal with a local car firm, Dagenham Motors.

AUGUST 13: In his regular 'Galey's Gossip' column in the *Newham Recorder*, defender Tony Gale admits: 'Players must accept responsibility when things go awry. But I found it no coincidence that the downturn [last season] began for us after the announcement of the Bond scheme that so enraged and alienated supporters. While we obviously did not feel the hostility which the Bond scheme provoked was directed at us, it was still very difficult to go out there and not let it affect us.'

AUGUST 15: Only 17,054 fans turn up for the opening fixture of the new campaign, a local derby against Charlton Athletic – the first of what was to be a season of low crowds. The visitors win, 1–0.

SEPTEMBER 1: With West Ham in financial difficulties, commercial manager Brian Blower and several other backroom staff are made redundant in a cost-cutting drive.

SEPTEMBER 5: A crowd of just 11,921 watch West Ham beat Watford 2–1, almost 8,000 fewer than saw the same fixture two seasons previously.

SEPTEMBER 20: Only 11,493 fans pay to see Hammers draw 1–1 with Derby County – the lowest league crowd at Upton Park for more than thirty-five years. 'Not since April 1957 have so few spectators watched a league game at West Ham, suggesting that the tradition of fans flocking there even after relegation is a thing of the past,' according to the *Daily Telegraph*. Peter Storrie blames the live TV coverage. The estimated lost gate revenue is £60,000.

OCTOBER 11: West Ham demolish Sunderland 6–0 at Upton Park in front of ITV's cameras. But the 10,326 crowd is a new record low. Bonds admits to disappointment that so few people have witnessed such a thrashing at first hand. Attendances are now 11,000 below last season's average.

OCTOBER 23: 'Board admits: We were Wrong' – the *East London Advertiser* headline. Storrie says: 'The club are responding to criticism from our supporters on admission prices. Bearing in mind the effect of the present recession and unemployment in the area, we have decided to reduce prices.' He does not acknowledge that Bond-inspired disaffection may be a reason for the low crowds. The cost of season and match-day tickets is cut by 15 to 25 per cent.

NOVEMBER 21: In a change of policy, *Over Land and Sea* says fans should call off their boycott. 'Enough is enough,' it urges. 'We have proved our point, and now it's time to go back before we ruin the one thing we care about – West Ham United Football Club. Go back to

Upton Park. Renew your season tickets, take your place on the terraces, let's give them a chance. Before it's not too late, let's make this a joint victory, not a fight to the death.'

Despite the rallying call, and discounted admission for HISA members and their children, a mere 11,842 fans see West Ham beat Oxford United 5–3.

NOVEMBER 28: There are 15,004 to watch West Ham defeat Birmingham City 3–1, their third home win in a week – and their third biggest crowd of the season. They move up into third place in the first division.

DECEMBER 4: 'Fans send out rallying call: "War is Over"' – *OLAS*'s plea to fans to go back induces a rather premature headline in *Hammers News*.

DECEMBER 10: A letter in the *East London Advertiser* from Hammers fan Amanda Dillane of Stratford explains why she and thousands of others cannot bury the hatchet: 'A lot of us disaffected followers have become born-again ordinary, rational people. We've discovered other ways to spend our Saturdays and our MONEY. We're no longer driven by blind faith to go to games we know we won't enjoy. In short, we've recognised the choice and we're not afraid to make it – the choice that Storrie said we didn't have.'

West Ham offer half-price admission to the unemployed and students, and transfer-list five senior players – Ian Bishop, Tony Gale, Colin Foster, Mitchell Thomas and Mike Small, the previous season's highest scorer – in a cost-cutting clear-out. The club admits it needs 16,000 crowds to break even.

JANUARY 10: The start of 1993 sees West Ham go second in the first division after beating Derby County 2–0 at the Baseball Ground, despite Julian Dicks's sending-off, his third of the season.

JANUARY 28: A Consumers' Association survey reveals

that, for admission prices, West Ham are the dearest club outside the Premier League.

MARCH 1: 'Hammers admit £1 million Bond flop' – *Evening Standard* headline. At West Ham's annual general meeting, the club's accounts for the year to 31 July 1992 reveal that only 576 of the 19,500 Hammers Bonds have been sold – seventy-six of the £975 Class A Bonds and 496 Class B Bonds costing £750 each – raising just £446,100. The total amount raised from the Bond issue, wholly or partly paid, plus bank interest, came to £52,348 by 31 July. In addition, £1,394,471 has been spent promoting the scheme, and the club lost £2,045,872 in that period. Storrie says the loss would have been greater but for the sale in August of Stuart Slater to Celtic for £1.5 million, and admits the club has scaled down its planned redevelopment.

In his chairman's statement, Terence Brown describes the previous year as 'without doubt one of the most traumatic in the history of West Ham United'. He warns of a serious financial predicament at the club and repeats that Upton Park will be a 25,000-capacity, all-seater stadium by August 1994 – but gives no indication of where the money will come from.

Reviewing the 'turmoil' of the previous season, he tells shareholders: 'As is generally accepted, our support is unique and, despite numerous disappointments over the past few years, has remained firm. We entered last season with an FA Cup semi-final defeat, under controversial circumstances, and the loss of the second-division championship with the last kick of the season behind us. We then turned to our supporters for financial assistance during what proved to be the worst economic recession this century and followed the launch of our appeal by failing to win any of the following ten matches.

'We ended the season being relegated in bottom place

with the second lowest number of goals scored in the Football League. The response of our supporters to this unfortunate set of circumstances is well-known to you and, with hindsight, perhaps not surprising.' He hopes that 'the trauma of last season will slowly slip to the back of most minds.'

Brown does not acknowledge the central role of the Hammers Bond in the club's disastrous season, and gives no hint of an apology for its launch.

Peter Storrie used to spend summer seasons as a Pontin's bluecoat, and he later trained to be an accountant; yet despite this in-depth experience of how to entertain paying customers and look after their finances, he nevertheless could not have expected that West Ham's depressing form, together with the Hammers Bond, would lead to such serious trouble. A West Ham fan since 1952, Storrie became the club's managing director in November 1991, and was instantly the front man deputed by his fellow-directors, including three members of the Cearns family, to weather the storm of protest that raged after the Bond scheme was launched in that month. For example, he dealt with all media inquiries about the Hammers Bond. He went to West Ham's Chadwell Heath training ground to impose a media gag on the players after Julian Dicks had told reporters that he opposed the scheme. And he was the one to try to appease a six-man delegation during the first Bond-inspired pitch invasion. Not Billy Bonds. Not Martin Cearns, the then chairman. And not Cearns's successor, Terence Brown. All three have preferred to steer clear of such tasks.

Peter Storrie, however, is torn between the instinctive sympathies of long-suffering West Ham supporters – which mean that he usually understands fans' complaints in a flash – and his duty as a member of the West Ham board not to criticise past or recent regimes. He is candid enough to admit that 'supporters generally feel that the club doesn't want success and that the board of directors aren't supporters of the club, that they don't care what happens to the club as long as the money's coming in.' Both beliefs, he says, are widespread but are 'myths – two of the greatest untruths I've ever come across in my life'.

Sitting in his office on the second floor of the West Stand at Upton Park, Storrie admits that the club had expected some opposition to the Bond, but nothing like the level which quickly materialised. Despite the protests and the tiny number of Bonds sold, though, he did not believe that the scheme had been an error. 'I wouldn't say it was a mistake. Perhaps the timing wasn't right. It obviously hasn't been successful, but it's still selling slowly. It's a long-term prospect.' For a man whose reputation is for staying in touch with feeling on the terraces, these are remarkably complacent – almost amnesiac, comments. He appears unable or unwilling to acknowledge the true extent of the damage done to the fabric of West Ham in the space of a few short months. It is not altogether clear what other trauma was necessary to convince him that the 1991–92 season had been a disaster.

Similarly, Storrie does not believe that what he himself identified as West Ham's secret weapon, the phenomenal loyalty of their fans, is now a thing of the past – and that he is partly to blame. He even talks about breaking with tradition by seeking bank loans secured on the basis that West Ham's attendances are 'stable'. After the destructive débâcle of the bond, nothing could be further from the truth. And he mentions the club's traditional spirit – the East End notion that 'if there's a crisis or something's gone wrong, people stick together, it's all for one' – as something that will persist whatever the problems that beset Upton Park.

Storrie hopes that, for the sake of the club's future, the fans will forgive and forget, and once again get behind their team in the inspirational way that they have done so many times before. The fans, for their part, hope that sooner rather than later, Storrie's ambitious plans for the club start to materialise. He has now helped to institute a five-year rebuilding scheme at Upton Park, much of which depends on unearthing exciting young talent through a revived youth and scouting system, as used to happen. Storrie's mission is clear: get West Ham back in the Premier League, then end the yo-yo effect so that they stay in the top flight, and emerge as one of England's top six clubs. That, he says, is where West Ham belong.

With his business acumen, excellent PR skills and highly constructive attitude towards relations with the claret and blue faithful, and his lifelong love of the Hammers, he may just pull it off. The avowedly ambitious new regime of Storrie and Terence Brown certainly represents the best hope of pulling the white rabbit out of the hat.

Now, if West Ham are ever to regain the affection which was unquestioningly theirs for almost a century, if they are to avoid the 'Burnleyisation' that many fans feared they were sinking into even *before* the arrival of the Bond, they should start by saying one word – *sorry*. Honour, history and their incredible fans demand it.

ELEVEN

Spurred into Action

From fanzines to full-time lobbyists: the rise and rise of fan power

In the smoke-filled upstairs room of a club in Central London, a group of people are meeting to plan the overthrow of the British government. It is an invitation-only, hush-hush affair, strictly limited to like-minded idealists; this job won't be easy, so there's no room for non-believers. The plotters number around thirty: mainly young men, but there are also a few women new to this game, and a sprinkling of old campaigners. Most of those present are casually dressed, but some are even wearing business suits; *very* clever. The evening's agenda over – the details of a headline-grabbing 'action' during the forthcoming general election decided upon, and roles assigned – there is just one item left for discussion: a name. They need a title for their grouping, if only so the media know who they are dealing with. 'Any suggestions?' True to subversive tradition, the plotters spend almost as much time debating that as on organising the tricky business ahead. 'What about FU, Fans United?' says somebody. 'It'd be nice and provocative.' 'How about the Independent Supporters' Association, ISA for short?' 'I suggest CASTRATE,' offers another voice. 'That's for Campaign Against the

Section of the Taylor Report About Terrace Elimination.'
Very imaginative, but a bit unwieldy. Eventually they vote on it. IFU, Independent Fans United, wins.

OK, the game's up. These people are neither staunch Irish Republicans nor far-right Tory activists seeking to oust lily-livered John Major and install Margaret Thatcher as a supreme ruler. In fact, they are a much less threatening breed: football fans. Just football fans. But they are football fans with a difference. Unlike many of their ilk, they believe in forgetting historic enmities and co-operating with their rivals for the good of the game's followers as a whole. That is why, tonight, you've got representatives of the faithful from Arsenal and Spurs, West Ham and Millwall, Chelsea and QPR, all sitting round the same table sharing stories, advice and know-how. There are Crystal Palace, Watford, Brentford and Southend United fans here too. It's hard to imagine any other forum producing such fraternity.

Most of those present are already involved in fan activism at London clubs – producing a fanzine or running an independent supporters' association – so they are well used to tussling with football's powers-that-be and not shy of fighting to improve the lot of the game's paying customers. Which is just as well, because the meeting has been called to solicit ideas about how the government's insistence that soccer grounds have to become all-seater stadia – which is feared by fans everywhere as posing a grave threat to the future of football – can be overturned. If there is an atmosphere of crisis, it is because it has already gone past the eleventh hour to halt the plan. Appeals from the chairmen of leading clubs for a rethink, or at least for more time to find the multi-millions needed to comply, have been rejected by ministers. Now these fans are going to undertake their own last-ditch attempt at persuasion, and the period of the election campaign seems the ideal time to do it.

The issue is deadly serious – the fans' fear that all-seater stadia will price traditional supporters out of the game, and possibly bankrupt smaller clubs – so the need for an imaginative, media-friendly pre-election protest is agreed. It will be IFU's first ever stunt, so it has to be good. Permission for a demo by football fans in Trafalgar Square or Downing Street is likely to be refused point-blank by Scotland Yard, reports a West Ham-supporting lawyer, because the police wouldn't want left- or right-wing campaigners joining in and maybe causing trouble. Someone suggests a symbolic gathering, with representatives from dozens of different teams in full colours, at a club which is in financial difficulties, such as Northampton. Liquidation-threatened Aldershot had already been approached as a willing 'target', it emerges, but said that, while they were flattered at the suggestion, sadly it was too late: they were already slowly expiring courtesy of a series of visits to the High Court.

After animated discussion, a proposal for a few fans from each club to picket the FA's smart HQ in Lancaster Gate, West London, all wearing their team's full kit, meets unanimous approval. Three themes of the protest are agreed: democracy, to stress that fans have not been consulted about all-seater stadia; fans in unity; and, particularly, safety at grounds, that seats are not *necessarily* safer than standing, no matter what Lord Justice Taylor has said. Hence the banners are to carry slogans such as 'We Stand Together', 'Standing Up For Football' and 'We Practise Safe Standing '– the parody on the official AIDS warnings dreamed up by irreverent Manchester City fans and displayed during a recent televised game. Scarves are welcome, too, and fanzines from all over Britain will be invited to send one.

In addition, an eight-foot by four-foot ballot paper is to be mocked up, with a huge X put in a box marked 'Vote for Safe Standing', and sent to the FA and HQs of both the Tory and Labour parties. An accompanying letter will point out that fans feel let down, that they want the consultation recommended by Taylor in an apparently overlooked section of his report, and that terracing *can* be safe, as the influential Institute of Structural Engineers recently said in a report. Then someone suggests changing the picket to an all-night vigil, and holding it on the last Saturday before polling day, which just happens also to be the night before the two FA Cup semi-finals – so it should attract TV, radio and press interest. Immediate approval is given, and arrangements for a shift system are made. Finally, tasks are allocated: Ross from Chelsea will look after the ballot paper, Trevor from QPR the vigil, and Colin from Southend United the scarves. Telephone numbers are exchanged, the meeting breaks up, and everyone heads downstairs to the bar.

A few weeks later, the event passed off as planned. The protest was symbolic, timely, and even attracted some media coverage. It was, on its own terms, a success. And as a model of collective organisation by rival football fans, it was remarkable, if not unique. However, politically, the biggest campaign undertaken by fans since the Thatcher government's plan to introduce compulsory ID cards for all spectators ultimately achieved nothing. During the ensuing election run-in, Labour pledged to exempt the third and fourth divisions from the all-seater requirements and to review Taylor's obligation on the first and second, but did not get the chance to make good its promise. Instead, the Conservatives were re-elected and pushed ahead with implementing the controversial proposals.

Before long, IFU – conceived as a fresher, more radical version of the Football Supporters' Association, the body recognised as the voice of the fans by Lord Justice Taylor in his report – had faded into obscurity, defeated in its main aim. Although intended to be a national pressure group which would bring together independent supporters' groups from all over Britain, it did not stay in existence long enough to broaden the base of its loose membership beyond the thirteen London teams and a handful of others in the south-east. That wacky, well-planned vigil at FA headquarters would prove not just its finest hour, but its only hour.

On the surface, the dissolution of the group and, even more so, the defeat for supporters everywhere in their attempts to have the dreaded all-seater requirement rescinded, suggest that frustrating impotence remains the natural state of football fans. In fact, the 1990s have witnessed an unprecedented growth in the influence of supporters at dozens of individual clubs in England, including many in London. Whether that influence is essentially negative (such as the campaigns by Arsenal and West Ham supporters against their respective bonds) or positive (such as the vital role played by the Charlton faithful in endlessly lobbying for, and then part-financing, the club's return to the Valley), there can be little doubt that it has been unleashed as never before.

While the 1980s had seen supporters at several London clubs record notable victories – a speedy response from QPR and Fulham fans in February 1987 quashed the proposal to merge their teams and call the result 'Fulham Park Rangers', for example, and Spurs die-hards campaigned successfully to save at least part of their beloved Shelf – it was not until the 1990s that the idea took hold that fans should be organised on an ongoing, not just a one-off, basis. The majority of London clubs now have a supporters' organisation which is entirely independent of the official body sponsored by the club. The two campaigns just mentioned, for example, led directly to the formation of the QPR Loyal Supporters' Association and TISA, the Tottenham Independent Supporters' Association. Both are still going strong today, several years after the events which created them, sustained by new issues of local or national importance. In May and June 1993, for example, dozens of TISA activists, angered at Terry Venables's sacking by Alan Sugar, demonstrated outside the High Court in the Strand to support their fallen idol in his vain battle against the computer tycoon they called 'Judas'.

There are encouraging signs that a much more enlightened attitude is fast taking hold among the clubs' administrators. The harsh economic realities of the 1990s dictate that smaller outfits, such as Millwall, must carry their supporters with them, particularly on an issue as vital and potentially rancorous as moving to a new ground. But things are changing at the big clubs too. Under the Irving Scholar regime at Tottenham, for example, the influential *Spur* fanzine was frozen out of the discussions about the club's troubled goings-on. But when Terry Venables and new chairman Alan Sugar called a press conference to announce their take-over, editor Stuart Mutler was invited to attend alongside representatives of publications with slightly larger circulations. It was a welcome break with the frostiness of the past and set the tone for relations which, Mutler says, 'now mean that John Fennelly, the club's chief press officer, treats me just like any other journalist when I ring up.' Interviews with players, seats in the press box and gossip have duly followed. Not only that, but Mutler is now able to refer to Mr Venables: 'Yes, I can – and do – call him Terry to his face,' he laughs.

Clearly, some clubs are still stubbornly rooted in the Dark Ages as far as relations with their fans go. At Barnet, for example, fanzine writers and prominent supporters recall a climate of fear, paranoia and self-censorship because, as one said of former chairman Flashman, 'everyone's scared stiff of Fat Stan'. Happily, such cases are the exceptions, the last remaining outposts of the traditionally bullish attitude which, if exhibited in any other line of business, would be severely punished by the concern's paying customers. Football, however, has long been the only entertainment industry somehow able to ignore the most basic rule of all, that the customer is not a mug. Almost everywhere else, clubs and their fan bodies are inching slowly towards a situation, if not of mutual respect, then certainly of mutual understanding. The reasons for this gradual *glasnost* range from the cynical – 'we might be able to persuade them that the bond's a good idea, so we'd better have them in' – to the surprisingly open-minded. After all, 'constructive discussions' with the fans keep everyone happy – and keep the turnstiles clicking.

The irresistible rise of the fanzine movement, begun by publications such as *Foul!* and *Off The Ball*, and given its most significant impetus by the more recent and large-scale success of *When Saturday Comes*, was the first indication that fans were starting to get organised. Instead of simply grumbling on the terraces and in the pub with their mates, they began to put those complaints – about facilities, prices, the team's appalling form – into print and share them with a wider audience. There was also a lot of humour too, which helped. Impressed with the mixture of caustic comment and high comedy being produced by people just like themselves, other fans responded; sales took off, and fanzines quickly became an integral part of the football experience in Britain. They are now so well established that it is virtually impossible to go to any league ground in the country and not pass fans peddling at least one club fanzine.

The total number of fanzines in England has been estimated at 400. But this may even be a conservative figure: judging by the number of new launches in the 1992-93 season alone, the decade's deep recession does not seem to have deterred would-be editors, writers and cartoonists from putting their thoughts, wit and erratic talents into print too. Even non-league clubs have fanzines these days: Wealdstone, for example, boast two. And the size of the team's crowd is clearly no deterrent either: Wimbledon, legendary for abysmal home attendances of barely over 3,000, somehow sustain an incredible six publications. That's one for each fan, as some wag remarked.

In 1992-93, the season after the bond fiasco at West Ham, the team behind *Over Land and Sea* recorded a novel first in the fanzine field when they started to produce *Home Alone*, a fanzine-style alternative to the club's rather predictable official match programme. Initially, the quality was variable, doubtless because of the difficulty of finding twenty-eight pages of original material for every home fixture in a crowded forty-six-game season. Nevertheless, *Home Alone* offered all the basic ingredients of *Hammer* – team-sheets, match reports, match previews, interviews with West Ham players, and ticket and travel details for forthcoming games – plus a few features the club would never have entertained. Its intention was bold: 'We want to become the match-day magazine that everyone wants to read,' editor Gary Firmager wrote in the debut issue. Selling for £1, which was fifty pence cheaper than the official programme, its early success led to suggestions that fans of at least one other big London club, Tottenham, were planning to copy the idea up in N17.

Perversely, perhaps the greatest testament to the influence of the fanzine movement is the fact that their original targets – the worthies, dreamers and hard-nosed businessmen who run football clubs – are now among their most avid readers. Irving Scholar thought that *Spur* was wantonly destructive of the club, yet devoured each issue. Arsenal's David Dein has been known to pull up in his Bentley round the corner from Sportspages bookshop on the Charing Cross Road and emerge a few minutes later with an armful of fanzines; mind you, a libel action against *One-Nil Down, Two-One Up* for what he called 'a campaign of personal abuse and untruths' perhaps suggests that his interest is less thick-skinned than most. And John Ellis, editor of the Palace fanzine *Eagle Eye*, tells the very funny story of how, when he and co-editor Tony Matthews were summoned 'to be scolded like naughty schoolboys' by Ron Noades for alleged subversion, they were amazed to find the chairman kept a full set of their subversive organ under lock and key in a filing cabinet in his office.

It was hardly surprising that a group of West Ham supporters had broken new ground in fan activism. The season before, the spontaneous popular revolt against the Hammers Bond created an organisation, the Hammers Independent Supporters' Association, which was soon displaying organisational ability, resourcefulness, imaginative protest-making and support among the faithful which were previously unseen among English fans. Followers renowned for their legendary fanaticism suddenly began channelling their insatiable energy into activism, in order, as they saw it, to protect the true spirit of the club they loved. The club's officials, already appearing embattled and besieged, found themselves further isolated from opinion at the ground because the supporters now had their own representative body to act as much more than a glorified lightning conductor for dissent, but as an authoritative negotiator. In the highly-charged atmosphere of red cards and pitch invasions, HISA attracted hundreds of members immediately and recorded its 1,000th participant before the end of that traumatic season – the largest paid-up membership of any independent supporters' organisation then known in England.

The powers-that-be would have been well aware that the professional qualifications of the inaugural HISA committee probably outstripped those held by the members of the boards of directors of many clubs. HISA's representatives were not elected for having lots of letters after their name but, just for the record, they included: an architect, a construction manager, an associate director of a merchant bank, a lawyer, the owner of a security company, and the director of a firm dealing in company searches and formations. It was a fearsome collection of talent, and their primary use of their professional training was to examine in detail the financial and legal implications of the Bond scheme and the plans for the new all-seater stadium, and to establish an organisation which would exhibit many of the characteristics of a trade association or one of the more respectable political pressure groups. That meant a computer database, excellent PR skills, sophisticated campaigns. No football club in England had ever been confronted with such an array of disparate though complementary talents – all of whom were, needless to say, totally committed West Ham fans.

Since then, HISA has shown another way forward. It has become, in effect, a shadow organisation to the club itself, offering many of the same services: merchandise, coach travel to away games, social events. Its Ironworks Initiative showed that it was comfortable dealing with financial experts in the City to try to produce an alternative fund-raising scheme to the Bond. The only avenue firmly closed off to it is putting out a team every Saturday afternoon; so far, it has had to limit its ambitions in that direction to friendlies against supporters of other clubs.

'At first, West Ham looked on HISA as an enemy, pure and simple,' recalls founder-member Shane Barber, now the group's chairman. 'That was based on the fact that we could destroy the Bond, which they had staked so much on.' Although the policy of openness instigated at the club by MD Peter Storrie meant that it already had healthy enough relations with its three fanzines – whose editors, when given a sneak preview of the Bond initiative, had denounced the scheme, only to be assured that it would be a roaring success – the formation of HISA posed a more difficult problem. Ignore it and hope it proved to be a short-lived, flash-in-the-pan protest group, or meet head-on the fears and anger of its growing membership?

Storrie, to his credit, followed Plan B. He and Upton Park stadium manager John Ball decided to brave the inevitably intense hostility and attend HISA's second meeting to try to persuade fans that there really was no alternative to the bond scheme. Despite the gulf between the sides, he continued to meet HISA representatives regularly, both parties tentatively seeking to identify some common ground. Initially, there wasn't much to be found. Storrie assured HISA several times that he would help them if he could. And early on the following season, the organisation presented him with a list of practical ways in which the club could honour its surprising suggestion. But nothing subsequently came of it, fuelling HISA's suspicions that the club saw the meetings as little more than a talking-shop and useful sounding-board about fan feeling. Gestures which would have been of symbolic as much as practical importance, such as allowing HISA merchandise to be sold alongside official products in the club shop, and granting HISA a small office in the main stand at Upton Park, were not acted out.

Clearly, the situation at West Ham that traumatic season was particularly fraught; only Barnet's ongoing tragi-comedy received more back-page headlines at the time. But the rise of HISA also highlighted what is perhaps the most significant recent development in the growing power and influence of ordinary supporters: the emergence of a generation of fans who are fast becoming the footballing equivalent of the political lobbyist at Westminster. At Upton Park, Storrie & Co. now know that the aloofness and high-handedness practised by previous regimes will not be allowed to work in future; and that, if any new initiative is to be successful, or at least received with an open mind, then they must first consult the fans' representatives in the shape of the three fanzine editors and the HISA chairman, Barber, who also doubles as editor of *On A Mission From God*. In June 1993, for example, the club proudly unveiled its home and away strips for the following season, which involved a pleasing return to an orthodox use of its traditional colours of claret, light blue and white. Unbeknown to the national media present at the unveiling, however, the three editors had been invited in several months previously for a sneak preview. In return for signing a confidentiality clause – Storrie understandably did not want the shirts' official launch spoiled by advance publicity – the trio were able to see that the very first of the litany of complaints to have surfaced at Upton Park in recent times, that the club's classic shirt had been distorted beyond recognition, had finally been satisfied.

A similar phenomenon has been repeated during the birth of other ISAs. When Arsenal were designing their new North Bank Stand, for example, the IASA commissioned their own architect to come up with what they regarded as fan-friendly plans. And the Millwall ISA did the same thing for the club's New Den, producing an impressively detailed sixty-page document outlining their ideas. Barry O'Keeffe, chairman of the Millwall ISA, says 'club chairman Reg Burr took our proposals very seriously.' The inescapable implication of all these developments is that fans no longer trust football clubs to look after their interests so, where possible, they will just have to do it themselves. Loyalty to teams is as absolute as before; clubs, though, are living on borrowed time in that department.

Amid all the stories of rancour and division and despond within football, it would be easy to assume that fans, when they get together, tend to have a negative influence – being *against* everything all the time. Nothing could be further from the truth. Reducing it to its simplest, fan activism is usually directed against things only when they are clearly prejudicial to their own interests: price rises, all-seater stadia, bond schemes.

Much of the time and energy and commitment they display is, in fact, invested in campaigns either to preserve existing features, such as the club's separate identity or a favourite strip of terrace or, in the case of the Fulham fans, their home ground; or gradually to improve conditions, such as toilets, catering or policing practice. There is a third category, however: that of fans agitating to ensure that, at a time when uncertainty is the common currency of English football, their club's future is secure.

The struggle of the Wimbledon fans to relocate the club back within the boundaries of the borough of Merton has already been described. But the best example of fans fighting for the future surely came at the Valley on 6 December 1992, when Charlton staged a glorious, emotion-filled return to their spiritual home after seven years as nomads. The fans had done everything: raised over £1 million towards rebuilding work through a bond-style Valley Investment Plan scheme; even stood as candidates in the local elections on a Back To The Valley ticket. Inspired by such devotion and determination, incoming chairman Roger Alwen pledged to make returning to SE7 his goal.

The day, when it finally came, was magnificent. The football wasn't brilliant, a 1–0 win over Portsmouth; but then it's rarely world-class at Charlton anyway. No. The thing that mattered was that a dream had come true. It was the footballing equivalent of a miracle, except that everyone could see who was responsible. Derek Hales, one of the Valiants' old stagers from the 1970s, got it right as he was mobbed on the way into the homecoming game. Surrounded by autograph-hunters resplendent in red, he kept saying: 'You did this. This is your day.'

TWELVE

London Football in the 21st Century

Survival of the fittest?

The much-vaunted 'Whole New Ball Game' started on 15 August 1992, insisting that English soccer was suddenly going to become the best it had ever been. Fans were invited to succumb to the fantasy that, almost by magic, games in the top flight would now be the most exciting and fulfilling that anyone had witnessed. It was a ludicrous claim, of course – more hype than hope. No amount of glossy, sixty-second peak-time commercials courtesy of BSkyB could convince the footballing public that every game – yes, even Wimbledon v Oldham Athletic – was a big game, a crunch match, a vital fixture. But if football's new rulers were hoping to perform a conjuring-trick, they were soon embarrassed to find that there was no white rabbit in the hat. As sporting hoaxes go, it was just about as credible as the idea that every beefcake in the Olympic shot-putt final trains on nothing more than raw steak and pints of milk, and that Frank Bruno will one day become undisputed heavyweight champion of the world.

Within weeks, as we have seen, the sham had been exposed. After just six Saturdays of the Premier League, there were 11.7 per cent fewer spectators at the Premier League fixtures compared to the same time a year before in the old first division. Coming after six years of continuously growing crowds, the drop in gates was quite an achievement. Their instincts honed by seasons of spotting clear offsides and players feigning injury, fans had quickly seen through the illusion: matches were still as frenetic as they had ever been; goals were still created as much by mishap as mastery; and flair was still found more often on *Match of the Day* videos of the 1970s than on the resurrected show each Saturday night. Even by the lazier criteria of home viewing, the new set-up was a failure: a series of dismal viewing figures for live games seemed to bear out an unusual lack of early-season interest.

There were, perhaps, logical explanations for this phenomenon: a hangover from England's dismal failure in the European Championships in Sweden; the swingeing price increases imposed almost everywhere despite deepening recession; and the fact that, after the shortest close-season ever, many stalwarts were simply 'footballed-out'. But there was another reason: an intangible feeling among fans that, for the first time, the game's powers-that-be would not be too concerned if the regulars failed to turn up as faithfully as before, because they had already taken BSkyB's money and run. It was a restless unease about their true place in the game born of frustration, exasperation, exhaustion – and a little bit of fear.

As English football belatedly started to embrace the discredited 'greed is good' philosophy of the 1980s, the game's followers were right to be anxious. The civil war between the Football Association and the Football League had thrown up a radically altered balance between the two bodies; although fan power had enjoyed several successful manifestations in the smaller spheres of individual clubs, they were, in the broader scheme of things, more impotent than ever before. For almost a century, the sport had been sustained by the notion that everyone involved was a member of an extended family; that, besides the legal kinship of belonging to the ninety-two-club Football League, there was also an historical bond between Arsenal and Aldershot, Chelsea and Chesterfield, based on an alleged unity of interest. Now, though, having formed a self-governing élite which saw no common interest with the rest of football, the breakaway twenty-two certainly did not intend to let mere fans interfere with their plans. Thus, when the fixture-list was dismembered and some matches every weekend moved to Sundays at 4 p.m. and Mondays at 8.05 p.m., supporters were given a simple choice by the BSkyB schedulers: take it or leave it. After all, if there aren't enough spectators in the ground to generate the real thing, crowd noise comes on pre-recorded tapes these days.

If the fans were being increasingly regarded as irrelevant to the live occasion, BSkyB and the Premier Leaguers were not the only offenders. As the season wore on, outbid by the satellite station and the BBC, and outflanked by Channel 4's scoop with *Serie A*, ITV mounted a late and desperate lunge into the football fray with a policy apparently based on a simple principle: if no one else has snapped it up already, wave a cheque in front of it. Still reeling from the shock of losing their four-year monopoly on screening live action from the top flight, ITV were now reduced to pretending that attractions as dubious as the Smiths Crisps International, an Under-15 clash between England and Scotland, and gems from the first division of the Barclays League such as Southend v Millwall – live and exclusive from Roots Hall – were a worthy substitute for Arsenal, Manchester United and Spurs.

Despite the limited appeal of many of the games

broadcast in their Sunday-afternoon *London Match* slot, few of which would have been anywhere near sell-outs in the first place, ITV appeared to be competing with BSkyB in the amount of fan-unfriendliness generated by their tampering with the fixture-list. For example, West Ham followers turning in mid-February 1993 to the *Newham Recorder* for the latest news on the Hammers learned from a two-paragraph item that, over the next seven weeks, no fewer than five of their team's key promotion matches had been moved from their original dates. Two had been shifted so that ITV could show them live, two others to avoid clashing with live screening in London of the Coca-Cola League Cup semi-finals, and the fifth on the advice of the Metropolitan Police, keen to avoid conspicuous consumption before the traditionally tense West Ham v Millwall derby. The Upton Park faithful should, perhaps, have been prepared for all this; after all, ten dates had already been changed before this latest batch, including the fourth-round FA Cup-tie at Barnsley which went ahead at noon on a Sunday – a replayed third-round encounter the previous Wednesday having left Hammers fans with only four days to plan complicated travel arrangements. Fanzine *On A Mission From God* vented their frustration when it blasted: 'That's fifteen games which have had their original date changed. It makes printing the fixture-list a complete waste of time, doesn't it? Now how about asking us, the fans, how we feel for a change?'

Under both the BSkyB and ITV deals, those clubs forced to switch dates and times were at least compensated for the inconvenience caused. The 'inconvenience', however, was a tacit recognition that thousands of fans couldn't – or wouldn't – get to the rearranged kick-off, so the tens of thousands of pounds offered were meant to make up the shortfall in gate receipts. From the start, the Premier League was required to stage a game every Sunday afternoon and Monday evening; in the Football League, the policy was Sundays-only, but ITV's variety of regional demands meant that, some weekends, an entire clutch of games was transplanted to the Sabbath. When it came to television planning its live coverage, the wishes of the punter paying at the gate simply did not figure in the calculations. A few clubs went through the motions of wringing their hands and saying sorry of the bother, but their apologies rang hollow coming from the same mouths which had happily said yes to the offers of loadsamoney from TV.

In an era when everything in football was meant to be 'new and different', the explicitness of this two-fingered gesture towards fans was certainly novel. Amid all the selfish schedule-shaping, a Rubicon had been crossed: the armchair audience was, for the first time, more important than the live one. It was a dangerous and wilful disregard of the very people who had been the game's financial backbone since the inception of the Football League in 1888. To football's new rulers, 15 August 1992 marked the start of Year Zero. Like Pol Pot, they wanted us to believe that history never happened.

By the end of year one, however, the Premier League had manifestly failed to fulfil any of its three original promises. The fixture-list was still as hopelessly congested as ever: Sheffield Wednesday were forced to play four games in the last week, while Arsenal were obliged to postpone the ritual end-of-season champagne celebrations because there was still the little matter of a rearranged North London derby to be fitted in the following Tuesday, three days after everyone else's programme had ended. The quality of football was showing few signs of improvement: the fact that the title-chasing teams all season had been attractive, passing sides could not disguise the frenetic, physical nature of so many contests. Most important, England's chances had not been improved one iota. While the Italian authorities had declared a willingness to axe two clubs from *Serie A*, had they been drawn in a World Cup qualifying group with seven teams, in order to improve the nation's chance of reaching the 1994 finals, the exacting demands of the club game in Britain had saddled Graham Taylor with a recurring selection headache brought about by injuries to key players. Deprived of his strikers Alan Shearer and David Hirst before the crucial World Cup qualifier against Turkey in Izmir in March 1993, for example, the manager admitted he had called up 'from nowhere' Sheffield Wednesday's centre-half-turned-frontman Paul Warhurst. For a 'whole new ball game', it all sounded depressingly familiar.

* * *

Where association football was once administered by the butcher, the baker and the candlestick-maker, it was directed in 1992–93 by an accountant and a banker, the latter of whom was totally up-front in stating the terms on which the game would in future be run. 'Professional soccer ought to be regarded as a business,' said the Barclays Bank and Premier League chairman, Sir John Quinton. 'It's very much like the theatre, where you have to put on a good show; if you don't, then the entire thing will turn into a financial disaster.' Among Premier League supremos, only David Dein of Arsenal admits to seeing the NFL across the Atlantic as the model for how the top flight in English football should develop. However, another sports entrepreneur, Frank Warren, shares a similar admiration for the American way. The Islington-born boxing promoter established his reputation when he upset the sport's old guard by adopting a showbiz approach to the previously mundane business of getting bums on seats at bouts. A lifelong Arsenal fan, it was surely significant that Warren first started to show interest in the financial potential of football at precisely the time that it was throwing off the shackles of the past.

'David Dein's approach to football is very commercial, which is the way you've got to be if you're going to succeed. He was one of the big driving forces in creating the Premier League, and in fact I believe it should go a stage further and become a European Super League, which would be the equivalent of the NFL. I think that is both inevitable and desirable. Big money. *Big money*. That's the way the game's going to have to go. Like in the NFL, people who own a club will basically have a licence to print money.' In Frank Warren's eyes, the destiny of England's top clubs belongs in the realms of money-spinning European TV deals and international sponsorship by multi-national companies. That, he believes, is the game's future: 'It must be, because it would improve the quality of football at the top level.

'If Spurs were in a European Super League, and they were going to play Inter Milan or Barcelona or Real Madrid, I'd want to buy a ticket for the game, not as a Spurs fan – because I'm not, I support Arsenal – but as a *football* fan.' However, Warren is uncertain that this will ever happen, because English clubs failed to see the obligation to comply with the Taylor Report as an opportunity to dispense utterly with the past. He is convinced that, unable to develop their inner-city grounds to the capacity of the San Siro or Nou Camp, Arsenal and Spurs should have forsaken Highbury and White Hart Lane and shared a new, purpose-built stadium nearby. 'They should have gone for Alexandra Palace. I mean, there's a perfect site there that's easy to get to; it's had a racecourse there, so it's used to coping with crowds; and it would make a perfect neutral spot. Or, alternatively, why not take it off to the M25, move it out further again to where it should be. That's what the clubs should have been looking at. When my dad was a kid, Spurs was in the country because Tottenham was still a suburb, and Arsenal was a greenfield site. But now they're not. Their grounds are bang in the middle of built-up residential areas, and they're probably a nuisance to the local people.' Only by making such bold moves, asserts Warren, can they hope to gain the same financial muscle as their European counterparts. Sticking with grounds which have small capacities by European standards will inevitably restrict access to those able to pay through the nose for the privilege.

Frank Warren's early forays into football – trying to buy Luton Town FC, and organising the money-making players' pool for Liverpool's 1992 FA Cup final appearance – are doubly interesting in the light of the revolution in the staging and promotion of boxing matches that he has helped bring about. Until the late 1970s, boxing was a sport in apparently terminal decline. But by importing marketing techniques from American showbiz such as flashing lights, loud music, theatrical entrances and the creation of 'personalities', and from sports such as wrestling and American football, Warren managed to persuade the sport's predominantly working-class followers to part with three-figure sums to attend big fights. He believes that the leading football clubs in England could usefully study both the presentation and financing of sport across the water. To do so, he considers, would help avert their otherwise inevitable fate as the perpetual also-rans of the European soccer scene.

Warren is convinced that, because clubs failed to grasp

the historic opportunity offered by the Taylor Report to think big and bold, opting instead to rebuild their present stadia but with lower capacities, the basic laws of supply and demand dictate that clubs such as the North London rivals will rapidly start to display the chief characteristic of American sport: the affluence of its live audience. Although he is regretful that working-class fans will be priced out, sentiment has no part to play in Warren's vision of the future of football. Clubs will simply charge what the market will bear. 'Clubs' capacities have been reduced, so if they've got to make the cheapest ticket fifteen or twenty quid, say, then that, unfortunately, is a problem the government has imposed on them.' But how can that be reconciled with any desire to see football remain a mass, popular entertainment? 'I don't think it can.' And for clubs not to charge their limited audience top whack would further reduce their potential by rendering them non-starters in the race to sign the best players in Europe.

With a wry smile, the promoter tells a funny story which illustrates the ultimate paucity of ambition preventing English clubs from realising their true potential. 'Ken Friar, Arsenal's managing director, once told me about a time when the Gunners played in the Joe Robbie Stadium in Miami at some international invitation tournament. The Miami club president said to him, 'How many parking spaces have you got?' Ken answered, 'Seventy-five.' 'Jeez,' the club president whistled, 'we've only got 60,000 . . .' He obviously thought Ken Friar meant Arsenal had 75,000 spaces! In fact, they only had seventy-five.'

With the exception of David Dein at Highbury, senior officials at leading clubs have expressed little public support for the deliberate emulation of the NFL. Nevertheless, two important developments at big clubs in recent years suggest that, cheerleaders and popcorn apart, the process is already under way. First, there is the increasing gentrification visible at the top two dozen grounds, as remarked upon by Tony Willis at Arsenal. Second, a clutch of clubs are operating the American system whereby, because of the rapid growth of season-tickets and membership schemes, every game is all-ticket – the catch being that you will only have a ticket if you bought it in a book with twenty-nine others the previous summer. Newcastle United, for example, were expecting to start the 1993–94 season with every seat in St James's Park occupied by a season-ticket holder, thus becoming the first ground in England with the unenviable distinction of being permanently barred to the casual fan; money, not loyalty, is in danger of becoming the only acceptable currency there. This transformation is also well advanced at the Uniteds of Leeds and Manchester – and at Tottenham, where some 25,000 of the fans inside a 34,000-capacity stadium pay £12 each for a flimsy plastic membership card and, crucially, the right to priority booking for glamour ties. A further 10,000 hold season tickets. Hence, on a Sunday morning in late March 1993, a queue more than a mile long snaked around White Hart Lane as thousands of supporters sought tickets for the forthcoming FA Cup semi-final against Arsenal at Wembley. Every one was a member. Until recently, fans bought season tickets primarily for the convenience and the 10 per cent discount in the club shop. Increasingly, however, they are motivated to do so by something approaching fear – at the very least an anxiety that the day is fast approaching when committed followers will be frozen out unless they can part with their cash in advance.

It would be unwise to read too much into the lesson of the Sky Strikers: inspired by Americans, imported by Australians, and booed by the English. The derisive reception the cheerleaders have received at grounds across the country suggests that football is not yet ready for the razzmatazz of Stateside sport. However, the number of spectators using their flexible friend to pay for an entire season's football long before the first ball is kicked shows that a quiet Americanisation is steadily, if more subtly, taking hold.

* * *

These developments should not be too surprising, bearing in mind that the thrust of English soccer since the mid-1980s has been inexorably towards élitism, with the emergence of a clutch of powerful, rich clubs calling all the shots. A process which began with the formation of an informal pact betwen the 'Big Five' – a term never present before in the football lexicon – ended with the arrival of a Premier League. Perhaps the only surprise was that it took so long to happen. It was a truly historic rupture, marking the first time any cartel of clubs had dared declare their superiority and separate interests to those outfits left behind. It was no coincidence that the long-rumoured breakaway finally occurred within months of Lord Justice Taylor's insistence on all-seater stadia; chairmen already restless for more power had recognised that this effectively spelt the end of football as entertainment for the masses, and decided to make the most of this heaven-sent opportunity to woo a different class of punter.

Throughout its protracted dumping of the Football League, the Premier League swore blind that its plan would still maintain some links in the form of promotion and relegation and participation in the FA and League Cups. It was rather like a husband divorcing the wife he no longer cared for in order to move in with a younger model, but insisting that he would still like to stay in touch with the kids after the separation. David Dein, for example, vowed that the lower divisions would not be cast aside: 'That was never our intention. We simply wanted those who generate the most income to be able to determine the direction of the Premier League. I want the good things to be available to everyone. If a club like Barnet get from the third division to the Premier League, they're entitled to reap the dividends of their labours. And if someone else dominates their profession, do they not deserve a greater share of the dividends? Is that not fair in life?'

The major weakness of the new set-up, however, was that it was plainly *not* a strategy which would benefit the whole of football. And that's the trouble. A phenomenon such as Barnet or Wimbledon happens only once a decade. The implicit 'winner takes all' rationale behind the Premier League was little comfort to the clubs outside the twenty-two involved at the outset, the seventy-one for whom survival each year was more often a matter of luck than judgement. Denied the multi-million pound subsidy of a satellite TV deal, sponsorship by brewers and hi-fi giants, and banner headlines on the back pages of the papers, they were effectively condemned to a permanent future as the second-class citizens of football. Yet the prospect of many such outfits going to the wall appeared not to concern the Premier League conspirators, who were surely gambling by disregarding the role played by their now distant cousins in nurturing the stars of tomorrow. Like the concept of the Premier League in total, this move showed that the go-it-aloners had demonstrated appalling lack of wisdom in elevating the importance of short-term wealth for the few above long-term health for all.

Another flaw lies in the uncomfortable nature of

an alliance which has thrown together Arsenal, aspiring European Super League champions, with Wimbledon, whose crowds would probably be disappointing in the Turkish second division. Although apparently united by common interest, in fact, the sole bond between the twenty-two – the urgent need for some sort of coup – disappeared as soon as that mission had been accomplished. The notion that a new, élite league would finally banish the constant bickering which had long plagued football was rapidly exposed as another example of misplaced idealism. The row over the right of the self-styled 'Platinum Collection' clubs to sign an extra advertising deal for themselves merely underlined the wishful nature of such thinking. In fact, the furore, over the eight's intention to capitalise on their added glamour without reference to the other fourteen partners gave the game away – that 'maximising their commercial potential', as they put it, presaged the creation of an élite within an élite. The Platinum Collection's relationship with the Premier League was rather like that of the Militant Tendency to the Labour Party: an organisation pursuing its own separate agenda, ideals and aims behind a public façade of fraternity. Although those clubs' commitment to the breakaway was certainly wholehearted, it was also clear that they saw their long-term ambition lying in a European Super League which would mean much less domestic football.

At Arsenal, for example, manager George Graham and vice-chairman David Dein disagree only over the detail of how English and European competition should be dovetailed. Seething with frustration at the domestic disease of 'too much football' – a complaint which obliged the Gunners to play five games in the last ten days of the 1992–93 season – Graham favours a sixteen-team Premier League and the elimination of the League

Cup. Dein, on the other hand, would be happy with the eighteen teams in the top flight originally envisaged in the FA 'Blueprint.' Either slimming-down, however, involves junking a handful of clubs which are seen as a hindrance. 'Personally, I think a European Super League will happen,' says the manager. 'Nothing stands still in life. One domestic cup competition is enough for Arsenal to meet second- or third-division sides in; having two competitions is a bit much. The fans would like to see Arsenal play Real Madrid rather than a home-and-away tie with Chester. I don't think there's anything wrong with pitting your wits against the best in Europe. I believe the public will start to demand that.' Without the further restructuring he envisages, Graham believes that the whole of English football will suffer. 'I've heard people say in the past, "George Graham has got big ideas. It's OK for him to say that, he's manager of Arsenal." But I used to be manager of Millwall. My philosophy then is the same as it is now: if you want to go to the top, go for it – but don't hold the high-flyers back.'

As the inaugural Premier League season progressed, the bigger clubs became more convinced that their ambitions were being thwarted, both in the commercial sphere and on the pitch by the sheer grind of the forty-two-game campaign they had sought to leave behind. Prevented from signing a lucrative deal on revolving advertising boards and nostalgic for the days when the ITV deal guaranteed them the bulk of the booty, they came increasingly to resent the egalitarian principles of the breakaway league. The cake was now cut into twenty-two equal slices where previously it had been divided far less equally. With a predictable handful of self-consciously superior clubs frustrated at not getting things their own way – and at seeing humbler outfits such as Ipswich Town and Norwich City near the top of the table – it was hard to imagine them putting up with such injustices for long.

Despite the fraternal smiles of the twenty-two Premier League chairmen when they are signing yet another money-spinning sponsorship deal together, it is no secret that the bigger clubs have an inbuilt dread of having to play teams such as Wimbledon, Crystal Palace and Coventry City home and away. They regard it as an ordeal, not a pleasure. Not only is there fear of failure on the pitch, but also there is less revenue generated by the type of fixture where otherwise loyal fans always seem to have a wedding to go to. George Graham insists that the door into the top flight must always be left open for successful smaller clubs: 'Take Wimbledon, for example: good luck to them. The ambition and opportunity should always be there. But,' he adds ominously, 'it [admission to the élite] should be gauged on ability allied to facilities.' And it is that rider, 'allied to facilities', which may well become the means by which the smaller clubs are jettisoned. David Dein, for example, is in charge of a three-man FA Premier League criteria committee, which wants to establish minimum standards off the pitch. Although he declares that any recommendations will be geared towards giving spectators value for money and complying with the Taylor Report, it is not hard to see how an insistence on, say, a minimum 20,000-capacity all-seater stadium could be used as an excuse to dispose of poorer clubs unable to carry out the work.

Ironically, however, to implement such change – which was, after all, the justification for the supposed revolution in the first place – a further upheaval in English football will be necessary. This is unlikely to happen by consent, though, because of what could rightly be called 'Cross-Channel Cup Syndrome' – the belief of so many club chairmen that their team should be in action every weekend and, if there isn't a league game scheduled, to play such an unnecessary fixture as Chelsea v Le Havre. It is almost impossible to conceive of the required fifteen Premier League power-brokers voting for the footballing equivalent of Christmas coming early for turkeys: for the axeing of four or six of their number to achieve a sixteen- or eighteen-club league and thus forfeiting a substantial chunk of gate revenue. Given that, history will have to repeat itself and the momentum for change come from the few. No one knows if David Dein and Martin Edwards are currently organising a cabal of like-minded colleagues at secret retreats in country hotels to take control once and for all, but the impetus for a final showdown will almost certainly come from such figures. Six or eight chairmen might well force the issue by threatening to resign *en bloc* from the Premier League, and take their glamour elsewhere if a timetable for a dramatic slimming-down is not agreed. Without voluntary change, this is likely to happen sooner rather than later.

If such a scenario develops, doubtless Dein & Co. will argue that the resulting upheaval is for the good of the game, in the interests of football *as a whole*. Similar claims were made for the Premier League, that its wealth and prestige would benefit every club in the land and its altruism assist the national team. It sounds wonderful: an England manager able to pick his eleven first-choice players, all fit, fresh and with skills honed by regular European encounters. Nor should this be pie-in-the-sky idealism which is never realised. No other country forces its national coach to operate under such pressure; instead, they build a domestic programme geared towards international success. Although the cancellation of Premier League matches before a major international has belatedly become standard practice, following the débâcle of the 1992 European Championships, the notion that the needs of the

England team should be at the apex of the entire footballing pyramid is still only paid lip-service. Absolutely everyone in soccer agrees that this is the goal. The Premier League has not delivered it. So the thorny question remains: how can it be achieved?

The answer is that the twenty-two Premier League chairmen must relinquish some of their power and learn to sacrifice their habitual self-interest for a new concept of the common good. A Commissioner for Football, charged with advancing the interests of the game as a whole, needs to be appointed. If left to quarrelsome soccer administrators to elect, this NFL-style innovation – the best of all ideas which could be copied from America – might never happen. Perhaps the government should step in and impose a commissioner who, when consensus cannot be reached, has the power to dictate policy. It is a proposal which recognises that football is a national asset, and needs to be administered as such. Instead of the game being run by separate bodies such as the FA, Football League, Football Licensing Authority, Football Trust, Football Grounds Improvement Trust and the PFA, this would give overall responsibility to a Football Commission to which the other organisations would report. Each would continue in its traditional role, but their historic power-struggles would become pointless, as impasses would be resolved by the higher body. Implicit in the proposition is the accusation that football's current rulers cannot be trusted with safeguarding the game's interests as a whole; with ensuring that football at each level from the national team down into the GM Vauxhall Conference receives the attention it deserves. Instead of pulling together, they are pulling soccer apart. After all, English Heritage, the Arts Council and the BBC's board of governors operate fairly successfully at arm's-length from Whitehall or Westminster.

It sounds like a job for a trouble-shooter. Why not call on the services of the man best known for diagnosing the ills of industries and putting them straight, former ICI chairman Sir John Harvey-Jones? Or a long-standing football figure associated with previous mould-breaking moments in the game's history, such as Jimmy Hill? Or an articulate ex-player such as Garth Crooks, now active in the PFA? The best choice of all for the commissioner's job, though, is the sole personality with the appropriate authority, negotiating skills and recognition that football is as important in Torquay as Tottenham. That individual is Gordon Taylor, the PFA chairman.

Taylor is surely right to identify short-term planning as the greatest threat to football's future prosperity. The immediate financial gain to the top clubs of the BSkyB deal and rapidly rising admission prices is all very well, he argues; but it may be at the cost of eroding interest in the game and pricing fans out of being able to say, 'I was there'. He is encouraged by the overdue investment in youth schemes, the recognition by a few clubs that admission charges have risen too sharply, and the increasing liaison between fan groups and administrators. However, the game still exhibits the self-destructive myopia which has ruined so many other British industries: a failure to see beyond this year's balance sheet.

Alone among football's leading voices, Taylor insists that the fans must be central to any strategy because of their unique contribution to the game, past, present and future. They alone have the power to turn a mere match into an occasion; an army of dish-owning couch-potatoes cannot manage that. Most important, despite BSkyB's largesse, they remain the sport's biggest sponsor, through both the ticket office and the souvenir shop. Should a European Super League ever come about, the expected multi-millions will doubtless help a few leading clubs compete more equally in the global transfer market. But for the vast majority of English outfits, their survival depends on nothing more complicated than keeping the fans happy. As Taylor himself puts it, 'As an entertainment industry, the last thing you need to do is to disenchant the public.' In the same mysterious way that Tube passengers suddenly became 'customers', too many football club chairmen have portrayed themselves simply as the providers of a service, but at the same time abused the special loyalty of their supporters. The inaugural Premier League season showed that fans were slowly starting to vote with their feet. Nobody minds being treated like a punter; few enjoy being treated like a mug.

With football's turmoil showing no signs of abating, London will remain the best testing-ground of the game's health because of the sheer diversity of its thirteen clubs. Come the year 2000, the glory of Arsenal topping a European Super League could serve as a beacon for a soccer city. But it would not increase attendances at picturesque Craven Cottage, where the 3,500 die-hards will still turn up for their regular lower-division fare. The shame is, Fulham's prospects for advancement will be frozen in stone, the fluctuating fortunes which are essential to the romance of football replaced by an ever starker division between the haves and the have-nots. After all, wealthy benefactors determined to upset the balance of power do not grow on trees. As the Blackburn Rovers fans delight in reminding us, 'One Jack Walker/There's only one Jack Walker.'

EPILOGUE

The Final Whistle

If, as Harold Wilson said, a week is a long time in politics, then a season is an eternity in football. But if events during the ten-month campaign were not enough – promotions, relegations and cups aplenty – then the weeks afterwards proved even more dramatic, with London's managerial merry-go-round spinning faster than ever and two of the capital's clubs tearing themselves apart in court.

WEST HAM UNITED: Having nestled comfortably in second place behind Kevin Keegan's formidable Newcastle United from January to early April, a nasty run of away defeats thrust the Hammers out of an automatic promotion spot. But an unexpected implosion by Portsmouth and a dramatic Hammers win against Glenn Hoddle's Swindon set up a tense final game at Upton Park. With Pompey going 2–1 up against Grimsby, Billy Bonds's men desperately needed to put a second goal past Cambridge to guarantee elevation to the Premier League. In the 90th minute, a Clive Allen tap-in did it. Many of the sell-out 27,399 crowd staged the customary pitch invasion. MD Peter Storrie believed the afternoon's events marked a vital turning point on the club's long road to recovery: 'We shouldn't be looking for miracles next season', he advised, 'but the first stage of the rebuilding process has been achieved.' However, with just

£700,000 to spend on new players, survival looked as tough as ever.

LEYTON ORIENT: The O's, too, appeared well-placed for promotion for much of the season. Cruising smoothly in the top six until a late-season 1–2 home defeat by soon-to-be-relegated Wigan precipitated a sudden drop from even the play-off zone, 1992–93 proved to be yet another frustrating season of unfulfilled promise. Missing a play-off place solely on goal difference left O's fans bemoaning an appalling total of thirteen defeats away from home. Worse, mid-May saw the Brisbane Road MD and all-round inspiration Frank Clark decide to take on the unenviable task of replacing Brian Clough in the dugout at the City Ground, Nottingham. Ironically, his first signing was Orient's England Under-18 defender Mark Warren, another product of the club's youth development scheme.

ARSENAL: Confounding widespread expectations that they would walk away with the inaugural Premier League championship, the Gunners finished in a surprisingly lowly ninth place. Instead, they consoled themselves with an unprecedented double in domestic knock-out competitions, winning both the Coca-Cola League Cup and the FA Cup, the latter after a replay, both against Sheffield Wednesday. The uninspired nature of their successes, however, did not augur well for Arsenal's renewed assault on manager George Graham's Holy Grail – Europe. In recognition of the Scot's achievements during seven years at the helm, the Highbury board commissioned a life-size waxwork of him to occupy pride of place in the museum in the new North Bank Stand.

TOTTENHAM HOTSPUR: Predictions that Spurs minus Lineker, Gascoigne and Stewart would struggle were borne out by early-season results. The £2.1 million acquisition of striker Teddy Sheringham filled the most obvious gap. In addition, Darren Anderton flourished after an uncertain start, Neil Ruddock proved an inspiration in defence and barrel-chested forward Nick Barmby emerged as English football's undisputed find of the season. Once in their stride, the team turned in a series of scintillating performances, scoring freely, and progressed to a second Wembley FA Cup semi-final showdown in three years against Arsenal, losing a forgettable match to a Tony Adams header. No wonder MD Terry Venables spoke of them winning the Premier League next time round, and dominating the domestic scene for a decade to come. Then, Tottenham being Tottenham, disaster struck. Less than two years after the 'dream ticket' of Venables and Alan 'What's the double?' Sugar rescued the club from the twin perils of bankruptcy and Robert Maxwell, the partnership was torn apart. The Amstrad tycoon sacked Venables, accusing him of commercial incompetence and, worse, financial impropriety; the man acknowledged as Spurs' saviour countered that Sugar was more interested in profits than trophies and had betrayed football's best interests by covertly helping BSkyB to win the Premier League contract. Talk of a boycott by fans and a mass exodus of players left morale at White Hart Lane at its lowest-ever ebb – and that really was saying something.

BARNET: 'Well, they did it,' wrote Geoff Brown in the *Independent on Sunday* on 25 April. 'Despite the slings and arrows of outrageous Stan Flashman, despite the loss of their much-put-upon manager, Barry Fry, to Southend United a few weeks ago, despite investigations into their finances by the Football Association, and despite not being paid for periods of the season, the players of Barnet FC won promotion to the second division.' Joy at the incredible feat of their second elevation in three years was short-lived, however. Within weeks of the season's ending, Barnet again found themselves attracting unwelcome headlines. Talks with prospective buyers broke down and the true extent of the club's debt was revealed to be £1.3 million. 'The legacy left by Stan Flashman has proved too great. It's chaotic', fumed Fry's despairing successor, Edwin Stein. Liquidation loomed, and with it the prospect of expulsion from the Football League. Then a hefty cash injection from a five-man consortium saved the day – but for how long? Perhaps not for very long. Stein resigned at the beginning of July and all the players were given free transfers. So have we really reached the last chapter of the saga at Underhill?

QUEEN'S PARK RANGERS: Gerry's pacemakers didn't stay at the top of the Premier League for very long, but they were never far off it and ended the campaign in fifth spot. That placing not only made them London's top side, but also guaranteed them £666,990 of Premier League merit money. If a mid-season injury crisis had not wiped out their midfield, Rangers might well have challenged seriously for a place in Europe. Francis's ongoing minor football miracle prompted inevitable newspaper speculation about his future at the club: would he replace Graeme Souness at Anfield, or even Graham Taylor? In the end, he scotched such rumours by signing a one-year extension to his contract – but, as is always the way at Rangers, appeared doomed to lose his twenty-goal, emerging England striker Les Ferdinand and, possibly, talented winger Andy Sinton.

CHELSEA: Their future at Stamford Bridge now secure, the Blues could concentrate on activities on the pitch – which, given yet another mid-table placing, was now urgent. Ruthless as ever, Ken Bates decided that his friend David Webb was not up to the manager's job after his three-month trial, an axeing which prompted former

Chelsea hero Ron Harris to declare: 'Bates should be the first manager-chairman. He wants someone to train the team which he picks'. Rejecting the challenge of keeping newly-promoted Swindon Town in the top flight, Glenn Hoddle forsook pastures green for pastures blue and took what many regard as the most tenuous job in the Premier League. After two dismal decades at the Bridge, the future suddenly looked, at the very least, interesting.

FULHAM: Like the club whose ground they were touted to share, Fulham's only achievement during the 1992–93 season was to secure their future at Craven Cottage. Their on-the-field endeavours earned them no better than twelfth position in the second division, sandwiched between Rotherham and Burnley. Unfortunately for their fans, the only trophy remotely associated with Fulham was a ceramic model of the Cottage, another of the enterprising Fulham 2000 campaign's fund-raising schemes. Despite the group's ambitions for the club's future, it appeared that its devotees had nothing more to sustain them than memories.

BRENTFORD: The Bees' fortunes changed dramatically with the turning of the year. From a comfortable mid-table position at Christmas, they sank to the depths of the first division – in one particularly woeful spell going 810 minutes with just a solitary own goal to their credit. Survival was still possible on the last day of the season, but a 1–4 blitzing at Bristol City sent them back to the division from which they had escaped only a year earlier. Heads duly rolled. Manager Phil Holder was sacked – and replaced, ironically, by the man made redundant in West London football the very same day, David Webb. 'The battle is on here and everyone has to commit themselves to the cause', warned the new boss. Brentford's one achievement attracted fewer headlines, however: winners of the Jewson/The *People* Family Football Award, worth a useful £25,000.

WIMBLEDON: Life went on pretty much as normal for the Dons. Vinnie Jones copped the largest-ever fine handed out by the FA for his promotion of the infamous 'Soccer's Hard Men' video, and they temporarily engaged in verbal warfare with Tottenham when the home team objected to Fash & Co. playing their notorious 'boogie box' before the sides met in the fifth round of the Cup. But Wimbledon continued to claim the scalps of the big boys, such as a double over champions-in-waiting Manchester United and the removal of Aston Villa from the Cup, while players such as Warren Barton, Robbie Earle and John Scales appeared next in line for conversion into million-pound internationals.

CRYSTAL PALACE: After struggling all season, the inevitable happened – relegation, alongside Middlesbrough and Nottingham Forest. Nine years after arriving, manager Steve Coppell resigned, saying: 'I created a monster – a Premier League club, paying Premier League wages and with Premier League players. The only problem is that Palace are not in the Premier League any more.' Promising continuity, his former deputy Alan Smith got the nod. Facing an anticipated £3 million drop in revenue, chairman Ron Noades quickly made the decisions from which Coppell had blanched: Eddie McGoldrick went to Arsenal for £1 million and Geoff Thomas to Wolves for a curiously low £800,000. With goalkeeper Nigel Martyn also the subject of transfer speculation, the prospect of a downward spiral of decline loomed large.

MILLWALL: After all the optimism generated by their move to Senegal Fields, Millwall's tenure at the Den came to an inauspicious end when Lions fans began the ground's planned demolition a little early – at half-time during the final game against Bristol Rovers to be exact. Supporters dug up the pitch, threw turf towards the directors box and, at the final whistle, stole the goalposts. 'This is a tragedy for people who feel passionately about the club, because nobody has done more in the community', stated Chief Superintendent Ken Chapman. The incident, one of the worst outbreaks of hooliganism in a notably peaceful season, overshadowed the stylish football which Mick McCarthy's team had played for much of the term, before defeats during the vital run-in condemned them to seventh place, just outside the play-off zone.

CHARLTON ATHLETIC: The fifth of December 1992 proved to be Charlton's most famous day for decades – but was the only highpoint of a season which, judged strictly on footballing terms, was another non-event. The vigour of the early-season performances under new joint-managers Steve Gritt and Alan Curbishley quickly disappeared, and the Addicks' surprising appearance at the top of the first-division table was shown to be a flash-in-the-pan. The euphoria of the return to the Valley produced a series of sell-out crowds, but the consequent 'all-ticket' policy was abandoned three months later as interest began to wane and the team finished in twelfth position. More positively, Greenwich Council gave the go-ahead for a £2 million, 6,000-capacity all-seater stand on the old East Terrace.

If ever proof were needed that English football was sick at heart, it came a week after the season ended with the mind-numbing sterility of the Arsenal v Sheffield Wednesday FA Cup final, the poorest showpiece anyone could remember. The replay was just as tedious, the players again failing to serve up anything approaching entertainment. Domestic soccer's general gloom darkened even further when England, confidently expecting four points from two crucial World

Cup qualifiers, which manager Graham Taylor had stated 'we cannot lose', scraped a 1–1 draw in Poland and were then totally outplayed in Norway, going down 0–2, a trip also scarred by the re-emergence of the English disease: hooliganism abroad. If all that were not embarrassment enough, Taylor's jaded squad then travelled to Boston to take part in the US Cup, a four-nation friendly competition designed as a dry-run for the World Cup – a tournament in which England now seemed unlikely to be appearing. In their opening game against the part-timers of the host-country, defeat led to the headline 'Yanks 2 Planks 0' and a general recognition that English football, once synonymous with style and success, had become the laughing stock of the world. Graham Taylor still did not resign – nor, more interestingly, did the mandarins of Lancaster Gate ask him to do the decent thing. Mind you, the man who could have had the necessary quiet word was Peter Swales, chairman of both Manchester City and the FA's International Committee. Echoing Admiral Lord Nelson's reply when asked if he could see any ships, Swales refused to believe that the English game was already being dashed against the rocks. Crisis, what crisis? He simply could not see one.